Tourism, Travel & COVID-19

The new narrative for Southern and Eastern Africa during a crisis vortex

Copyright © KR Publishing and Shanaleigh Hebbard

All reasonable steps have been taken to ensure that the contents of this book do not, directly or indirectly, infringe any existing copyright of any third person and, further, that all quotations or extracts taken from any other publication or work have been appropriately acknowledged and referenced. The publisher, editors and printers take no responsibility for any copyright infringement committed by an author of this work.

Copyright subsists in this work. No part of this work may be reproduced in any form or by any means without the written consent of the publisher or the author.

While the publisher, editors and printers have taken all reasonable steps to ensure the accuracy of the contents of this work, they take no responsibility for any loss or damage suffered by any person as a result of that person relying on the information contained in this work.

First published in 2020.

ISBN: 978-1-86922-854-5
eISBN: 978-1-86922-855-2

Published by KR Publishing
P O Box 3954
Randburg
2125

Republic of South Africa

Tel: (011) 706-6009
Fax: (011) 706-1127
E-mail: orders@knowres.co.za
Website: www.kr.co.za

Printed and bound: MegaDigital, 24 Kinghall Avenue, Eping 2, Cape Town, 7460
Typesetting, layout and design: Cia Joubert, cia@knowres.co.za
Cover design: Marlene De Lorme, marlene@knowres.co.za
Editing: Valda Strauss, valda@global.co.za
Proofreading: KR Team: krpublishing@knowres.co.za
Project management: Cia Joubert, cia@knowres.co.za

Tourism, Travel & COVID-19

The new narrative for Southern and Eastern Africa during a crisis vortex

Edited by

SHANALEIGH HEBBARD

2020

DEDICATION

To ....

Jayde, Ethan, Danielle and Jonathan.

Your future is just around the corner.

"One's destination is never a place, but always a new way of seeing things"

–Henry Miller

TABLE OF CONTENTS

ABOUT THE EDITOR	iii
ABOUT THE CONTRIBUTORS	iv
INTRODUCTION	xiv

Part 1: The power of collaboration and crucial conversations through visioneering 1

Chapter 1: Helping brands survive and Build Resilience
– *Mariette du Toit-Helmbold* 2

Chapter 2: SA Tourism's strategic objectives for tourism recovery
– *Sisa Ntshona* 9

Chapter 3: Initiatives to support the tourism industry
– *Johan Hattingh* 15

Part 2: Building a New Model: Acceptance, Adaptability and Opportunity 23

Chapter 4: Rainmaker: Digital Transformation is key to success and economic sustainability – *Thomas Müller* 24

Chapter 5: Resilience Action Planning: Attracting Domestic Guests & Social Distancing Measures – *Sarah Habsburg* 31

Chapter 6: Revenue Management: Perfecting key elements to positively influence business growth and sustainability – *Derek Martin* 39

Chapter 7: Fixing the weak links in the Tourism Value Chain to ensure trust and strong relationships – *Illana Clayton & Kate Bergh* 45

Chapter 8: Tourism versus Poorism – *Mandisa Magwaxaza* 53

Part 3: The Future of Aviation and the Traveller: Ensuring Safety & Peace of Mind and Tourism Crisis Recovery Checklist 61

Chapter 9: COVID-19: A catalyst for change in African Aviation
– *Derek Nseko* 62

Chapter 10: The rise of sanitised travel: A day in the life of an airline passenger – *Simplyflying* 67

Chapter 11: The sky has limits for the African Aviation Industry
– *Joan Vilardell* 79

Chapter 12: A Tourism crisis recovery checklist during and post COVID-19
– *TRINET* 95

Part 4: Crisis Leadership Excellence   **106**

   Chapter 13: Crisis leadership excellence: Navigating in, beyond and through a crisis – *Theo H. Veldsman*   107

   Chapter 14: Managing uncertainty, complexity and chaos in a crisis vortex – *Sonja Blignaut*   123

   Chapter 15: Promoting personal and workplace mental health in the age of COVID-19 – *Navlika Ratangee*   129

   Chapter 16: Positive mental mindset versus COVID-19 upset. Winner takes it all – *Kobus Scholtz*   137

Part 5: Embracing the challenge and finding solutions to do our part for humanity, conservation and tourism   **144**

   Chapter 17: How Rhino Africa is navigating COVID-19 through Thought Leadership – *David Ryan and Grant Rapaport*   145

   Chapter 18: The story of African Bush Camps and the impact of COVID-19 on tourism, conservation and community – *Beks Ndlovu*   161

   Chapter 19: The story of Care for Wild: Keeping rhinos safe in a time of crisis – *Sharon Gilbert-Rivett*   167

   Chapter 20: #TOURISMINMYBLOOD: United in purpose to share, inspire and help one another during the crisis vortex – *Greg Smith & Richard de la Rey*   171

   Chapter 21: Rise of the Warrior – *Shanaleigh Hebbard*   175

REFERENCES   **183**

INDEX   **187**

ABOUT THE EDITOR

Shanaleigh is driven by her passion to help people live their best life. As a life, business and strengths-based personal development coach she utilises her strengths to uplift communities through volunteering outreach programmes, supporting conservation projects and helping people find peace, purpose and connection by escaping the fast-paced life of the concrete jungle and being immersed in activities and destinations that allow for life-changing experiences and a story of the African dream to inspire others. This passion is realised through Shongile – Future Self Journeys, by finding the best opportunities and solutions to bring people, places and events together to achieve maximum enjoyment, inner healing and a lasting impression of increase through effective collaboration, storytelling and purposeful travelling.

Shanaleigh believes that real joy lies in the journey to one's destination. With that said she will move mountains to make her clients' journey truly memorable. As a young adult Shan started her career in lodge management within the Kalahari Desert where she soon became an expert in managing the logistical challenges of such a remote establishment. Within a short time, she managed the central reservations office and finance department at the company's head office in Windhoek, Namibia. Her journey in the lodge industry took a turn when she opened her first franchise with over 700 monthly members. She soon realised that she needed additional resources to better assist her members and embarked on becoming a life and business coach. In 2010 she attended one of Bob Proctor's seminars in America and invited Bob Proctor from the movie *The Secret* and Sandy Gallagher to South Africa where they delivered two seminars in Johannesburg in collaboration with Makes You Think. Inviting Noor Hibbert, a successful life and business coach from the UK to inspire female entrepreneurs in Cape Town has added to her resumé of recruiting and working alongside international thought leaders and business coaches. Although Shan offers an impressive skill set, her experience in life coaching is most intriguing. A firm believer in utilising one's talents and identifying talents in others, her love of life and people along with her meticulous attention to detail culminate beautifully in her role. Although a strategic thinker and self-starter, Shan is inspired by beautiful stories, the wonders of our southern sky and our alluring African landscapes. It's here that she feels Africa's very heartbeat and this she hopes to share with all who visit our soil.

Living out her purpose would have been impossible without the support and encouragement of her family. As a mom of four, she is committed to inspire, create and advocate a brighter future for them and generations to come through her example and belief that you might not be able to change the world, but you can change the world for someone if you are motivated by love, compassion and kindness.

ABOUT THE CONTRIBUTORS

MARIETTE DU TOIT-HELMBOLD

Mariette du Toit-Helmbold is the Chief Destineer at Destinate. She established Destinate in 2013 after 10 years as CEO of Cape Town Tourism. She has a real understanding of both the private sector and the public sector, having navigated a complex environment as CEO of Cape Town Tourism and establishing and managing a successful business for the past six years. She has extensive experience in destination brand development and management. Her work in place marketing received international recognition. Du Toit-Helmbold is also in demand internationally as a strategist and speaker on tourism, trends in marketing and the role of digital and social media in destination and tourism marketing. She is strategic advisor to a number of hospitality brands and works with multinational commercial corporations as a strategic communications advisor.

SISA NTSHONA

Sisa Ntshona is the CEO of SA Tourism and is the former Head of SME Banking for Absa/Barclays Africa responsible for the Enterprise Development strategy, operations and activities as well as the development of competitive and innovative propositions for emerging Small and Medium-size Enterprises across 12 countries in Africa.

He held various positions in banking, gaining experience across various functions initially in the Investment Banking Division, Africa cross-border remittances (Western Union), Small Business and Specialised Finance Divisions. Prior to banking, Sisa held senior positions across various industries including, FMCG and Aviation.

An accountant by training, Sisa holds an MBA from GIBS and has studied an International Executive Programme from INSEAD in France and Singapore.

JOHAN HATTINGH

Doctor Johan Hattingh is the HOD Tourism and Events Management department at the Central University of Technology (CUT), Free State.

Johan graduated from the University of the Free State and Central University of Technology, Bloemfontein holding a doctorate in tourism and involved in academia for the last 10 years. He is a skilled and experienced senior lecturer in tourism development and marketing with a demonstrated history of working in the higher education industry. Prior to his career in academia he was the Tourism Manager of

Senqu Tourism (Lady Grey and Rhodes), Mangaung Tourism (Bloemfontein), ex-board member of Free State Gambling and Tourism board, tour guide and researcher at the Anglo Boer War Museum, Chair and partner in a tour operator company. He is a recipient of the Golden Shield Heritage awards: Heritage Education from the National Heritage Resource Agency (NHRA).

Contact information jhatting@cut.ac.za

THOMAS MÜLLER

Thomas Müller is the founder of Rainmaker Digital. He is actively involved in the African Hospitality and Tourism Industry and enjoys coaching and mentoring entrepreneurs.

He established a Hotel Management company in Namibia and successfully executed the turnaround of two hotels. He was involved in the building project of the new Strand Hotel in Swakopmund, Namibia and the Chobe Water Villas before he started his company, Rainmaker, in 2016 as an African TravelTech company.

Thomas lived and worked in eight countries when he was working with TUI and Thomas Cook. He has 37 years of experience in IT, Software Development, Systems Integration, Product Management, Consulting, and Business Development.

Thomas has been honoured with many awards for his technology inventions and its effective impact on businesses. He is a keynote speaker at hospitality and tourism conferences. He passionately advocates to keep more tourism spend in destinations through democratising technology. This technology promotes sustainable development for hospitality and tourism businesses throughout various destinations.

SARAH HABSBURG

Sarah Habsburg has spent the last two decades immersed in the tourism industry. Originally from the UK, a bachelor's degree in Hispanic Studies at Liverpool University took her to Chile for a year abroad and the country became her adopted home. First it was a base for tour leading across the Latin American continent, then as the birthplace of her own backpackers' hostel at the foot of a live volcano in the south. A masters in Responsible Tourism Management led her into customer service and marketing consultancy for hotels and hostels in Chile and beyond. A major family move from southern Chile to the Austrian countryside in 2019 allowed her to stand back and watch the impact this pandemic has had on the industry. This gave her the energy and inspiration to produce a series of resources aimed at small hotel, lodge, B&B and hostel owners and managers.

Sarah now consults in tourism resilience and achieving excellence in customer service and hopes that her resources inspire and promote sustainable action.

Info@sarahhabsburg.com, www.sarahhabsburg.com

DEREK MARTIN

Derek Martin, BCom, started his career in hospitality in 2006. He has held several senior property-based and corporate Revenue Management roles with regional and international brands, including one of Asia-Pacific's leading hotel management companies. In 2015 he moved to Asia-Pacific as Director of Revenue with one of the region's leading hotel management companies. Derek founded TrevPAR World, a global consulting firm specialising in Total Revenue Management. TrevPAR World does daily commercial, revenue, sales & marketing and social media management for over 50 hotels ranging from large international corporate brands to local independent hotels and lodges. Derek Martin is a member of the Stenden Advisory Board, University of Johannesburg School of Tourism Board as well as the aha Hotels and Lodges Executive Board and is currently involved with hotel strategies and strategy development at executive levels across a number of hotels on a daily basis.

Derek holds a Bachelor of Commerce degree in Hospitality Management from Stenden University's School of Hotel Management in South Africa. His passion for Revenue Management led to the establishment of a Revenue School and the development of the very first Revenue Management degree on the African continent, in partnership with Stenden South Africa.

ILLANA CLAYTON

Illana is the CEO of Travel Smart Crew and shareholder in TSC Africa. She has spent over 20 years in Inbound Destination Management and began her tourism career with Thompsons, before moving on to Travel Smart Crew.

Illana has worked in various specialist areas, including customer-facing positions in International Sales and supplier-focused positions in Product Procurement and Systems. In the last five years at Travel Smart Crew, Illana has changed its face and focus, adding to and bedding down its shareholder support functions and focus on product and supplier partnerships. She has also been instrumental in setting up a unique new business within the group, TSC Africa, and in addition to her role at Travel Smart Crew, overseas the daily management of TSC Africa.

Illana currently holds a seat on the board of SATSA and heads up the Western Cape Chapter.

KATE BERGH

She is the owner and Managing Director of Cedarberg Africa, a specialist DMC company for the last 25 years. The company focuses on high-end tailor-made private tours and safaris combining unique experiential travel with interesting excursions, soft adventure and gastronomy at boutique hotels and game lodges. She is also a director of Cedarberg Travel in the UK, an overseas wholesaler governed by the EU package travel regulations.

She owns Cederberg Ridge Wilderness Lodge and is a shareholder in a number of game lodges. Prior to emigrating to South Africa, Kate worked at Bain & Co, a management consultancy in London, and Glaxo Smithkline Beecham in International Strategy.

She has an MBA from Insead in France and an MA from Oxford University.

MANDISA MAGWAXAZA

Mandisa Magwaxaza lives in Port Elizabeth, South Africa. She manages P.R. and content for Mantis, a hotel management and development company representing luxury hotels, lodges and houseboats all over Africa. She is the Chairperson of the Eastern Cape Chapter of the South African Tourism Services Association (SATSA). Mandisa began her career in tourism while she was studying at Rhodes University and left her studies to pursue full-time employment at Kichaka Game Reserve where she started as a reservationist. She moved to Cape Town in 2010 and forged a career in content marketing over a decade of progression at the Cape Grace, Steenberg Hotel, Booking.com and Classic Portfolio. Mandisa is an active community builder who raises funds and resources for environmental and tourism education and experiences for schools in the townships of Motherwell and New Brighton in Port Elizabeth.

https://www.mandisamagwaxaza.co.za

DEREK NSEKO

Derek is a Ugandan born commercial pilot, aviation expert, analyst and the founder and managing director at iFly Aviation. He is also an aviation development ambassador for Africa at AviaDev.

Based in South Africa, iFly is a multi-national Africa-focused aviation solutions company. iFly conducts unique and broad social responsibility initiatives in Africa by spearheading transformation, promoting women empowerment and STEM programmes, and driving participation between government, big corporate and the wider industry, thus enabling the next generation of aviators.

Derek started his education in Uganda at Makerere University, pursuing computer science before deciding to chase his aviation dream. He started his Ab-inio training at the East Africa civil aviation academy before moving to South Africa where he completed his Commercial Pilot licence at Border Aviation in East London.

In 2018, he was named a global goodwill ambassador and iFly aviation was nominated as a finalist for the award of outstanding contribution to transformation in South African aviation at the inaugural civil aviation industry awards.

In 2019 Derek was awarded the Panache Man of Valour visionary award by Panache International.

Email: derek@ifly-global.com,

SIMPLIFLYING

SimpliFlying is the world's leading aviation marketing consulting firm. The team is 100% remote – based in Singapore, India, Spain, UK and Canada – providing airlines with a global and a 24/7 presence.

Since 2009, SimpliFlying has worked with an enviable list of aviation brands and also built a unique work culture that appeals to the disruptors in the industry.

The team is young, energetic and brimming with ideas on how to make airlines remarkable. These are ideas based on over eight years of working with over 80 aviation firms and analyzing over 500 airline social media pages every 60 days.

www.simplyflying.com

JOAN MIQUEL VILARDELL

Joan Miquel Vilardell (Masters in Business Administration and Ph.D & MSc in Civil Engineering) is partner at ALG – Africa & Europe Advanced Logistics Group, SAU.

He has more than 20 years of experience in managing and overseeing transport and transaction projects from international organisations as well as national ministries, being a renowned expert for Ministries of Transport in Africa, Europe, Eurasia and Latin America, and for the main International Donor Agencies. Currently, he is responsible for business development in the African market, having developed projects in more than 20 countries in the region in the last years.

He has developed a broad knowledge and has long-standing experience within the whole air transportation economy, having led numerous business/economic consulting and infrastructure financing projects. He is well-acquainted with Civil Aviation reforms and has a long track record in drawing Strategic Plans for several institutions and stakeholders within the aviation industry (CAA, airports, airlines and ANSP). In particular, he has extensive experience liaising with stakeholders associated with PPP project processes; he has been involved in three of the most recent airport transactions in Africa. Joan Miquel is currently working on market access and liberalisation of air transport in Africa.

TRINET

TRINET, the Tourism Research Information Network, is an electronic discussion forum that connects over 3 000 international tourism researchers and educators worldwide. Its purpose is to promote an open exchange of ideas, information and opinions that are relevant to tourism scholarship, including theory, research, education, policy development and operational matters.

PROFESSOR THEO VELDSMAN

Professor Theo Veldsman is a Work Psychologist, a Strategic People Effectiveness Advisor, and a former Professor and HOD at the Department of Industrial Psychology and People Management in the College of Economics and Business, University of Johannesburg (UJ.) He is currently a Visiting Professor at UJ and an Extraordinary Professor at the University of Stellenbosch Business School.

Theo is regarded as a thought leader in South Africa with respect to people management and the psychology of work. He has demonstrated his ongoing ability to proactively identify emerging people and leadership needs, and arrive at fit-for-purpose innovative solutions that are simultaneously theoretically and practically sound. He has a proven ability to move seamlessly between theory and practice, and vice versa. He has led the profession of Psychology and Industrial Psychology nationally as President on several occasions, and was awarded Fellowship status by the Society of Industrial and Organisational Psychology of SA (SIOPSA.) Theo was given an Award for Lifelong Achievement by the South African Board for People Practices (SABPP) in 2012.

SONJA BLIGNAUT

Sonja Blignaut, the founder of More Beyond, has been working in the fields of narrative and complexity since 2002. Before founding More Beyond, she worked as a consultant for PWC and IBM. She left the formal consulting world in 2004 and has since consulted locally and internationally with clients including the Sasol Group, Sasol Inzalo Foundation, Barclays, MMI, Anglo American, Harmony Gold, Nedbank, Standard Bank, Liberty, FNB, Gautrain Management Agency, PWC, IBM North America, DSTV, Eskom, SANParks, the Water Research Commission and many others.

Sonja trains locally and internationally in complexity and related topics at various academic institutions, including the University of Pretoria and GIBS. She is a sought-after speaker in a wide variety of industries and conferences, including Agile Summits, OD conferences and TedX Pretoria.

NAVLIKA RATANGEE

Navlika Ratangee is currently the Clinical Operations Director at ICAS SA. She is a clinical psychologist who has diverse experience in Human Capital Management, Behavioural Risk, Change Management, Managerial Consulting, Global Management Consulting, Leadership, Organisational Resilience and Organisational Strategy. She also has many years' experience in dealing with mental health in the workplace, and has consulted to many South African corporates in this regard.

Navlika completed her MBA at GIBS in 2016 with distinction, and was awarded the prize for top graduate on the programme. She furthered her executive education at Harvard Business School, regularly acts as a guest lecturer at GIBS, is a group mentor for PGDip and MBA programmes, and was selected by McKinsey & Company for their WomEnpower event, which aims to develop future female leadership for the global community.

KOBUS SCHOLTZ

Kobus Scholtz is the Founder and Main Member of The Human Equation where he and his team offer unique solutions to behavioural competence training. He has been involved in training & consulting since 1984 across diverse business sectors in mining, manufacturing, education, government and private enterprises in South Africa, and internationally in Singapore, Peru, Botswana, Mozambique, Namibia and Zambia. His success as a Business Owner, Consultant, Trainer, and Evolved Coach is underpinned by his entrepreneurial mindset.

Kobus obtained a Higher Diploma as an Education, Training & Development Practitioner. After spending the last two decades furthering and sharing his knowledge and skills around Leadership, Management, Behavioural Skills, and Mind Power, Kobus became especially inquisitive about various brain sciences to enhance brain performance, including the field of Neuroscience, mindfulness and personal growth. He then went on to study Evolved Coaching, NLP and Neuroscience.

Kobus may be contacted on kscholtz@xsinet.co.za

DAVID RYAN

David Ryan is the founder and CEO of Rhino Africa, Africa's leading online travel company. Established in 2004, Rhino Africa has distinguished itself as a pioneering company, continually seeking to disrupt a traditional industry by constantly exploring innovative approaches and new web technologies.

Rhino Africa was the pioneer in Search Engine Optimisation and Digital marketing in promoting Tourism products online. Rhino Africa has grown into a billion-Rand company welcoming over 17 000 guests per year across 30 source markets and 5 languages. One of Africa's largest B2C's and a R50-mill annual investment into online lead generation, Rhino Africa's success is attributed to a sustained, innovative approach to Digital Marketing in a rapidly changing digital landscape.

David takes particular pride in the social responsibility aspect of his business. Heavily involved with several NGOs that focus on conservation and education, David is also the IGLTA African Ambassador and has received multiple Pioneer and Entrepreneurial Awards through Rhino Africa's 15-year history. In 2017 David was voted a finalist in the Ernst and Young World Entrepreneur Awards.

GRANT RAPAPORT

Grant Rapaport grew up in Cape Town attending UCT and completing business, accounting and economics focused degrees and later split his career between Cape Town and New York over the last 15 years. After starting out as a Chartered Accountant and later CPA working primarily in the private equity and real estate space he moved into various finance, strategic and operational roles with Rhino Africa leading various areas of the business including sales, technology, marketing, finance and human resources in his roles as CFO and COO of the tour operating business. Grant also led the development and project management of the successful custom built 400 seat Rhino Africa HQ as well as 5 star Camissa House and Silvan Safari openings in recent years and the property portfolio's ongoing operations. Given his diverse background crisis management certainly falls into his ambit and COVID-19 has certainly been keeping him busy in 2020! Luckily Grant thrives on a challenge in the office and across the globe and has a passion for travel, wildlife and adventure and sharing knowledge and time with interesting people that all enrich the path along the way.

BEKS NDLOVU

African Bush Camps was founded in 2006 by Beks Ndlovu. Ndlovu is a professional safari guide who was born and raised in the village of Lupane on the outskirts of Hwange National Park in Zimbabwe. From the start of operations, Ndlovu's mission has been to operate a portfolio of luxury tented camps and lodges across Botswana, Zimbabwe and Zambia that reincarnate the fantasy of 'Old Untouched Africa,' while treating guests to authentic and adventurous professional guide-led experiences that can only be found in the bush.

He also started the African Bush Camps Foundation in 2006 which has since pioneered 72 community projects.

Prior to his African Bush Camps' involvement, Beks lead 'Beks' Safaris', a business he ran from 2001 to 2006. Prior to this, he cut his teeth in guiding while at Wilderness Safaris.

SHARON GILBERT-RIVETT

Award-winning writer, journalist and filmmaker. Tourism and safari consultant. Sustainable tourism expert. Conservationist.

Experienced consultant and award-winning writer and filmmaker with a demonstrated history of working in the African tourism industry and specialising in sustainable tourism. A recognised African safari industry expert and conservation commentator. Skilled in content production for digital platforms with considerable marketing acumen. Former tour operator and tourism industry stakeholder.

GREG SMITH

Upon completing his studies as a school teacher, Greg turned to the corporate world and by the age of 28 was appointed as the sales and marketing director of a listed company. A few years later opportunities arose for Greg to start his own business and since then he has never looked back. Now, with over 25 years of tourism-related marketing experience, he has established a firm foothold within the digital marketing segment. As the only South African nominee, he was selected to be part of the best digital marketing global awards in 2014. In 2015, two of his digital projects were selected for the top ten digital campaigns in South Africa. Currently Greg is fully immersed and involved in local and international tourism marketing which has led to a mutually beneficial friendship with Richard de la Rey as they share the same ethos of giving back to the tourism industry. As a result, their united efforts and passion for the industry have led to the formation of the ***#tourisminmyblood*** Facebook group. This initiative has blossomed into a credible platform of like-minded individuals supporting one another and providing tourism-related information during a time of unprecedented challenges brought about by the COVID-19 pandemic

RICHARD DE LA REY

After matriculating at Potchefstroom High School for Boys, Richard followed his passion for wildlife and spent four years as a guide at Londolozi Game Reserve. He then went on to fill various sales and marketing roles across several industries, at the same time completing his IMM Diploma in Marketing Management and an MBA in Strategic Marketing. In 1998 he founded Dark Giraffe Marketing, which brought together his love for tourism, marketing and sales. Dark Giraffe Marketing is a marketing consultancy and sales representation company, which represents a portfolio of 4- and 5-star game lodges and hotels across South Africa and Mozambique. During his travels he met Greg Smith and together they have worked on many projects, including co-founding #tourisminmyblood, which has brought together thousands of tourism professionals from around the world during an incredibly challenging time in the industry.

INTRODUCTION

On 2 March 2020, I wrapped up nine days of site visits at various lodges in the Sabi Sands Reserve and Wildlife Rehabilitation Centres in Mpumalanga and North West Province of Southern Africa. My journey introduced me to various lodge owners and their families. Each meeting left me humbled and eager to learn more about the communities and conservation initiatives they support. I was scouting for a suitable retreat destination for an intimate group of international travellers. Nineteen days later, on 21 March 2020, we entered lockdown Level 5 in South Africa. As a Key Account Manager for an overseas tour operator, I was finalising the logistics and planning for all our international student group travellers throughout 2019 and 2020. Suddenly, with less than three months short of their arrival, our biggest account, our student travel bookings, was cancelled. On 5 May 2020, I joined the ever-growing number of "unemployed" statistics due to 90% of the 2019/2020 revenue of our company being wiped out as a result of the COVID-19 pandemic. Up to that point, my career and account looked promising with future business expansion and exciting projects lined up. In an instant, I was sitting without a job and looking at starting all over again in a new world of uncertainty and unknowns. This was a whirlwind "adventure" that I would not choose for any of my clients and one I did not sign up for. Then again, neither did anyone else in the hospitality industry. Everything changed in the space of 2 months. In moments like these many thoughts cross one's mind: I chose the words of Buckminster Fuller, "we are called to be architects of the future, not its victims" to be my inner voice and daily mantra.

Before the emergence of COVID-19, the year 2020 looked promising for the tourism & travel sector in Southern and Eastern Africa. The reality is that everyone was caught off-guard, and every industry has been impacted financially and environmentally. However, the mental well-being of employees has also suffered greatly with many who now find themselves without employment. This in itself echoes catastrophic consequences for their families, communities and the economy for years to come. More specifically, this has never rung more true than for the vulnerable sectors supported by tourism, our communities, and wildlife conservation efforts on land and sea. All businesses that were not part of essential services throughout Southern & Eastern Africa, by law, had to close their doors at some point within a matter of days, being left in the dark and not knowing when operations would resume. Sadly, the reality for many establishments meant that their doors would never open again.

All industries are grappling with the uncertainty of, 'what now'? How do we manage this crisis? No one seems to have a definitive answer. With the introduction of lockdown level 5 and social distancing measures implemented by the government, COVID-19 has equalised the playing field for all in the value chain, whether involved in travel planning, transport, or accommodation and tourist sites. The industry embraced the only lifeline extended for business interaction outside of one's personal dwelling: technology. This brought on an avalanche of webinars and zoom meetings arranged from government and associations all the way to ground operations. It has become the norm to have suffered from webinar hangover and/or being zoomed out on a daily basis. These webinars and zoom meetings, along with other social media initiatives, have created a platform to keep the sector united with one purpose in mind: What can be done to help the industry survive and, by extension, assist business owners to retain their employees for as long as possible? However, the pursuit of answers and the perfect recovery plan is ongoing. There is an overwhelming call for ALL to reach out to each other and offer suggestions, strategies and solutions that will continue to build confidence and develop positive solutions and sustainable recovery plans offering the inspiration that we all need so desperately in these uncertain times.

Under the umbrella of Shongile: Future Self Journeys, I have taken on a project of editing and publishing a book in collaboration with a reputable publishing company, Knowledge Resources. By reaching out to various industry experts, thought leaders, business owners and ambassadors supporting conservation and communities, they kindly agreed to contribute articles towards this book called *Tourism, Travel & COVID-19: The New Narrative for Southern and Eastern Africa during a crisis vortex*. This book offers strategies, stories, insights, key objectives and actionable steps that businesses can start implementing now in preparation for when the flood gates open again, and we welcome back local and international guests in an atmosphere of feeling safe and secure whilst enjoying all that we have to offer under the name of hospitality. Future tourists planning on visiting Southern and Eastern Africa will benefit greatly from reading this book, as it will give them an opportunity to understand the impact that COVID-19 has had, and continues to have, on the industry as well as the solutions offered to make sure that their next visit is not only enjoyable but will give them peace of mind as regards health and safety measures, and what to expect when domestic, regional and international travel resumes again.

This book is not intended to be the "be all and end all", nor the final say or the last chapter, as the journey ahead is still uncertain and ongoing. It's not just a compilation of theoretical information but offers practical guidelines and actionable steps. This book also forms part of the New Narrative for tourism and travel. A Buckminster Fuller quote states: "You never change things by fighting the existing reality. To change something, build a new model that makes the existing model obsolete." If we are forced to accept the "new normal" then we are called to be the architects and create a new model for doing better business too. Are there any weak links in the existing model of the hospitality sector that need addressing and fixing, thus assisting and developing in building that "new model?" Trinet, which is an electronic discussion forum of over 3 000 tourism researchers and educators worldwide, articulated the following: "This re-birthing of tourism will require new sets of values, new paradigms, and a dramatic shift from the over-tourism, overconsumption and excessive greed that defined much pre-COVID-19 tourism."

This book hopes to assist in the re-birthing of tourism and thus form part of a 'New Narrative' for tourism and travel. I sincerely hope it serves as a launching pad for engaging in crucial conversations and assisting in ongoing efforts to create, enable, execute and optimise a new business model that will be beneficial for all in the value chain.

The book opens with a chapter by Mariette du Toit-Helmbold, previous CEO of Cape Town Tourism and well-known destination marketing and tourism thought leader, where she shares practical ways in which the sector can get through this crisis and build a more resilient and future-fit business. She has developed a bouquet of tourism support services to help small businesses navigate the COVID-19 crisis and become future-fit. She highlights two alternatives for moving forward: "We can get sucked into the depth of doom, or we can rise to the challenge and ride out this storm."

Sisa Ntshona, CEO of SA Tourism shares how SA Tourism is using this period to shape the sector for the future and developing a sector recovery strategy to prepare for the post-COVID-19 era. In this chapter he discusses the three strategic objectives central to South Africa's recovery which are re-igniting demand, rejuvenating supply and strengthening enabling capability. This strategy is inclusive of the entire sector: large, medium and small businesses.

In Chapter 3 Doctor Johan Hattingh: HOD and Senior Lecturer Tourism and Event Management at the Central University of Technology mentions that "between **five and seven years' worth of (tourism) growth will be lost** due to COVID-19" as estimated by the United Nations World Tourism Organisation (UNWTO). He also highlights the various initiatives and industry-specific protocols delivered by SATSA and other associations together with a recommended recovery plan and a plethora of tourism products which can aid in the *new growth* of tourism.

Chapters 4 and 5 focus on how Digital Transformation and Building Tourism Resilience is key to success and economic sustainability. Thomas Muller, the owner of Rainmaker, an African TravelTech Company, explains how companies can obtain new market opportunities by adopting new digital technology. He further elaborates on the different stages of the traveller's mental model each time they think of travelling. Sarah Habsburg, a dedicated content writer and having a Masters Degree in responsible tourism management has compiled a series of Tourism resilience resource files of which attracting domestic guests and social distancing measures form part of the narrative of this book. She shares how to communicate with your guests with the emphasis on when and what to say during the travellers' journey. She exclaims: "Selling peace of mind is your number one priority!"

Derek Martin, founder of TrevPar World, a global consulting firm specialising in Total Revenue Management discusses in his chapter how the revenue management functions have changed dramatically from revenue generation to stopping revenue bleeding now and in the future. He further elaborates on how revenue managers and commercial managers need to come to terms with and embrace a few fundamental realisations to the "new normal" of the industry. Not all is lost as he shares key elements that, if perfected now, will have a long-lasting impact on business, thus resulting in a competitive advantage when demand returns.

In Chapter 7 Illana Clayton CEO of Travel Smart Crew and a shareholder in TSC Africa together with Kate Bergh director of several businesses in the Tourism Industry which includes a DMC, a wholesaler and a product owner, discusses the traditional transaction flow and how open communication between every player is more important than ever before. An in-depth look at every stage of the transactional flow lends itself to recognize and adapt to areas that need improvement, thus creating a new model that will optimise the effectiveness and efficiency of the value chain. As mentioned by Illana and Kate "The pre-COVID-19 terms and conditions do not serve us as an industry, and certainly won't in our new future."

In Chapter 8, Mandisa Magwaxaza, a communications professional in the tourism industry as well as a creative writer, voice artist and thoughtful public speaker, discusses in her chapter a vision for South African townships. She mentions that the "majority of unemployed South Africans live in townships and what they need are economic opportunities". Township tourism lends itself to authentic experiences and community upliftment with opportunities to embrace the collaborative business environment and the individualistic business environment. She advocates towards the growth and perfection of the cycle of value-added services and consultation.

Chapter 9, 10 and 11 focus on the future of Aviation and the traveller. Derek Nseko, a Ugandan born qualified commercial pilot and founder and managing director at iFly Aviation, discusses the "Significant changes required to drive the African aviation industry to a more sustainable future" A report and infographic from Simplyflying create a visual representation of "The rise of sanitised travel – A day in the life of an airline passenger". In Chapter 11, Miquel Vilardell, Partner at ALG – Advanced Logistics Group, compiled a comprehensive Aviation briefing for the African Aviation industry. Discussing different recovery scenarios and expected recovery rate segments of African regions.

Chapter 12 discusses Trinet's Initial response to COVID-19. As the rebirthing of tourism takes new shape the "Travel and Tourism Transformed" platform shares resources for a new tourism future. Their second initiative that will be shared in this chapter provides a detailed "Tourism Crisis Recovery Checklist" for During the Event and Post Event. The checklist includes the following:

- Strategic Actions
- Operational Issues – Marketing, Finance, Staffing, Operations,
- Consumer Confidence – Community, Communications, Government Relations
- Policy
- Sustainability
- Integration and
- Tourism Crisis Management Strategies

How do you lead in a crisis like the one we're facing now? In Chapter 13, internationally recognised leadership expert, Professor Theo Veldsman, offers leaders a framework for understanding the current context, as well as leadership options to respond to the crisis, and the necessary capabilities and competencies to perform optimally. He advocates that in handling a crisis, leaders have to enable and empower as many members of the organisation as possible to handle the localised rollout of the solution, as well as the knock-on effects, fallouts and blowbacks of the crisis. He also highlights how important it is to craft a *real* solution, whatever the cost, and not a make-believe PR-friendly one that is aimed at smoothing one's own conscience and/or appeasing stakeholders.

Organisational development expert, Sonja Blignaut, highlights how we have believed for too long that we are in a nicely linear world, where we can manage change and create multi-year strategies… until now. The knowledge and skills that brought success in the past are now becoming irrelevant at a mind-bending pace. As situations are emerging and evolving from moment to moment, and as we fluctuate between chaos and compassion, Sonja offers various approaches to help us cope with this changing reality.

In Chapter 15, clinical psychologist and Clinical Operations Director of ICAS, Navlika Ratangee, makes the crucial point that this lockdown period is not a normal way of life, which may cause increased anxiety levels. She suggests that in order to reduce the negative effects of this on your mental health and cope better, it may be useful to try and see this as a different period of time in your life, and not necessarily a bad one, even if you didn't choose it.

Whenever humans face a crisis, like the current COVID-19 pandemic, the fight-or-flight response gets activated. Kobus Scholtz, Business Owner, Consultant, Entrepreneur,

Trainer and Coach explains that "Unless you are able to control the threat of your outer environment, the sub-branch of your Autonomic Nervous System, the Sympathetic Nervous System, kicks in. When you are feeling constant fear, anger, aggression, panic, etc. you are living by the hormones of stress due to the release of adrenal hormones. This results in stress not just seriously impacting your immune system, but you start to become a victim of your environment". In this chapter Kobus provides a practical guide on how to create a positive mental mindset. For creative juices to flow and give birth to recovery solutions for the tourism and travel sector and to have the stamina to implement these, taking care of what one can control, and having a positive mental mindset, are crucial if you want to have a chance of winning in the COVID-19 arena.

Chapter 17 introduces key factors and beliefs that will form the basis for any forward planning. The chapter discusses the treatment and vaccine horizon. It also asks: What factors are required for key source markets to recover, how the crisis plays out on structural differences between flights, beds and activities and tour operations, and highlights the recovery tailwinds? David Ryan, founder of Rhino Africa and Grant Rapaport, a finance professional, have been tracking and identifying the major trends and structural elements assisting them to compile a scenario assessment which is further discussed in their chapter.

African Bush Camps founder, Beks Ndlovu, takes you on a journey of what life on lockdown has been like for the company, community and conservation. Throughout his chapter one is left inspired and motivated by the example of leadership, resilience and a firm and unshakeable attitude to preserve livelihoods, upskill staff, the continued efforts exerted throughout the years to explore and support conservation initiatives together with the ever-growing community projects surrounding the African Bush Camps properties. "Although Zambia and Zimbabwe might not be rich in capital, they are rich in resources." Beks further mentions that "Our fauna and flora belong to the world and we can only continue to urge people to travel and help us sustain the means to protect it."

In Chapter 19 Sharon Gilbert-Rivett, award-winning writer, journalist and filmmaker, compiles the history, facts and the effects of the COVID-19 pandemic, which present enormous challenges for those caring for orphaned and injured wild animals in rehabilitation centres across South Africa, but at Care for Wild Rhino Sanctuary there's a confidence that both the wildlife and people they work with will weather the storm. A remarkable story that will inspire you to support the ongoing efforts of sustaining and protecting the vulnerable and compromised forms of life – our endangered wildlife and the people who make up our communities.

Greg Smith, owner at Zebra 360 Online Marketing and Richard de la Rey, owner at Dark Giraffe Marketing, founded the Facebook group #tourisminmyblood which has exponentially grown to well over 13 000 members within a very short period of time from its inception. Its rapid growth is testament to an industry coming together to support and share COVID-19 news, marketing plans and destination-related issues. In this chapter, you will get to hear how the platform is doing and what gems have come from it to help the industry.

The last chapter reminds us that our stories matter and that vulnerability is essential for innovation, creativity and change. We are all on a journey and along the way we get to pause, reflect and do introspection to hopefully never be defeated by our environment or our story which will, in the end, be the legacy we leave behind. As our industry comes together during this crisis vortex, we all yearn to rise above the setbacks and challenges we currently face. To stand tall with our shoulders straight, our chins up and the glorious African sun shining on our faces and healing our broken parts. But what is feared more than never rising again is to stand, unchanged, never having risen to fight for the change you want to see in the world.

Bringing this book to publication and continuing to press forward despite receiving numerous rejections to contribute as authors towards the book, at the same time homeschooling four children, employed, unemployed, cleaning, cooking and making sure my family is safe and healthy made me think about throwing in the towel on numerous occasions. But what kept me going was imagining the ecstasy and beauty of seeing the African dream through my children's eyes for the first time. Returning from site visits and sharing my experiences through my photos or trying to explain what a lion kill smells like is not enough for me anymore. I want my children to not just hear about the African dream, I want them to experience it for themselves and in order for that to be a reality, there is no such thing as giving up!

I would personally like to thank each contributor for taking the time to share their extensive expertise, capability and knowledge, especially at such a difficult moment in our history. I have no doubt that their contribution will help to steer the new narrative for tourism and travel in a more strategic and sustainable direction in the coming weeks. I would also like to thank Wilhelm Crous, Cia Joubert and the Knowledge Resources team for agreeing to guide and help me get this project off the ground and assisting me throughout the journey of editing and publishing my first book. I am forever grateful for your support.

A special word of thanks to my parents, Kobus and Elise, whose unconditional love and unwavering support has been the constant feature in my life. The kindest, most compassionate and selfless people I have the privilege of calling my parents.

To my dear husband, James Hebbard, for introducing me to a life of game drives, bush walks, sundowners and sunrises. An adventurous life with a storyline that movies are made of. My love affair with Africa and all her glory started with you and may we forever dream and be together for all eternity.

> *"A winner is a dreamer who never gives up"*
> —Nelson Mandela

Part 1

The power of collaboration and crucial conversations through visioneering

Chapter 1

Helping Brands Survive and Build Resilience

Mariette du Toit-Helmbold

When we were thinking about the biggest global trends impacting people's travel behaviour earlier this year, we could not predict that we would find ourselves in a global travel shut-down three months into this new decade.[1]

We knew that with economic pressures, political and social upheavals and a growing awareness of our contribution to climate change, the industry would face significant shifts. As travellers look for slower, more meaningful and deliberate ways to explore, we were expecting to see an uptake in people swapping over-crowded, mainstream destinations for more unique and unknown places.
Like many, we predicted that people would continue to travel in the new decade and that we can expect tourism to continue growing, albeit at a slower pace and with dramatic changes as to how, when and where we travel to.

Fast forward to 13 March 2020 and the world's most crowded destinations are deserted as governments ground planes, shut borders and scramble to deal with the biggest impact on our world in recent history — COVID-19.

A lot has been written about COVID-19 and the importance of flattening the curve with great tips shared on how to protect yourself and what to do when you think you are infected. Social media is awash with horror stories, fake news, bad news, hopeful accounts of recovery, humour in the face of panic and those who still think it's better to build walls than to build bridges and show a little humanity and kindness.

A crisis always reveals our true character

We should think about the impact our actions have on others. You might be young and healthy, eager to travel and exploit the many flight specials on offer or, like many, you are blasé about the seriousness of COVID-19. Others are not as privileged as you are and your ignorance and selfishness can fuel the spread of the virus and help to prolong its impact.

---

[1] Du Toit-Helmbold, M. (2020). COVID-19: A time to reveal our true character and resolve. Retrieved from: https://www.destinate.co.za/blog/entry/covid-19-a-time-to-reveal-our-true-character-and-resolve

Now is the time to be responsible and to think very carefully about the impact of our actions, our words and yes, our utterances on social media. Now is the time to show kindness, courage and strength of character. Now is the time to support those who are not as strong or capable and cannot see a way through the current crisis.

I have always been an optimist and an advocate for travel. Travel is a vehicle of peace and an engine of economic growth. It challenges perceptions, enlarges our world, expands our knowledge and understanding and brings the world closer together. It uplifts the poor and it is an easy entrance into the job market and formal economy, providing entrepreneurs and small businesses with an opportunity to compete for market share. It is the livelihood of millions with a value chain that extends much further than the hotel or visitor attraction. Without travel and tourism to sustain us, many people lose their ability to survive.

COVID-19 has put the spotlight firmly on the travel and tourism sector, highlighting not only just how significant its contribution is to the global economy, but also greater tolerance and opportunity for some of the most vulnerable in society. For many, travel is a basic human right and to take that away is to lose a part of your identity and your freedom.

One of the things I love most about working in travel is my global network of friends, who are like family. Our lives and careers have all been profoundly impacted within a matter of weeks. Whilst most of us will be severely inconvenienced and struggle financially over the months to come, many more will see their businesses fail and their livelihood lost. The economic impact of COVID-19 will be far-reaching.

Whilst we are confident that we will overcome this crisis and that we can return stronger and more resilient than before, we must realise that tourism and the world at large will never be the same again. The Corona outbreak will forever be a watershed moment.

There are no quick fixes and one thing is clear – our industry will be changed forever. Whilst many yearn for normality to return, normal no longer exists and neither will it be enough to safeguard us or help us recover fast enough when this crisis finally abates.

Nobody can predict how long the industry will remain under lock-down or to what extent we will be affected in the medium to long run. We need to make sure we can ride out this storm and be ready to operate in a post-Corona world.

Whilst we don't know for sure how things will pan out over the next few weeks and months, domestic tourism will most likely show the first post-lockdown green shoots of recovery. Many people are craving the simple pleasure of a walk in nature, a shared meal and a weekend away with a few of the people we've missed the most during lockdown. Many will want to reunite with loved ones in a beautiful and quite remote or secluded place, not too far from home.

It is clear now that the lockdown will be eased gradually allowing some businesses to start operating whilst the vulnerable remain in some sort of extended lockdown. Either way, once we are allowed to travel, even with restrictions, people will be keen to venture out. The ability to escape home with loved ones whilst being safe will be important and my prediction is that rural towns and getaways within an hour or two radius from cities will be popular as people yearn to get away and reunite with their loved ones after weeks of lockdown.

Rural destinations have an opportunity to position themselves as attractive post-lockdown destinations but will have to be well prepared and ready to offer the new post-lockdown traveller exactly what they crave. Destinations and the tourism industry will have to respond with very specific information, build trust with customers and assure travellers that their safety and health will be prioritised. Transparency, flexibility, added value and the ability to show potential customers exactly what they can look forward to through the use of virtual tours, visual content that tells a compelling story and shows how our trips support a value chain of small businesses will be important. Participants in the industry should prepare themselves to respond with suitable offerings and the kind of information required, organising themselves in networks that can offer one-stop travel information and experiences to travellers who are hesitant to jump from one platform to another. It is now all about simplicity, transparency and TRUST and the opinion and recommendations of friends and people we trust will become even more important.

The message for the next few months must be clear. Few countries offer its citizens the kind of experiences and getaways that South Africa does. We don't need to go far, we can stay home in South Africa.

Whilst travel will recover over time, it will forever be changed. The tourism industry will have to respond with very specific information, build trust with customers and assure travellers that their safety and health are prioritised.

Helping Brands Survive and Build Resilience[2]

Our world has been turned upside down by the Coronavirus and the COVID-19 outbreak. It calls for innovation and smart solutions as we brace ourselves for the economic and social impact of the outbreak and the much-needed social isolation.

I wanted to reach out to destinations and tourism businesses to share some of the practical ways in which we can help you get through this crisis and build a more resilient and future-fit business.
Some of you only know me as a strategist and previous CEO of Cape Town Tourism, but I am also an entrepreneur and a business owner navigating this crisis.

With 40 years of combined experience in tourism, business and crisis management, the Destinate team has helped steer destinations and tourism organisations through challenging times. In recent years we've worked with a number of multinational companies on strategic and crisis communication, helping them navigate some challenging situations.

We sat down and thought long and hard about what the industry needs now and how we could help businesses be more resilient now and successful in the long run.

There are no quick fixes and one thing is clear, our industry will be changed forever by COVID-19. We will not return to a state of normal. Normal no longer exists and won't be enough to safeguard us in the short term or help us recover fast enough when this crisis finally abates. So, what do we do?

You are most likely caught up in a panic wondering how your brand will survive this crisis. Potential customers may not be planning trips or visits right now, but now is the perfect time to create and strengthen the bonds your customers have with your brand. Now is the time to show your customers that you are ready to ride out this storm, even if you feel you are not, and that you will be there to welcome them back when they are ready to venture out again.

It is much harder to reach new customers than to keep current customers. If you go silent now, you will be forgotten by the time COVID-19 is under control.

We are all in this together and our customers want to hear how we are doing and what we are doing to get through this crisis. Let's show them our resolve and what they can look forward to from us in the near future. We will beat COVID-19, of that I am certain.

---

[2] Du Toit-Helmbold, M. (2020). Helping Brands Survive and Build Resilience. Retrieved from: https://www.destinate.co.za/blog/entry/helping-brands-survive-and-build-resilience

The travel industry has proven itself to be resilient, recovering valiantly from many global challenges and disasters over the past decades, showing continued growth despite adversities faced.

I know we will overcome this crisis. How we behave now and the choices we make can have an impact on how long the crisis lasts and how many people are affected.

It is time to adapt or our businesses will die and our industry will suffer for far longer than what it takes to get the pandemic under control. Rather than postponing or cancelling meetings at the last minute, opt and plan proactively for virtual meetings, check on each other, support small businesses and put together an army of solution finders that can get working on business resilience strategies and plans.

Destinate has been working with a number of tourism businesses providing business support and hosting a series of COVID-19 business sessions helping small businesses navigate the time ahead and prepare for a post-Corona travel era.

These include:

- Help develop a resilience plan to survive the next few months.
- Develop a communications and social media plan that will keep customers informed and hooked into your brand. You need a good 6 – 12 month content plan for implementation across your communication platforms, including direct consumer communication.
- Identify new business opportunities and income streams.
- Help you develop your recovery plan now so that you are ready and able to hit the ground running when the crisis abates.
- Assess your brand's online presence and customer journey to make sure it is fresh, user-friendly and effective not just for the weeks to come, but for the future.
- Assist you with social media management and content creation.
- Provide you with business mentorship and strategic marketing support over the next three months as you navigate your way through the crisis and into a new post-lockdown travel era.

In conclusion the predictions are that 2020 will mark significant shifts in the travel and tourism industry. Fuelled by technology and innovation, as well as a growing sense of responsibility and deeper connection with the people and places we visit, we are on the brink of a completely new travel era.[3]

---

3   Du Toit-Helmbold, M. (2020). Travel Trends Report for 2020. Retrieved from: https://www.destinate.co.za/blog/entry/travel-trends-report-for-2020

Previous years have been all about the perfect Instagramable destination, but as more and more travellers look for a slower, more meaningful and deliberate way to travel, big changes are afoot. Travellers are expected to swap over-crowded, mainstream destinations with more unique and unknown places. There is also a tendency to invest in experiences they can learn from or that will not have a harmful impact on host destinations.

With a whole new generation of travellers coming of age (Gen Z – aged 10 to 25), there is a mass awareness of climate change. The devastating fires raging in Australia and other recent natural disasters are putting the spotlight on the fragility of our world and the terrible impact humans have on the planet.

Besides the impact of COVID-19, the growing awareness of our contribution to climate change will be the single biggest catalyst of the transformation in travel behaviour. Simultaneously, it is also driving innovation through technology like never before. It might all be too little too late, but we can expect to see large and small travel operators and destinations make dramatic changes to their travel offering as consumers demand a more transparent and responsible travel experience.
There is no denying that people will continue to travel in the new decade and that we can expect tourism to continue growing, but one thing is sure, travel as we knew it is gone.

We can get sucked into the depth of doom or we can rise to the challenge and ride out this storm. I am ready and look forward to working with my global travel family and clients to find solutions that will not only build resilience, but will shape a whole new chapter in the travel and tourism sector.

For a full report on the Future of Wine Tourism please visit https://www.destinate.co.za/blog/entry/report-the-future-of-wine-tourism-webinar

Chapter 2

SA Tourism's strategic objectives for tourism recovery

Sisa Ntshona

Background of South African Tourism

South African Tourism is a Destination Management Organisation (DMO), the tourism arm of the South African government. Simply put, our job is to promote the country domestically and internationally, whether for leisure, business or events tourism. We employ over 200 people and operate in 44 countries around the world with 10 country offices.

As an entity of government, we have the responsibility to improve the lives of South Africans by contributing to the inclusive growth of the country's economy through tourism. Tourism injected R116,9 billion into the South African economy in 2018/19 through the direct spend of both international and domestic tourists.

The sector accounts for 3% of GDP, supports over 700 000 jobs and generates some R82.5 billion in direct foreign spend. 2019 saw 10,23 million international arrivals and 4,59 million domestic trips. African markets account for nearly three-quarters of arrivals but, however, less than half of the spend. Other international markets outside of Africa yield just 1,2 million arrivals, but a quarter of total spend.

Of course, with the COVID-19 outbreak, we cannot rely on past performance and statistics. It may take a while before we see pre-COVID-19 numbers.

COVID-19 impact on the tourism sector for Southern & Eastern Africa

COVID-19 has been devastating for the tourism sector around the world and South Africa and the rest of Africa are no exception. There will be a significant negative impact on our sector at all levels in the short to medium term.

Tourism was among the first sectors to immediately feel the impact of COVID-19 as we saw the cancellation of conferences, meetings and bookings. The sector came to a standstill when borders closed, and flights were suspended.

COVID-19 has been particularly devastating to small and medium enterprises. The reality is that many businesses will struggle to survive, and numerous jobs will be at risk.

As we go through this pandemic, which has an unknown end date, it will be important for tourism business to be informed and aware of all the initiatives put in place to aid their survival. Thus belonging to associations and industry bodies become a key source of information as this can be a very lonely period.

Tourism businesses need to consider that the post-COVID-19 tourist may have different needs and expectations. And they will need to cater accordingly.

How is SA Tourism coping and what strategies have been implemented during this period?

SA Tourism shares the sentiment that the priority now is saving lives and livelihoods. That is why we encourage people not to travel now to halt the spread of the pandemic. Encouraging people to stay at home goes against the grain of what we stand for. But we must make short-term sacrifices today for long-term recovery. We must all play our role to combat the pandemic and flatten the curve.

The travel restrictions cause uncertainty, disappointment and challenges for our sector. But we need to act responsibly to put our people first. If people do not travel and move around, the virus does not travel.

Despite the numerous challenges we face, I believe that there is always an opportunity in a crisis. That is why we are using this period to shape the sector for the future. To that objective, we are developing a sector recovery strategy to prepare for the post-COVID-19 era. Our strategy is inclusive of the entire sector – large, medium and small businesses.

As we develop this plan, coordinated response and collaboration are key as we develop what will be the blueprint on how we reposition ourselves domestically and internationally. To this end, we have hosted a series of webinars to gain insights and ideas from key thought-leaders in our sector, covering hotel chains, airlines, tour operators and other stakeholders. Sometimes it takes a crisis to bring about unity. Tourism is government led, but private sector fulfilled. We have to all work together as a sector in terms of pricing and geographic spread.

What is going to be the new normal post-COVID-19? We cannot assume that the sector will revert to what it was before the outbreak. The re-set button has been pressed. The sector has to re-shape itself. We must allow ourselves to be driven by what the traveller wants. We must be attuned to consumer trends and preferences.

The recovery plan is an appropriate instrument to influence the change that the sector wants to see.

What are the recovery plans/strategies after COVID–19 for the industry?

Government has implemented a risk-adjusted strategy to provide, a transparent methodology to guide decision making. Tourism has been allocated a rating on the risk-adjusted framework.

There is no silver bullet and there is no single answer. There are so many variables and permutations to be considered simultaneously. Thus everything is dependent on something else. COVID-19 presents us with ever-changing challenges and scenarios.

An emerging theme in industry engagements is that the recovery is going to be led by domestic tourism, then regional and ultimately international tourism.

We will emerge from this crisis as a strong resilient player in the global tourism market and will have the opportunity to once again celebrate our country as the home of humanity. The time will come when we can safely "visit each other and welcome the world".

There is no doubt about our competitiveness as a tourism destination. South Africa is geopolitically distinctive, possessing natural and cultural diversity that supports a globally compelling tourism proposition.

Initiatives set up during this period

This pause gives us an opportunity to address many of the sector and country's shortcomings and also implement new technologies that improve our global tourism competitiveness and enhance the visitor experience for tourists. This is also a period for us to address legacy challenges such as visa processing, as well as safety and security, whilst enhancing geographic spread so that the benefits of tourism go beyond the popular urban areas. This also allows us to address seasonality to ensure tourism activities happen throughout the year.

Therefore, we must ask ourselves: How can South Africa outcompete in a market where every destination will simultaneously be chasing recovery? By extension, "recovery" cannot just mean a return to pre-crisis levels, but rather the attainment of a growth trajectory capable of realising the country's vast tourism potential.

It is also clear that the pandemic's trajectory will differ across countries and regions. How and when key source markets and competitor destinations emerge will strongly influence the shape of South Africa's recovery. Our approach will consider when international markets open and may require looking at new source markets aligned to the global lift on travel.

While each set of conditions is unique, a number of features are common to successful recoveries. In this regard, I can single out the importance of market diversification. When core source markets become constrained, the focus must shift to growth territories. Successful recoveries often achieve structural change because they force investment into new regions while traditional markets return organically over time.

We must also give enough attention to barrier messaging. Since currency depreciation often accompanies a crisis period, recovering destinations have successfully combined price and value for money propositions with high-intensity, always-on communication campaigns focused on safety and security barrier messaging. Safety and security have become factors for all travel destinations across the world, in terms of health. This has somewhat levelled the playing field, and it is up to us to seize this opportunity. How South Africa carries itself out of it, will be a key differentiator.

Differentiation is a key feature. As we explore new source markets, new visitor preferences and product development opportunities will emerge.

While it is tempting to look for a single high-impact intervention – for example, ramping up marketing spends or dropping visa restrictions – such actions alone do not get the job done. A comprehensive strategy that takes all available levers into account and drives across-the-board reform is required. The successful features of the crisis response should be preserved for the recovery. Similarly, transformation initiatives that have long been planned should be accelerated.

There are three strategic objectives central to South Africa's recovery. These are re-igniting demand, rejuvenating supply and strengthening enabling capability.

Protecting the supply side of tourism

Without rejuvenation of supply, the sector will come under immense pressure as revenues and profits will fall. In this case, inbound mobility, specifically air access, will be a key point of friction. With many airlines unlikely to survive the crisis and much more certain to scale back operations, schedules will be reset, and new incentives and agreements will have to be concluded. The visitor experience mandate can be strengthened to curate an integrated service to visitors, including the provision of information, quality assurance, access to booking services, safety initiatives and crisis support.

There will be a focus on the visitor experience of South Africa to reposition itself as a standards regulator, complementing the market rather than trying to compete with it. Inbound operators, accommodation, and attractions and experiences should be invited into an industry-wide data-sharing agreement, deepening available market intelligence and facilitating coordinated efforts towards capturing new product development opportunities, supporting SMME growth, speeding sector transformation and revitalising state-owned tourism assets.

Re-ignite demand

How do we reignite demand? As the recovery unfolds, we are going to see varying rates of recovery in source markets. We must, therefore, conserve marketing investment. The marketing investment framework should be evolving to incorporate multi-year investment cycles to optimise scarce resource deployment.

South Africa as a travel destination is stronger on international travel, as opposed to domestic. This is an opportunity for us to build our domestic travel capacity, ensuring that we have a strong and robust domestic tourism sector.

Strengthen enabling capability

Key to our success is better inter-governmental coordination to secure tourist sites and prioritise visitor affairs which can bring credibility to efforts to shape international market perceptions of safety and security. We must also continue to relax visa and immigration policies and ensure ease of travel.

COVID-19 has generated solidarity within the industry. Successful coordinating forums established to navigate the crisis conditions should be preserved for the recovery. As we rebuild South Africa's reputation as a destination of choice, we must all explore collaborations and partnerships.

Chapter 3

Initiatives to support the tourism industry

Johan Hattingh

The South African Tourism context

The current COVID-19 pandemic has undoubtedly hit tourism as one of the most negatively affected economic sectors. In an assessment of the likely impact of COVID-19 on international tourism, the World Tourism Organization (UNWTO) expects that international tourist arrivals will be down by 20% to 30% in 2020 when compared with 2019 figures.[1] This is in stark contrast with recent international tourism figures which sustained year-on-year growth for eight consecutive years.[2]

This was also the case in Africa, more specifically South Africa. The number of tourists visiting South Africa exceeded ten million in 2016, indicating an increase of 12,8% compared to 2015. International tourists also recorded a 2,4% increase in visitation numbers during 2017, compared to 2016. In 2018 a total of 10 472 105 tourist arrivals was recorded which was a growth of 1.8% compared to 2017. South Africa derived 2.8% of its GDP directly, and 8.2% of its GDP indirectly from the travel and tourism sector whilst tourists spent more than R425-billion in 2018. Nearly 4.5% (726 500) of jobs directly and 9.2% of jobs indirectly in the country are in the travel and tourism sector.[3]

On 7 April 2020, the UNWTO declared that "Due to its cross-cutting economic nature and deep social footprint, tourism is uniquely positioned to help societies and communities affected return to growth and stability after COVID-19. Over the years, the sector has consistently proven its resilience and its ability not only to bounce back as a sector but to lead the wider economic and social recovery".[4] With these words in mind, the South African tourism sector, although reeling under the COVID-19 pandemic, are covertly optimistic towards possible tourism growth in the country. It

---

[1] World Tourism Organization (UNWTO). (2020). International Tourist Arrivals Could Fall by 20-30% in 2020. Retrieved from: https://www.unwto.org/news/international-tourism-arrivals-could-fall-in-2020

[2] World Tourism Organization (UNWTO). (2018). UNWTO Tourism Highlights: 2018 Edition. Retrieved from: https://www.unwto.org/global/publication/unwto-tourism-highlights-2018-edition, p4.

[3] National Department of Tourism Republic of South Africa (NDTRSA). (2018). Tourism Destination Planning Manual National Department of Tourism. Retrieved from: https://www.tourism.gov.za/AboutNDT/Branches1/Knowledge/Documents/Destination%20Planning%20Manual-%20September%202018.pdf

[4] World Tourism Organization (UNWTO). (2020). International Tourist Arrivals Could Fall by 20-30% in 2020. Retrieved from: https://www.unwto.org/news/international-tourism-arrivals-could-fall-in-2020

is widely agreed in the industry that international tourism will take at least a year to recover – it will be domestic tourism that will need to be stimulated, supported both by the private and public sector and embraced to be able to act as enablers of growth post-COVID-19.

South Africa has a plethora of tourism products which can aid in the *new growth* of tourism in the country. Within its nine provinces, natural, historical and cultural products abound. Joining these traditional types of tourist attractions are adventure activities in particular which are operating from a strong base. Examples of the strong tourist attraction base are arguably Table Mountain, Cradle of Humankind, wine tourism, big five game reserves (i.e. Kruger National Park), tourism routes like the Garden and Panorama Routes, Clarens/Golden Gate, UKhahlamba Drakensberg mountains, specific tourist areas like the Midlands in Kwazulu-Natal and the West Coast. Other tourist attractions include the annual sardine run, whale watching, shark cage diving, zip lining and white water rafting. Meetings, incentives, conferences, events (MICE) and sports tourism like the Comrades ultra-marathon and the Cape Town cycle tour also add to the wide variety of tourism activities and attractions on offer.

How has COVID-19 impacted Tourism?

The impact of COVID-19 is devastating to tourism, not only in South Africa but worldwide. The United Nations World Tourism Organisation (UNWTO) indicated on 27 March 2020 that they expected international tourist arrivals to be down by at least 20 to 30% compared to 2019 figures. This translates into a decline in "…international tourism receipts (exports) of between US$300-450 billion… This would mean that between five and seven years' worth of (tourism) growth will be lost to COVID-19".[5]

In South Africa, industry expert Onne Vegter, Managing Director of Wild Wings Safaris, indicated that the result of the current meltdown in tourism will have a total impact of arguably -11% on South Africa's GDP whist the total impact on employment will be down by at least 9.2%.[6] Gillian Saunders, Tourism and Hospitality consultant, indicated that "tourism represents directly (before the multiplier effect) some 8% of the retail industry in this country. Travel and tourism also drive sales of petrol, diesel and jet fuel (travel needs fuel), manufacturing of textiles (towels, linen, blankets, duvets, décor fabrics, uniforms), furniture, crockery, cutlery and kitchen equipment, cleaning products and guest supplies, services such as banking (credit card fees are a big element for banks), marketing, laundry, and security etc. And finally, agriculture. Not

---

5   UNWTO. (2020). International Tourist Arrivals Could Fall by 20-30% in 2020. Retrieved from: https://www.unwto.org/news/international-tourism-arrivals-could-fall-in-2020

6   Tourism Update. (2020). Letter to the editor: Government's flawed tourism model. Retrieved from: http://www.tourismupdate.co.za/article/199251/Letter-to-the-editor-Government-s-flawed-tourism-model

just the wine and beer industries but all agriculture....".[7] It is thus clear that tourism and the multiplier effect thereof, plays a very important role in the economy of South Africa and that the pandemic has a huge negative effect on the South Africa Tourism sector.

The nationwide lockdown has led to tourism coming to a complete halt in South Africa. In effect, this meant the total suspension of any travel and tourism-related activities with the resultant direct and indirect loss of income of role players in the industry – large and small. In reality, it means that many small business owners and SMMEs who are dependent on a steady flow of tourists for their income and livelihood has now been denied that income stream. Overheads remain, albeit that Government announced a number of relief programmes aimed at tourism. In effect, the tourism industry is experiencing many businesses closing down, or at best, downsizing. Furthermore, the opening of the tourism sector is only expected to be in a very late stadium of 2020, making it even more difficult for tourism businesses to survive without tourists.

How is the Tourism sector coping and what strategies have been implemented during this period?

Stemming from the pandemic the current consensus is that the tourism industry as a whole is more inclined to work together in unity to overcome the immense problems facing the industry. It is only through **collaboration** that Southern Africa as a destination can survive **and thrive** in the future. An industry organisation like Southern African Tourism Services Association (SATSA) took the lead in gathering relevant information and played a leading role in dissemination of tourism information to the industry. Although it's an industry member organisation, in the time of crisis it shunned its "members only" directive and jumped on board, representing the whole of the industry. This initiative seemed to gain the respect and admiration of the industry at large – in particular if one looks at social media comments about their role and on their website itself.

SATSA started with a number of webinars which quickly became popular and were enthusiastically supported by industry. Through the role they played, the Tourism Business Council requested SATSA to provide industry-specific protocols regarding the following six categories:

1. Tourist Transportation
2. Accommodation

---

[7] Tourism Update. (2020). Little awareness of tourism's economic effect, says Saunders. Retrieved from: http://www.tourismupdate.co.za/article/199269/Little-awareness-of-tourism-s-economic-effect-says-Saunders/17

3. Tourism Products and Attractions
4. Education
5. Volunteering
6. Guide Training (www.satsa.co.za)

Through a series of webinars for industry, the protocols were identified by industry role-players and are thus the voice of the industry. It is believed that these proposals will play a meaningful role in the outcome of industry-specific protocols for the future post-COVID-19.

In a similar vein, South Africa Tourism (SAT) acted on the pandemic and fulfilled its mandate as representing the industry at large. A series of three webinars were held named: **Tourism Industry Recovery Plan by South African, Travel and Events**, and various industry leaders and role players participated as panellists. The feedback of not only the panellists but also of other participants via Q & A were used to assist SAT in a proposed recovery plan.

The role of social media cannot be ignored and as such, the industry rallied behind the #tourisminmyblood initiative. Within a very short space of time, the Facebook group grew to 10 000 members. Its main focus is on COVID-19 news, marketing planning and destination-related issues.

Some other strategies referred to by industry role-players are Virtual Regional Product Exposure (Mega Fams, etc.), Virtual International Product Exposure and Destination positioning in a post-COVID-19 world. These strategies are aligned with the needs of tourism product owners to be heard and more importantly, to be seen by prospective tourists. It's also important to note that the tourism product owners not only focuses on individual tourists but are also acutely aware of the role that Destination Marketing Companies (DMC) and Destination marketing organisations (DMO) play in the tourism value chain. DMO's and DMC's also have to revaluate their role in the tourism value chain and re-invent their role post-COVID-19. This can mean changing of commission structures, new ways of doing business i.e. shifting of online presence and targeting new channels and markets. It can also mean that profits and not growth, are probably going to be more important. A re-think of tourism will take place where quality will be more important in the future.

The rebuilding of companies from a low base will affect everyone, which means that everyone will have to start at ground level or start over post-COVID-19. Thus, taking care of customers now by businesses, will assist in keeping those customers. Some companies can even decide to go into hibernation now and then restart with more focus, and a much lighter company. Although this would mean the layoff of personnel, a refocus will assist companies to re-strategise and be ready for when tourism starts to grow eventually. It can even lead to the establishment of micro-entrepreneurs which can create unique experiences for the sector. However, the likelihood is that a large number of the population will not be able to travel beyond their own province for a long while, never mind internationally – we are just consumers – we need to add value to experiences.

What are the recovery plans/strategies after COVID–19 for the tourism industry?

It is generally expected that domestic tourism will start to grow first, although from a very low base. This will only start to happen when travel restrictions – both within provinces and then later across provincial borders – are lifted. A gradual phased-in Tourism Recovery Strategy regarding the reopening of tourism are being envisaged and proposed by the Tourism Business Council of South Africa (TBCSA). The data-driven Tourism Recovery Strategy advocates for a phased reopening of international tourism to South Africa as soon as September 2020. "As we see elsewhere in the world, the opening of domestic tourism is the first phase in ensuring that tourism starts to open slowly and leads the way in launching the various components in the tourism value chain. Business travel is the largest component in the formal travel industry. Its reopening provides us with an opportunity to see how we can further open domestic leisure within the context of the protocols in the very near future," explains Tshifhiwa Tshivhengwa, CEO of TBCSA."[8]

Luxury tourists, those frequenting upmarket establishments i.e. private big five game reserves, are expected only to start arriving end 2021. There is even an opportunity for new opportunities like adventure activities because of smaller outdoor groups and thus less chance of being infected.

People might travel less – therefore they will seek deeper enjoyment. Travellers will be more focused on Value for Money, and what they will get for their hard-earned money. During this challenging period, it's time for destinations to pause, hit the re-set button and re-think about smart, responsible tourism development – quality over quantity, with focus on responsible impact by respecting and contributing more to locals, all while travellers have a higher value transformative experiences. *Over tourism* might become something of the past as customers seek more personal space, immersing themselves in the experience and overall having a deeper tourism experience. The reason for travel will thus change significantly and the value proposition of each company will become far more important than before.

---

8   Tshivhengwa, T, (2020). TBCSA presents calculated, driven and gradual re-opening of tourism to parliament's tourism portfolio committee. Retrieved from: https://www.satsa.com/tbcsa-lobby-for-gradual-re-opening-of-tourism-to-parliaments-tourism-portfolio-committee/

Actionable steps and guidelines for companies

Check your business model, identify new products and identify new customers. Re-invent the supply chains, equitable spread of beds and more sustainable businesses. Source new markets, do introspection into company and/or businesses. How do we work with each other? Smaller companies need to start working together more.

An important post-COVID-19 factor will be the ease of doing business in the new reality. At the moment aspects such as the National Public Transport Regulator (NPTR) and obtaining operating licenses for coaches continue to be a huge stumbling block for businesses. If the red tape and backlog regarding transport permits can be negated, it will be a huge boon to tourism. The system needs to allow for a turnaround time of 60 days for accreditation applications, and 24 hours for new operating licenses for accredited operators (without a board hearing or gazette advertising).

Visas are also a major hindrance as visas fall under the Dept of Home Affairs, and the NPTR falls under the Dept of Transport, making collaboration to the benefit of tourism quite difficult in the reality of today. Although some relief was experienced recently, it remains one of the challenges for the industry and the tourism industry is of the opinion that further relief and the speedy approval of visas are paramount if the industry wants to grow.

The importance of air access needs to address the reality of SAA not continuing to operate after COVID-19 – and therefore, actively pursuing other airlines to fill the gap left by SAA and thereby ensuring that our source markets can get here in sufficient volume, is imperative. As a long-haul destination, we thus need more open-air access and cheaper rates. Airlines have another important role to play and that is to test pax (passenger) before they depart. It is believed that this pre-screening will become the new norm for air travel.

Travellers will want to know that they are safe to travel. The current situation provides the opportunity to re-look safety and security in the tourism sector and address hotspots accordingly. This leads to the promoting of brand SA. It must be aligned with the post-COVID-19 strategy of South African Tourism (SAT) and feed into those of the different provinces. It must be tourism industry-led! Not government-led.

Some industry role players identified responses to the health fears of the consumer. They propose that tourism can: reduce numbers on a game drive/touring vehicle; ensure day tours are operated on a larger vehicle to allow distancing; provide incentives for booking private services; offer midweek tours and weekend city tours;

provide increased restaurant floor space per head and replace buffet (or supplement) with à la carte options.

The following is a list of handy websites and Facebook pages. It's by no means comprehensive but we endeavoured to create a list of info that is easily accessible and of beneficial value to tourism product owners.

www.tourism.gov.za
www.southafrica.net
www.satsa.com
www.brandsouthafrica.com
www.tourismupdate.co.za
www.wesgro.co.za
www.supportbusiness.co.za
www.unwto.org
#VirtualTravelSA
#Tourisminmyblood
#TravelTomorrow
#StrongerTogether

Adding to the resource list of website to visit is:

https://cdn.nowmedia.co.za/NowMedia/TU/20200407SACovid-19ReliefSchemesSummaries.pdf

The South African Government has announced a number of relief funds, loan packages and other measures to businesses affected by the COVID-9 pandemic.[9]

- The special support has been implemented for small, medium and micro enterprises (SMMEs) as the COVID-19 Business Rescue Assistance (COBRA) and the South African Future Trust (SAFT).
- SAFT is administered by Oppenheimer Generations Trust and is an interest-free, five-year loan exclusively to pay permanent employees. Currently, this scheme is limited to clients of ABSA, FirstRand Bank, Nedbank, and Standard Bank.
- COBRA offers free daily and weekly webinars to share information to guide business leaders. The COBRA War Room will provide support to businesses to avoid business rescue at pro bono or discounted fees.

---

9   Tourism Update. (2020). COVID-19 relief – what the SA govt is offering. Retrieved from: http://www.tourismupdate.co.za/article/199253/COVID-19-relief-what-the-SA-govt-is-offering/5

- The South African Revenue Service has implemented COVID-19 Tax Relief for tax-compliant SMMEs. This can be a tax subsidy to employers of up to R500 per month for the next four months for employees earning below R6 500.
- Alternatively, SMMEs will be allowed to delay 20% of their employees' tax liability over the next four months and a portion of their provisional corporate income tax payments, without penalties or interest.
- Details of all the relief funds, loan packages and other financial measures the Government has announced can be retrieved from https://cdn.nowmedia.co.za/NowMedia/TU/20200407SACOVID-19ReliefSchemesSummaries.pdf

Part 2

Building a New Model: Acceptance, Adaptability and Opportunity

Chapter 4

Rainmaker: Digital Transformation is key to success and economic sustainability

Thomas Müller

Background of the company

As a social enterprise, it is Rainmaker's passion to keep more tourism spend in destinations for economically sustainable tourism development through the democratisation of technology. Fully aligned with the UNWTO Digital Transformation Strategy and contributing to the Tourism Sustainability Goals.

Rainmaker democratises technology that only large global organisations can otherwise afford. We make this technology available to the 200 000+ emerging, small, medium, independent hospitality, and tourism providers in Africa in an inclusive public-private partnership and freemium business model.

More tourism spend in a destination contributes to more and quality education, more and decent employment and work conditions, mitigates youth and women unemployment, and drives entrepreneurship for more sustainable and inclusive tourism development.

Rainmaker has been awarded for the impact provided – by the HSMAI (Hospitality Sales and Marketing Association International) with the Golden Adrian Award and from the World Tourism Forum Lucerne for its Destination impact in 2018 as well as with the African Tourism Leadership Award in 2019 and from the World Tourism Market 2020 in Cape Town.

How has COVID-19 impacted tourism development?

#StayHome, for now, is happening all over the world. The hospitality and tourism industry has been hit first and the hardest. The Corona crisis, the travel ban, the closing of borders, the lockdown, and all the other measures governments globally put in place, will change everything in this industry forever. Nothing will be the same as it was before. Almost the entire sector has lost 100% of its occupancy and revenues overnight while at the same time being pressured from online travel agents and tour operators to cash refund cancellations. It could not be worse.

Nobody knows for how long this situation is to continue, or when and how domestic, regional and international business and leisure travel will return. As it looks now, especially the emerging, small, medium and independent hospitality and tourism businesses (SMMEs) are fighting about pure survival.

This situation has the potential to change the hospitality and tourism landscape forever and it would be a disaster if the great variety, character, and personality of the many owner-managed hospitality and tourism properties would disappear while franchise and large global chains would take over as they seem to have the financial resources.

However, in a couple of months, every person and every business in the hospitality and tourism industry, whether it is an Airline, a Hotel, an Activity Provider, a Car Rental or Tour Operator, or Online Travel Agents will have to start again at the very same race line.

GROUND ZERO. This is an unprecedented opportunity for all of us.

How is your company coping and what strategies have been implemented during this period?

As a Travel Technology provider entirely focused and passionate about the hospitality and tourism sector in Africa, we have been inundated with emails, messages, and phone calls on all channels from panicking customers who were entirely overwhelmed by what to do.

At the same time, about 90% of our customers have been instantly unable to pay our services and long-term contracts. Many of them wanted to cancel, others wanted to stay, but for now, can't pay.

The first four weeks have been challenging on an unprecedented level never seen before and all our resources have been shifted and allocated to assist and help customers on how to deal with cancellations from direct customers, how to withstand the bullying approaches from online travel agents and certain inbound operators requesting instant cash refunds for cancellations instead of free rebooking or voucher options and whether or not they should close the business for now entirely and if so, what to do with the employees. Obviously the most important question asked is: "How do businesses cope financially and when will customers be coming back?"

As you can imagine, we could advise and assist them with many but not all of the topics. In the meantime, we have thought about how we could assist our customers even more, addressing their financial issues but also how we could retain them as customers.

As a social enterprise passionate about our industry, we have provided all our customers with a complete three months free of charge period while all services will be rendered as usual. Being a startup ourselves we could only do this by cutting costs in our own business, that is by moving team members from colocation workspaces in Windhoek, Cape Town, Johannesburg and other locations to the home office already on March 13.

At the same time, the entire team agreed to a reduced salary and the management team waived their salaries entirely. Also, we asked financially savvy or enterprise customers to pay for a quarter in advance to mitigate our pledge to the many emerging, small and medium sized businesses now in distress.

At the same time, we have contributed our technology to ubuntubeds.org who collaborate with accommodation providers of all kinds to enable them to manage the bookings of either free or very affordable accommodation for health and frontline workers in the direct vicinity of hospitals.

As entrepreneurs, and despite all the challenges everyone in this industry is currently facing, we, however, see the CRISIS as a once in a lifetime opportunity to change the hospitality and tourism industry for the better. We have attended numerous Webinars from all over the world, contributed to articles, videos, podcasts, and even this book to POSITIVELY contribute and show everyone in this sector the opportunities ahead.

What are the recovery plans/strategies after COVID–19 for the industry?

The word CRISIS means DECISION. And the industry is about to take tough decisions if we want to get out of this COVID-19 situation in a better way or with a better outlook than we have all entered it.

This unique opportunity and time is NOW while the entire travel, hospitality and tourism industry has reached the level of zero occupancies and revenue.

In a couple of months, and nobody knows whether this will be 3, 6, 9 or more months, everybody will be starting at the very same starting line. GROUND ZERO.

Since Online Travel Agents and others have become market-dominant (e.g. booking.com, expedia.com) and the long tail traditional value chains (e.g. the collapse of Thomas Cook) are no longer sustainable, Hotels have become very much dependent and have not only paid about 60% to 80% of their profits to such value chains, but have also handed over the customer ownership to those value chains. For quite some time this has no longer been sustainable for Hospitality and Tourism businesses, and therefore the entire destination.

However, since the Hospitality and Tourism Industry has been very slow for the last 10+ years in the adoption of new digital technology and to obtain new market opportunities while the customer behaviour changed to digital, Online Travel Agents took over and Hotels around the world have become dependent and have been paying a huge toll. In fact, in many cases, an OTA makes more money with a booking than the accommodation or activity providers themselves while hosting the guest, providing breakfast, etc.

When #TravelTomorrow takes place within a couple of months, it is high time to make sure that destinations and their hospitality and tourism businesses do not enter the same trap again.

Now is the time for hospitality and tourism businesses and destinations to take back the control of their visibility, their digital presence and reputation, their marketing communication and advertising, and, most importantly and foremost, their distribution.

There is absolutely no need for them to again lose the direct contact to their source markets and guests, to once again be dependent on foreign and market-dominating value chains where most of the tourism spend is not being contributed towards the destination, its businesses and people, but to global conglomerates having no interest in the destination and their suppliers, but only their own balance sheet and shareholder value.

Now is the right time for all suppliers such as Hotels, Lodges, Guesthouses, B&Bs, Activity Providers, In-Destination Tour Operators, together with Tourism Authorities and Associations in Destinations to make sure the sector is fully supported and enabled to keep more tourism spend in the destination and to take back control for sustainable tourism development.

Digital Transformation is the ideal way to achieve just this. Now is the time to engage and to create and provide the local capacity, education and training, democratising of the respective technology, to enable all hospitality and tourism businesses in the destination, and to take back control for sustainable tourism development when all are starting at ground zero again.

The UNWTO Digital Transformation Strategy provides a great framework and platform for their member states, destinations, and the hospitality and tourism industry globally.

Rainmaker Digital as a social enterprise, focusing on a positive impact through tourism, has invented and deployed the VISTA Destination Network. This is an Open Platform and Ecosystem democratising technology to seamlessly integrate all hospitality and tourism businesses in destinations. It was always our vision to keep more tourism spend in destinations for sustainable tourism development and to contribute to the Sustainability Goals.

As the largest industry in the world, tourism is everything and everything is tourism. Only with a sustainable and healthy hospitality and tourism sector, communities, regions, and its people, as well as many other industries, are positively impacted as tourism directly contributes 1 out of 10 jobs and about 10% to the GDP globally.

We believe that the time for #TourismGetsEnabled is now.

What initiatives are being set up during this period that you would like to promote or bring attention to?

We believe that now is the time for destinations and its hospitality and tourism businesses to undergo a digital transformation. The potential traveller is already digital to a large extent while the destinations and the hospitality and tourism industry have not yet adapted to provide the customers with what they want, demand and desire when looking, booking, experiencing and sharing about a journey. Each potential traveller goes through the traveller's mental model every time they think of travelling. The travellers' mental model consists of the stages below:

- **Dreaming** - Approximately 70% of all travellers are inspired through the internet in so-called micro-moments. Their next journey or destination is the direct result of any digital influence.
- **Planning** - Around 80% of holiday-makers use the internet as their main information source for planning their travels.
- **Booking & Paying** - Close to 60% of potential travellers book through the internet.
- **Experiencing** - Over 60% of travellers are using smartphones or tablets during their journey.
- **Sharing** - More than 50% of travellers share their experiences while they are travelling.

Currently, destinations and their hospitality and tourism businesses force a large number of potential travellers who otherwise would book directly with Online Travel Agents or through a high street travel office, while they are not genuine customers of those value chains in the first place. This is what Rainmaker is changing for destinations and its hospitality and tourism businesses.

Digital transformation is key to success and economic sustainability

In Africa, some 200 000 hospitality and tourism businesses exist. Only 15% of them are enabled by any kind of technology to run their business and only 10% have a decent and coherent digital presence. The majority has remained on pen and paper or is using Excel or such to run their business, not participating in the digital travel world and suffering from the above-mentioned problems.

A solution was required to "fix" the problem by focusing on the following key elements:

- Seamlessly connecting all hospitality and tourism businesses, amongst stakeholders in a destination, with each other
- Providing relevant rich content such as Images, Videos, 360° Virtual Tours, Descriptions, Facilities, Amenities, Policies, Room types, Rates, Terms & Conditions, etc. as well as real-time booking, and payment availability to all stakeholders in a simple unified way, thus providing instant gratification to their potential travellers
- Gaining back control of the visibility, reputation and distribution for the entire destination and its hospitality and tourism businesses in order to become less dependent on market-dominated online travel agents and unsustainable traditional value chains
- In conclusion, it is vital that WE KEEP CORE TOURISM SPEND IN THE DESTINATION. No longer do hospitality and tourism businesses need to give away 60% to 80% of their profits to the above-mentioned value chains.

The VISTA Destination Network and the 5 Stages of Success holistic methodology and managed services have been designed to offer all of the above, thus helping and assisting the hospitality and tourism businesses to confidently make the digital transformation leap and take their businesses to new heights.

Chapter 5

Resilience Action Planning: Attracting Domestic Guests & Social Distancing Measures

Sarah Habsburg

Social distancing measures

At the risk of sounding repetitive, the new marketing message for the travel industry is selling peace of mind. In these post-COVID-19 days that means assuring safety through the recommended social distancing measures.

How you communicate with your guests is crucial at this time. Despite it being counter-intuitive in an industry that is built on human interaction, there are creative ways to make your social-distanced service more personal.

One way to do this effectively is to send personalised digital messages before, during and after check-in. Research shows an astounding 98% open rate for SMS and only 20% for emails. Think about how you react when you receive an SMS as opposed to a WhatsApp or an email. SMS messages are read a lot faster than other methods of communication.

There is no reason not to give it a go. If the client does not read it then you will not know, just the same as if you sent an email. If the client is bothered by it, he/she will ask you nicely to refrain from sending more. If they reply, you have hit the nail on the head. It also makes sense to communicate important information to your guests in this way because you should have removed the booklets, leaflets, and hotel information sheets out of the bedrooms during this period anyway.

Here are some ideas of SMS content:

Pre-arrival message: Acknowledges their check-in dates and times and adds that the measures that you have taken to create safety and calm can be found at your webside. This will work super well if you create a dedicated page on your website containing COVID-19 information.

On-Arrival Message: Welcome your guest, share the property rules, WiFi password, parking information and highlight the COVID-19 measures such as using the hand sanitisers. Remind them they can collect a free bottle of hand sanitiser at reception that they can refill during their stay for example.

Mid-Stay Message: Ask if there is anything they need and if they would like any assistance in planning the rest of their time with you.

Post-Check-Out Message: Ask for their feedback about the service in general, and any suggestions and comments they may have about the new COVID-19 safety measures.

General Social Distancing Measures

Require that staff wear face masks or install protective shields between areas of guest-staff interaction. If guests are also required by local regulations to wear face masks in public areas, be sure to communicate that clearly before and during their stay. If you are concerned that your staff wearing masks affects the personal touch inherent to the business, consider printing photos of their smiling faces and pin them onto their uniforms.

Post your property's COVID-19 measures in reception, along with signage indicating the recommended public health guidelines (social distancing, hand washing, coughing into arm etc). The more prepared you look, the more trust you will generate.

Provide hand sanitiser dispensers throughout the hotel, particularly in all high-traffic areas.

Create social distance markers in your public areas to control check-in lines and general crowding.

Reconfigure your restaurant, lobby and lounge seating to maintain appropriate spacing between seated guests.

Remove unnecessary clutter from your check-in area. It will be easier to clean and will look much more hygienic.

If you have high-traffic check-in periods during the day, consider contactless and keyless check-in via the use of mobile apps. If you choose to continue to receive guests as normal, place their keys and anything else relevant to their check-in in a (sanitised) basket away from where you are standing. You can still talk them through the normal check-in information from behind your reception desk.

If you normally ask guests to complete a check-in form, consider sending this by email in advance, or leave it in the room for them to complete.

Allow guests to opt out of everyday housekeeping. You could even offer an incentive with a 5 dollar/euro voucher for your café/restaurant. They will for sure spend more when they redeem it.

For room service requests, give guests the option of contactless delivery, where items are left outside the door.

Ask guests to book in to use the sauna and jacuzzi. Social distancing markers should be placed on floors in pools, shower areas and spas. All massage services should be suspended unless specifically requested by the guest and agreed to by the massage therapist.

Breakfast Social Distancing

This will affect almost every type of property to some extent. These are the WHO recommended guidelines for ensuring adequate social distancing in areas where food is served:

> *"Whenever possible, it is recommended to have a maximum of 4 persons for 10 square metres. Tables shall be arranged such that the distance from the back of one chair to the back of another chair shall be more than 1 m apart and that guests face each other from a distance of at least 1 m".*

If your breakfast area is not large enough to do this, consider allotting specific times for breakfast to guests based on corridor, room numbers or check-in order. Buffet breakfasts should not be offered during this time. Consider taking breakfast orders the night before so the selection can be prepared in the kitchen and served directly to the table when the guests arrive. An alternative is to serve breakfast directly in rooms.

Make sure your kitchen and restaurant staff have all been trained regarding the additional hygiene measures that you put in place. They must be ready to answer any questions your guests may have about how COVID-19 has affected the breakfast service. It is also a good idea to make sure that all staff know how to contact the designated senior staff member who can answer any demanding questions from guests.

If you have always harboured a secret desire to omit breakfast from your offering, this is the perfect time to do it. Consider teaming up with a local café on your block and shout about the community spirit that the situation has generated.

As previously mentioned, it is critical that you communicate these changes to your guests before arrival. Selling peace of mind is your number one priority!

> "Nothing in life is to be feared, it is only to be understood. Now is the time to understand more, so that we may fear less." - *Marie Curie*

Building Tourism Resilience: Attracting Domestic Guests

> "I take to the open road, healthy, free, the world before me." – *Walt Whitman*

A recent survey by the International Air Transport Association (IATA) found that 60% of people questioned would wait for two months before booking flights after COVID-19 is contained – 40% said they would wait for at least six months.[1]

It is clear that domestic travel will be the main market for the accommodation sector over the coming months. Until people have clear information about the changes to air travel as they knew it, it is likely they will hold off booking, at least for now. Let's take a look at some ways to target your national market:

> First, do some **research on your past customers** and find out which cities or regions they came from in the last couple of years. You should have this record in your PMS system, or maybe in your email database. You can also get a historic overview into this by using Google Analytics data to track where people were located in your country when they viewed your website.
>
> **Update and modify the geographical location** on your Google and/or Facebook Ads. Pause or reduce spend for now on ads that are targeted to the international market and pool your resources into targeting the locations where your national arrivals come from. Spend a little more on the cities that are a little further away from your location but still within comfortable driving distance. Those are the clients who will potentially stay the longest. Create a specific offer for national customers on OTA sites that offer

---

1   Siret, M. (2020). Coronavirus: What global travel may look like ahead of a vaccine. Retrieved from: https://www.bbc.com/news/world-52450038

Geotargeting, such as Booking.com. Geotargeting allows you to offer discounts or add-ons, preferably the latter, to guests from specific geographical locations.

Team up with local restaurants to make your product look bigger than a standalone hotel room and then publish the details on your site and your social media channels.

Run a competition on social media to win a one- or two-night stay. Make it clear that to enter you must live in the country where the property is located. You could ask people to create and post a photo of their favourite cocktail, including the recipe, that they would like to drink during their stay at your hotel if they were to win. Choose the winner based on cocktail quality of course, and check you can get the ingredients where you are, so you can make it with and for them when they arrive. Then make sure you post a photo of the winners with their cocktails on social media.

Prepare and publish the actions you have taken to keep guests safe in regard to social distancing and hygiene measures (see separate Social Distancing resource at our site – https://www.sarahhabsburg.com/resources). If you have changed buffet breakfast to a room service breakfast, then publish that too. Managing expectations avoids negative reviews.

Who are they and where are they going?

Day trippers:
Ok, so you might be thinking "if they are day-tripping why would they be interested in a hotel or hostel?"… but if they live close enough to day trip to where you are, they could become a repeat customer in a flash if you can just get them through your door. If you have an on-site restaurant, this will be easier to market right now. However, maybe you can offer coffee and homemade cakes, fresh lemonade and free ice-cream for kids. Get these people in, show them your location, tell them about the birthday parties you have hosted there… next time they need a destination for a 50th party you will be on their shortlist.

Family and friend visits:
Many people will have a spare room to stay in when they visit their family and friends, but many will also not. Imagine a professional couple working in the city. They live in an apartment and are desperate to get out to the

country. One set of parents lives in a wonderful small picturesque town but in a one-bedroom house. They have been concerned about them during the lockdown period. One of the first trips they are going to take is to visit them. They will look for somewhere to stay nearby, and that might just be your property. Appeal to these people in your marketing and on your site. Whether they stay or not, you could offer free desserts for local families after a meal at your restaurant for example.

Getting into nature:
Of course, this point heavily depends on where you are located. If you just happen to be halfway between a main city and a national park, for example, make a point to talk about the name of that national park on social media, on your website, on Trip Advisor, on your OTA pages… and sell the idea of extending the trip with an overnight stay and a free hot tub session, for example. Or put a sign up selling your delicious herbal teas and free use of the sandpit for the kids in the garden!

Road trips:
Getting onto the open road after so many weeks in lockdown is a hugely desirable thought right now. Road trips are going to become part of our new normal travel trends, at least for a while. Consider your location in the context of four ways to do a road trip: **the hub, the loop, the trail and A-B** (shout out to Jan Hutton, GM Marketing Destination, NSW Australia, for the breakdown of these road trip types). Read on to find out more.

Types of road trips

The Hub:
Refers to a regional stay using one location as a base. Hopefully, this is where your property is located. Update, prepare and add to the information you give to guests in regard to day trips within 50 km, for example.

The Loop:
Implies a trip where multiple locations will be visited on the journey with stays of more than one night in each destination. Think about the location of your nearest city and any circular routes that can be taken that pass by your location. Offer ideas that help create the road trip itinerary including things to do while they are with you.

The Trail:
> Has a final destination and will include stops along the way. Think where road trippers might want to get to from the nearest city and get a message out there as to why they should make your location a mid-way stop-off point.

The A-B:
> Is just that. A trip that intends to start and finish without stops in-between. The destination is the point of interest. The people who take A-B style road trips are probably not looking for stays to break up the journey, but if you are located near a fuel station, for example, you could divert traffic from the road with that enticing fresh lemonade, homemade cake or free use of an outdoor child area.

This may be uncharted territory in terms of marketing, but attracting and converting national travellers into loyal customers not only makes great marketing sense, but it increases revenue in the long term.

However you go about reaching these new customers, remember to sensitively inform them about the actions you have taken to offer your guests a safe, hygienic and acceptably socially distanced stay or stopover.

> "I take to the open road, healthy, free, the world before me." – *Walt Whitman*

Sarah authored the following articles and a full list of her articles is available at https://www.sarahhabsburg.com/resources:

- Actionable COVID-19 Measures
- Social Distancing Measures
- Sustainable Practice Inspiration
- General Marketing Inspiration
- Social Media Marketing
- Attracting Domestic Guests[2]

---

[2] © sarahhabsburg All rights reserved. www.sarahhabsburg.com/www.tourismresilience.com

Chapter 6

Revenue Management: Perfecting key elements to positively influence business growth and sustainability

Derek Martin

COVID-19 has had a tremendous impact on the tourism sector as a whole. In terms of modern-day revenue management one can consider it as bad as a stock market crash. Most of the hotels that we look after showed a massive increase in short-term cancellations. As the lead time of a majority of hotels around the world is so short, the impact on cash flow has been devastating. Most hotels and restaurants require constant traffic in order to meet budget requirements and as a result of the lockdown, no cash flow could be generated, leaving the hotel with high fixed costs without the ability to cover them.

As a result of the various stages of lockdown the tourism sector will be hit extra hard. Restrictions in domestic and international travel will result in massive decreases in occupancies even when hotels are allowed to operate again, and this would once again mean lower cash flows and high financial pressures.

In terms of revenue management, the lower occupancies could result in a price war. In a normal market environment a lower price would stimulate demand. However, with the demand in all markets at an all-time low, lower prices would do nothing but eat into the hotels' margins. We are also expecting the cost of sale for rooms to go up as the various health regulations need to be met, things such a daily mask on turndown, deep cleaning of the room more regularly and other essential cleaning actions that would result in more expenses that need to be covered by the selling prices.

I feel that the extra cleaning efforts and actions put in place would not be seen as a value add but rather an expectation, which means revenue managers cannot increase the selling prices as a result of this and it would always remain a new fixed expense to consider.

Another impact of COVID-19 on revenue and commercial management is the fact that the historical data that has been collected by each hotel will not be applicable for many years to come. This means that hotels with revenue management systems that rely on historical data would not be able to generate the correct data, resulting in poor commercial decisions being made. A new approach to forward-looking data would need to be taken and this would be new for many revenue managers around the world as it is very difficult to gauge things such as pricing, demand and strategies when there is so much uncertainty. Poor revenue management decisions would result in additional revenue loss in a very difficult time already.

Revenue management is 100% driven by reservations and strategies to generate reservations and revenues for the hotel. As most hotels are under forced close-down, the revenue management function has changed dramatically, and the strategies have changed from revenue generation to how we can stop the revenue bleed now and in forwarding months? The daily tasks of a revenue manager have completely changed as if the hotels are closed there is no live data to analyse and use to tweak strategies. It is extremely difficult to watch all the hard work of building base business wash away to zero in a matter of days and something like this would never be seen again.

As revenue managers and hoteliers we have all realised by now that there will never again be a normal in the hotel sector, in any department, in any country. As this realisation is setting in, the revenue managers and commercial managers will need to come to terms with a few fundamental realisations, these being:

Capacity & Inventory will decrease – this will happen in two stages: Firstly, the number of rooms in your current market may decrease as some hotels will not reopen their doors after this. This means that the number of competitor hotels trying to gain market share during this low demand period would decrease, resulting in a higher chance of conversion for hotels that have survived this. Some hotels will close or be converted to alternative-use buildings or just simply remain closed for a longer period of time, all having a direct impact on the capacity and inventory of the market.

Secondly, the capacity of external industries that support the tourism industry may decrease, once again due to closures. Airlines will scrap older planes, be slow to bring back the grounded fleets and may even reject any new planes they have on order. Smaller corporate businesses that used to do the odd international or domestic travel may close down leaving a rather large gap in the hotel occupancies. Businesses that have adopted a work from home on video call strategy may remain doing this which means the amount of corporate travel, even when permitted, would be reduced as a drastic cost-saving initiative.

Closer to Home will define the new leisure travel landscape – travel by means of your own car would become the new safest way to take a getaway. This would mean that there could be an increased demand for destinations in and around major cities.

This could be good for the economy and hotel revenues but may pose a risk of overcrowding and exceeding government-stipulated rules. Even if we do see this, these demand hotels would still have to remain at reduced capacities in order to ensure that all the health and safety regulations are met. A combination of having fewer rooms to sell at lower prices is going to put added pressure on most hotels as achieved occupancy is often what drives the profitability of the business.

Health & Safety will be front and centre stage – post-COVID-19 will see many changes to the health and safety across the entire tourism industry with the airline industry being one of the most hard-hit – remember airlines bring us hotel guests, so this is not good! Hotels also face the same problem and potential opportunity as hotels will be forced to adhere to very strict cleanliness programmes which, if done right, could be used for potential marketing. However, without a set date of reopening or regulations around opening, any campaign would be nothing but a waste of money as it may run out of steam before consumers can travel again. As most guest review sites have the primary service rating cleanliness as a review score, much more importance would be placed on this, and who knows? We may even see a new guest review criteria develop.

Pricing will never be the same again – many regular travellers would have been directly impacted as a result of COVID-19, some may have had to take salary reductions and some may even have lost their jobs. As a result, many consumers would be expecting lower prices in the market, which would be seen as fair from a consumer point of view. Luckily, leisure travellers have shown that nothing beats a great deal time and time again. However, for hotels it means that an increased occupancy would need to be achieved for it to make financial sense. Consumer spending is going to be fragile and all prices are going to be deeply researched in order to get the best deals around. Travel will happen but it would be up to the hotel if the lower occupancies at a reduced rate would make commercial sense.

Some travel may never return – we all have to come to the realisation that every segment in the hotels business mix has been affected as a result of COVID-19 and we need to come to terms with the fact that some traditional travel may not return very soon, if ever. Domestic and International group travel numbers will be forced to be reduced, conferences, meetings and events will never be the same again with social distancing becoming the new norm. Any large chunks of business will now become much harder to get and filling a hotel with individual leisure or business travellers will become a lot more difficult if there is not base business to assist.

Trust may become the most important element before booking – as the restrictions are lifted and domestic and international travel opens again, consumer trust would need to be redeveloped. Many consumers would be scared to travel or stay in hotels, even at a great price. Hotels would need to focus on ensuring that any actions taken to ensure a safe environment needs to be top of mind when marketing the hotel as this could become the new determining factor when trying to convert lookers into bookers.

Affiliate partner marketing spend will slow down – with the demand at an all-time low and many hotels closed, the third-party affiliates that normally spend on SEO for your hotel would reduce this spend drastically. This means that any third-party marketing that was in place is now no longer there and will have a direct impact on the ability to be found when potential travellers are looking to book. This could allow for an opportunity to start driving direct traffic via search engines. However, this is based purely on the marketing spend that can now be allocated to online marketing.

Will hospitality education ever be the same? – many people who study hotel management or tourism require operational internships in order to graduate and now, with the low demand and high cost-cutting initiatives in place, would internships be considered? We may see a spike in the demand for interns as semi-skilled labour at a low price. However, only time will tell as to when hotels can be fully operational again.

Many in the industry cannot wait for COVID-19 to be a thing of the past. However, the impact thereof will be felt for a long time into the future. Right now many hotels are closed and even when restrictions are lifted we are expecting very low occupancies. Panic is a natural feeling. However, now is not the time to panic but the time to plan.

From a revenue or commercial point of view, there are a few key elements that can be perfected right now that would have a long-lasting impact on your business. Proper planning now would result in a competitive advantage when any demand returns.

Is your distribution footprint setup correct & maximised? – there are not many hotels that have a full in-depth understanding of where the hotel rates are distributed to or where the hotel can be found online. It is suggested that a full property management system audit is done as a starting point and then the same process followed across all API connection partners. The aim would be to ensure that all the available room types, rate codes and restrictions are applied across as many channels as possible in order to spread the hotel's reach. The more consistent the information distributed from the PMS system or the channel manager the higher the chances of converting lookers into bookers. It is also essential to ensure that the hotel has rates and availability distributed for as far into the future that the system used allows.

Understanding your value is critical – now is a great time to take a good look at the hotel offering and decide what and who you want to be post-COVID-19. It is essential to be brutally honest with yourself in terms of what kind of value offering will be put forward as this will have a direct impact on all benchmarking moving forward. A great data-driven tool to use for this is actual guest reviews from TripAdvisor, OTA channels and other review platforms. Often this data is not enough and now is the perfect time to use these actual guest reviews to align the hotel's new strategy and value offering moving forward.

Understanding your market is now more important than ever – After the hotel has decided who and what they want to be post-COVID-19 it is critical to establish a realistic competitor set that can be used for benchmarking purposes. Competitor and market benchmarking in terms of pricing, promotions and initiatives will now be more important than before as the lower demand will make it extra difficult to stand out in order to gain market share. Price will no longer be able to be used in order to stimulate demand.

Content Drives Conversion – a hotel has many 24 hour a day sales tools available at its disposal, direct web site, online travel agencies (OTAs) as well as wholesaler partners. All of these platforms require content to showcase the hotel to assist conversions. Now is a great time to take a look at how your hotel is presented to the everyday consumer, ensure that there is a logical flow to all content displayed and that the content is up to date and relevant across all online sales channels. There is a higher chance that a looker will turn into a booker if they can see the value of the experience even before arrival.

Guest Review Scores Count – now is the perfect time to go back and analyse your past guest review scores across the various revenue-generating platforms and determine the strengths, weaknesses, threats and opportunities that are presented using real guest data. If this is done correctly a clear trend would be identified and this would be able to be used to create a clear tangible plan per department with the focus on maintaining what has worked well in the past and putting measures in place to improve any shortfalls identified. A very quick win here could be the improvement of maintenance issues that may have been missed as well as any cleanliness issues that would now require much more focus.

Maximising existing marketing data – as it is a legal requirement to collect certain information from guests when they check in now is the perfect chance to deep dive into all the information collected. Guest information could be segmented in terms of geographical location, the reason for travel as well as the source used to book their stay. If this information is properly segmented it could be used to make contact with previous guests in a much more targeted manner. The conversion rates on targeted marketing are much higher than those of the spray and pray method. Personalisation is going to become a big aspect of travel and the hotels hold enough information about previous guests to develop a very strong communications strategy. It is essential that the hotel has permission from the guest before adding them to any marketing database. However, this should all be part of the guest information collection process at check-in and easily filtered.

Social Media is your friend – social media is your friend as a hotel right now, not in the way of spamming followers with hundreds of posts daily but rather in the way that you now have time to dedicate to a more streamlined strategy. Now is the time to understand what kind of content to share with your followers, think ahead, make them want to engage with your brand now and remember you when travel is allowed again. If you have any budget for social media marketing you need to ensure that this is spent wisely or at all. The key would be to generate conversions post-COVID-19 and if all the marketing budget is spent during lockdown, keeping top of mind it may be detrimental at a later stage when people are allowed to travel again.

Partner Up – It is crucial that the industry sticks together now more than ever. Every hotel or tourism business needs to find a way to partner up in order to maximise any dual marketing campaigns. It is now more critical than ever to find other businesses or service providers that can assist you in sales or brand awareness. Take every opportunity to maximise your product, promotions or even brand by playing smart and finding like-minded businesses. When looking for potential partners one needs to be realistic in who to approach and also be sure that all aspects can be maximised. Ask questions such as how many followers do they have on social media, are they able to do email marketing and even if they have any influencers that work for them. Now is the time to maximise on that network.

Chapter 7

Fixing the weak links in the Tourism Value Chain to ensure trust and strong relationships

Illana Clayton & Kate Bergh

The Road We Are Travelling

There is no question that the longer the global pandemic continues, the worse the future outlook becomes. The future scenarios change daily, the narrative is fluid. This means that open communication between every player is more important than ever.

Our industry is built on long-standing relationships between suppliers, Destination Management Companies (DMCs) and the overseas wholesaler. We are proud of this. Our behaviour has been guided by emotion; principled by respect and underpinned by passion and purpose.

Our foundation has to be stronger than ever. And we have to have a vision to emerge rock-solid on the other end.

It is only through **collaboration** that Southern Africa as a destination can survive **and thrive** in the future.

This is how we see it:

Every link in the chain wants postponement. But this is not always possible

The Traditional Transaction Flow

Whose money is it? Is there any money, and who has it?

The biggest misnomer in Inbound Tourism is that the buying channel flows smoothly. In reality each relationship, in terms of the financial transaction, is exclusive.

However, we all have to maintain our long-standing relationships with our immediate clients and be cognisant of everyone's issues (and pain) throughout the buying channel.

There is an important difference between PENALTY and TRANSACTION, so to break this down:

- **PENALTY:** The cancellation fee is ONLY a mechanism for applying a penalty to the transaction
- **TRANSACTION:** This is purely a financial aspect – deposits, pre-payments

The Consumer

Prior to COVID-19, the consumer intended to travel. They arranged a holiday through their tour operator overseas. The nuts and bolts of this holiday were then put together by the DMC in South Africa. The DMC booked the components of this holiday with each supplier (accommodation, tours, transfers, car hire etc).

The consumer put down a deposit to reserve the holiday.

It is important to remember that this deposit is not a penalty, nor it is related to the ability (or not) to travel. **It is NOT deemed payment until the services have been delivered**. It is the consumers' money until payment is due on consumption. Pre-payment is exactly what it says: 'before payment'. It is only to guarantee an intent to consume.

Generally, the remaining balance (for mid-May holidays onwards) remains with the consumer.
Now, rightly, this consumer is scared. There is a vast array of uncertainties facing him (or her):

- Will they will be allowed to travel?
- Will countries let them in?
- Will they be well enough to travel?
- Will there even be an international flight to that destination on their departure date?

The uncertainty continues…

- Will they have a job in three months' time?
- Will the company that they booked with (or any part of the buying chain through to the end supplier) still be in business in six months' time? And what happens if just one isn't?

Some can postpone. Some cannot…

- They may have been laid off.
- They may have been forced to take all due leave during lockdown.
- The holiday was for a specific date-related reason.
- OR – now – the EU is offering an alternative voucher scheme (see later).

April/Early May Clients

These clients had paid their full balance to the overseas wholesaler. In some cases (EU/UK clients booked by the trade) they were/are entitled to a full refund due to supervening impossibility. In other cases, they were not, but still expected a sizeable refund. As the global pandemic is a Force Majeure event, the clients are simply **unable** to travel (not "disinclined to travel") through no fault of their own.

Broadly speaking, claims for travel insurance refunds have failed.
Credit card transactions ***are*** *still being reversed by the client.*
And, in many/most cases the DMC has not received payment (see DMC later).

Mid May Clients Onwards

These clients have NOT paid their balances. And nor will they until:

a) There is a reasonable certainty of being able to travel (likely only a few weeks prior to travel).
b) They have postponed their trip (if this is possible for them, and the offer made for postponement is as attractive as possible).
c) They feel comfortable that a voucher system will deliver a future holiday or right to a refund (more on changing EU Law below).

Thus the reality is that **there is no money flowing from these clients** as there is vast uncertainty that the supply of the services (the holiday) can even take place.
And their commitment to travel was made in a very different world pre-COVID-19

Overseas Tour Operators (Wholesalers)

Overseas Tour Operators are under differing legal obligations depending on their location. Some *may* be able to keep some monies received yet whether they can **ethically** do so is a different consideration.

Many cannot. But **all** are under the now acted-upon threat of charge-backs from their clients via their credit card companies.

Generally, the financial relationship (transaction) between overseas Tour Operator and local DMC is via one consolidated monthly payment (as international banking is expensive). The Tour Operator pays the DMC monthly either 30 days after travel, in the month of travel or 30 days in advance of travel.

An Aside on the New/Proposed/Adopted EU Ruling (not yet ratified by the EU)

Some governments in Europe have made legal ruling around transactions. No government has made any law change on penalties.

What this means is that the Overseas Tour Operator (wholesaler) does not have to refund the consumer (yet). They can offer the consumer a credit or voucher (which remains the money of the consumer). This can be redeemed at a later stage **against any holiday**. (It can be for a different destination altogether. Or for different suppliers within the same country.) It is entirely the consumer's choice, and if they do not take it up within the stated time period (differing by country it seems), it will be fully refundable at the end date.

Governments in mature travel markets have made/will make law changes to support *their* Outbound Tour Operators. The sole purpose of the amendment is to keep the industry fluid and alive. **The consumer is still protected and if he wants the full refund, he just has to wait longer to get it.**
There are pros and cons for the Southern African Travel Industry:

- **PRO:** Our customers (overseas wholesalers) are more likely to stay in business
- **CON:** Our battle to support postponement over refund is now MUCH harder as the customer may choose the refundable credit over postponement with conditions

Because the world seems to now be supporting future credits for the consumer rather than encouraging postponement, we are seeing increasing volumes of request to cancel rather than to change dates.

So that doesn't help Southern Africa as a destination.

DMCs

Over the last few years, there has been a transactional shift as we have seen service providers asking for deposits or pre-payment. It has never made logical sense to pass this on to the overseas Tour Operator due to high international banking charges and increased administration. Thus, for many years now, DMCs have been floating deposits and pre-payments. Often international clearing of funds takes longer than local clearing does, so the DMC in a vast majority of cases pays out funds before having received them.
So it is not a case of DMCs wanting to refund. Rather, most often we have not been paid these pre-payments.

What Are DMCs Doing?

We are percentage profit-driven businesses. Every refund means that we make no profit. So:

1. First and foremost, we are 100% promoting postponement of bookings. We have had some success with this (70 to 80% of bookings). However, this is becoming and will become tougher, as mentioned.
2. In cases where we can invoice the agent, we **are** doing so.
3. However, there are cases where we cannot. In these circumstances, we need to discuss cancellation without penalty, refunds or other mutually acceptable options, with the affected service providers.

Remember: Even if the overseas Tour Operator can now offer a voucher to the client, there is no certainty that South Africa will be the chosen destination.

The Supplier (of the Services)

The supplier often has massive overheads to maintain and, potentially, debt repayments. We understand that. *(Some DMCs also have shares/ownership in lodges, and so understand the cost structure).*

However, the supplier's service is only consumed when the client stays in that hotel or game lodge.

The pre-COVID-19 terms and conditions often allow for a deposit or pre-payment at the time of booking and/or pre-payment or liability often starting 60+ days prior to travel. It is important to note that neither a deposit nor a pre-payment can legally be viewed or imposed as a penalty.

Yet:
a) The client has not consumed the service yet.
b) The deposit/pre-payment is merely a guarantee. If there is no certainty that the client can consume the service, this should ideally be refunded to the owner of the money. And certainly not "loaned" to fund future operational costs.
c) It is the DMC who is out of pocket in most cases, and thus if case-by-case mutual agreement is reached on any future credit, it should be to be in the name of the DMC, following the transactional flow.

Going Forward

Looking forward, we will receive overseas payments even later than before. The client will be hesitant to pay deposits (thus commitment) or final balances until much nearer to travel date.

Even when the overseas Tour Operator receives the balance, they will try to conserve any payment balances in case of supervening impossibility; especially in regard to costly international payments.

Any DMC now knows that he (or she) will have no guarantee of final payment from his overseas Tour Operator unless the holiday proceeds.

European governments have not amended their laws to protect South African businesses. Only their own businesses.

The pre-COVID-19 terms and conditions do not serve us as an industry, and certainly won't in our new future.

- Either we say that every confirmed booking is currently only a potential booking again, until such time that we **know** a client can consume the holiday. This would require DMCs to convert all confirmed bookings to provisional, at least for the next few months of uncertainty.
- Or the suppliers issue new and/or temporary COVID-19 terms and conditions which allow us to keep confirmed bookings in place **at no penalty** until much closer to the time of travel.

We would prefer the latter, as would suppliers.

We call upon suppliers to develop T&Cs which allow us to work through this period with the minimum of disruption and needless admin.

No-one knows if any client will be able to travel, say in June ... July ... August ...

The client will not pay his final payment. The overseas agent will not pay the DMC. Thus the DMC cannot have a prevailing contract/terms and conditions whereby they are liable for 100% at 45 days out! (to cite but one example.)

Existing Pre-payment, Deposits & Deposit Liabilities

When we can charge the overseas agent, we will.
However, in some cases, we cannot. In these cases, we rely on long-standing relationships, as well as emotional and intellectual understanding to underpin collaborative conversations between partners. This can be on a case-by-case basis.

Ultimately, what is important?

1. **Keeping jobs** in an environment where we have limited support.
2. **Exiting this crisis with as few casualties as possible** – we need product, we need DMCs, we need our overseas partners to nurture and encourage consumer desire to travel here.
3. **Ensuring that we have a marketing channel still invested in Southern Africa** – these very influential overseas Tour Operators do a huge amount of marketing in their destination, and we need to ensure that this does not dry up.
4. **Not making lawyers rich** at the expense of monies which could be used more productively.
5. **Ensuring a robust recovery strategy** – not 'talk' but actually, really, truly being OUTSTANDING. As Travel Smart Crew, we are working on a number of back-end initiatives around our systems, our API connectivity, specific earmarked projects which are going to save quantitative time when we get back up and running, contracting efforts to save time and limit losses, incentives for booking etc.
6. **Strengthening our relationships with our supplier partners.**

The consumer is at the heart of recovery – how do we get them here post-COVID-19? How do we talk to them through and with our Tour Operator partners? There are opportunities out there. We need to be thinking about and implementing them now. The Water Crisis taught us many lessons and new strategies. Most important, arguably, was the subtle art of a well-crafted campaign, "Nowhere Better".

Let's not lose this – we have all the marketing content and collateral. We need to start talking to our existing markets, as well as a new market which didn't even know they wanted to come to South Africa. And, more importantly, we need to do this now.

- Africa is always going to be a "bucket-list" adventure. It is not easy to give up on.
- Consumers are getting increasingly desperate to escape lockdown – physically and emotionally.
- Many overseas Tour Operators are holding guests' credits. What part can we play in convincing them to spend those credits in Africa? Many will be reconsidering their chosen destination. 'Social distancing' is a new consideration and many would have booked a mass-market destination. Many have booked seasonal holidays and six months later won't want to lie on a European beach in winter or visit the Alps in summer.

We need 2021 rates, early offers, marketing material, etc. to take to market as soon as possible.

We need to start the 'conversation' with the consumer now and ensure the message is simple and quick.

We encourage holding 2020 rates. These would be easy to implement and distribute quickly. They give a great message to the existing and new consumer. There's no messy admin, as well as half the risk of rate errors, etc.

We need your actions to respond to the health fears of the consumer and gain their trust:

- Reduction of max numbers on a game drive/touring vehicle.
- Day tours operated on a larger vehicle to allow distancing.
- Incentives for booking private services.
- Midweek winelands/Soweto tours and weekend city tours etc.
- Increased restaurant floor space per head.
- Replacing buffet (or supplementing) with à la carte option etc.

"Just because our path is different doesn't mean we are lost"

Are we reading the signs and using them to navigate our way?

Are they driving our behaviour?

Have we started implementing our recovery plans?

Chapter 8

Tourism versus Poorism

Mandisa Magwaxaza

The economic climate

This story tells of a vision for South African townships. I wish to see the parts of South Africa that are still marred by segregation become celebrated as the legitimate, authentic mirrors of South African culture which they are. As we grapple with the economic disability brought about by the COVID-19 pandemic, I watch the poorest citizens struggle more than usual. Handouts and social grants only go so far. The majority of unemployed South Africans live in townships and what they need are economic opportunities. On Friday 24th April South African Minister of Finance, Tito Mboweni, said that businesses hoping to open and thrive post coronavirus lockdown should consider amending their labour market policies to favour unemployed South Africans, but not discriminate against foreign nationals. He cited restaurants and spaza shops. Economic Transformation is a hot topic in South Africa, many forms of which come as a transfer of wealth, land and opportunities to disadvantaged groups of society. I am not as well versed as our Minister in these issues, but I am a South African who lives within and amongst various groups of society and takes their concerns to heart. I would like to have more conversations about the creation of new opportunities. Dignified activities that will generate new income streams, new ownership, and grow the money pie instead of cutting it into smaller pieces. I hope that my story will start one of these conversations for the tourism industry.

I recently enjoyed enlightening idea exchanges with four entrepreneurs, three of them from some of the most iconic townships in South Africa. I wanted to hear more about how they built their businesses and how they experienced tourism as an economic sector in townships.

- Semadi Ngwenya: Founder of The Hub Presents, a youth company that operates a tourism-based culturally authentic restaurant village in the East Bank area of Alexandra Township in the North of Johannesburg, South Africa. Alexandra is the oldest township in South Africa and a World Heritage Site.
- Thabo Modise: Artist, Founder and CEO of Shova Lifestyle Origin, a Soweto lifestyle experience which showcases local artists and entrepreneurs and includes a fashion boutique, art gallery, tours, events and exhibitions. Shova

Lifestyle Origin is in Vilakazi Street, Soweto – home of two Nobel Peace Prize winners – Desmond Tutu and Nelson Mandela.
- Mhleli Hallom, Carpenter, artist and CEO of IMG Designs and Managing Director of Raw Native Kreative. IMG Designs is a furniture manufacturer established in 2014 in New Brighton Township outside Port Elizabeth, South Africa. In 2019, Mhleli combined his artistic and carpentry skills with graphic designers, fine artists, computer programmers, and an illustrator from New Brighton to form Raw Native Kreatives – a skills transfer programme for township scholars.
- Rob Hetem, Deputy Chairman of SATSA and Founder of T-Cubed Consulting, a Transformation Through Tourism initiative which coaches, mentors and represents experiential travel options from the SMME (Small, Medium and Micro Enterprises) tourism segment for the market in a sustainable way.

The market

Many articles about how people will want to travel after COVID-19 say that the traveller will be looking for more authentic experiences that also create upliftment. When they eventually come to bask in our African sunshine and revel in the freedom of our wide-open vistas, township tourism ought to appear on more itineraries. By now our industry is aware that visitors from outside our borders will take some time to come back; some reports say up to 18 months. This gives us time to clean house and share our offerings with fellow South Africans. I hope that many will choose to learn more about the unfamiliar locations in their cities and find safe, fun, and affordable experiences to share with their families and friends.

Life in South African townships is a reality unknown to many South Africans and an exoticism enjoyed by few international tourists. The roads to these hotspots are not gated, yet travelled almost only by those who live there. How do we remove the invisible barriers to the townships so that all may see how the majority of South Africans live? Yes, poverty, crime and all their cousins live there, too. They can be alleviated. Local and international tourists can help make it happen by choosing to drive in and enjoy the culture, fun and history. Buy the art, shop the goods, eat the food. Stir localised micro-economies and open access to new income streams that can thrive within these urban subcultures. It is a trip, no guilt. Tourism. Not 'poorism'.

Let us look at how tourism provides income in South African townships, and how township tourism could be developed after COVID-19

The product

Township Tours: A slice of authenticity

There are colourful and vibrant urban hotspots all over South Africa. The people dress in self-determined remixes of the latest fashion trends. They ooze a rich swag. Aromatic smoke creates a haze of anticipation over the sidewalks. The air tastes like the goods on the grill. You're welcomed into a buzz of music and conversation with an icy drink. The faces around you laugh when they smile, dance when they walk, pose as they stand.

Alexandra to Zwelitsha, New Brighton to Gugulethu, Soshanguve to Soweto and Mdantsane to KwaMashu, Rhini to Mangaung. The *kasi*[1] energy is a subculture rooted in African indigenous practices, politics, sports, fashion, food, crafts, and community. Some of the dusty facades have been refurbished. Many streets are lined with modern, well-equipped, brick and mortar. Many zones are difficult to navigate. They are jigsaws of unorganised match-box-sized erfs with DIY dwellings that are meant to be temporary. The people are scattered on various points high-above, above and below the breadline.

Outdoor gyms, playgrounds and churches fill fields where political activists once gathered for freedom-fighting. Young boys race downhill steering old tyres with wooden planks; you'll cringe in fear for their front teeth, the thrill in their eyes is infectious. A mark of rushed settlement that is common in most South African townships is tall floodlights instead of regular street lamps. If you walk past a few, count how many have their concrete bases strewn with pebbles and chalked circles – ask your guide to teach you that game. I know it is *upuca*.[2]

Millennials with degrees hawk, dress hair and tutor their neighbours' children. Parents and grandparents till would-be sports fields to grow produce for school feeding schemes. Shipping containers become boutiques, barbers, tailors and shoemakers – trading at prices that will impress you. Alive with possibilities and economic hubs shaped by the needs of the people; by the lifestyle.

---

1   The word 'kasi' is an abbreviation from the Afrikaans word 'lokasie' which refers to townships. A derogatory term used during segregation and then adopted into urban slang in the democratic South Africa.

2   An indigenous game played with one hand, stones and a drawn circle. The player bundles many pebbles into the circle and tosses a bigger stone in the air. They score points on how many pebbles they manage to scoop out of the circle in one sweeping motion before catching the tossed stone again with the same hand.

This is the day-to-day behind the low lights on the news. The opportunities created by civilians who work to survive and live by the code of *ubuntu*[3].

The collaborative business environment

Township Tourism: It Takes a Village

When countries around the world started locking down and grounding their flight carriers, the booking cancellations started pouring into South Africa. We had not had our first COVID-19 positive test result, but we sat up and looked around. We looked to our associations, and they never averted their gaze but turned their sights down a barrel of darkness to create knowledge bases and guidelines. We turned to our local, regional and national tourism offices and they rushed in to reassure us. They created content of hope that fuelled our efforts to overcome the challenges. They spoke to those who work in tourism more directly and tried their best to understand the operational challenges on the ground. Our political leaders hurriedly put up barriers and funds to hem us in and protect all citizens from a rapid spread of COVID-19.

Leaders jumped off cliffs to build aeroplanes on the way down. The aroma of half-baked solutions comforted us all until we realised that we would still go hungry for a while. Relief efforts that were announced with no framework for implementation eventually started functioning. It will take a while, but we are grateful they are there, grateful for the effort that has been made for the South African people.

South Africa has rallied behind its leaders and supported them in full, even when they did not make the best decisions. We appreciate that our leaders communicated consistently, built solutions and asked for comment through private-sector-led communities and associations. That is at least true for the tourism industry.

Can South Africa please continue to grow and perfect this cycle of value-added service and consultation?

Private businesses to associations. Associations to tourism offices. Industry leaders to politicians. Politicians to communities.

Let us look at Township Tourism as an example of how this cycle of consultation can work.

---

3   An African concept of humanitarianism best illustrated by the Zulu Proverb "a person is because others are".

Tourism can become the lifeblood of township economies. The entire tourism industry accounts for a significant portion of South Africa's GDP and employment. It is a vital source of a wider network of contribution. This is more evident in the townships where you can see the chain in action. The tourism industry feeds into other sectors such as construction, agriculture, transport, and retail, to name a few.

Township tourism increases social relations and unity and helps to beautify the community's streets and facilities. The consequences of tourism benefit many people, and they become willing to participate in the improvement of their surroundings.

An exciting example of this kind of collaboration is in Alexander township where one cycle tour operator started his business with a brute determination to single-handedly bring the world to Alex. Semadi Ngwenya and his business partner started The Hub Presents in 2011. Their electric bike township tours added something new and exciting to the travel agent's product pack. However, the phone barely rang. There began the greatest business lesson for Semadi – he was not going to get far working on his own.

'You are who you are because of others' – A Zulu proverb that surmises social relations in townships and South Africa's underpinning spirit of ubuntu. Many things that are private in the mainstream are better done communally in township communities.

The Hub Presents project developed the first-ever tourism site for the Alexandra community (and the country as a whole) with Johannesburg as the immediate catchment market. Semadi and his team run an excellent total township experience with tours, traditional cuisine and entertainment sourced from in and around Alex – creating income streams for residents.

The people of Alex are an important part of The Hub's business model, and the reason Semadi established Greater Alexandra Heritage and Tourism Association (GAHTA), a local association geared towards growing Alex's economy and tourist experience. The association represents the Alexandra Greening Route, The Hub Presents, numerous craftsmen and economic players in Alexandra's tourism network.

Semadi hopes GATHA will soon be able to provide business support services such as training, admin services, I.T. resources, and access to mentorship programmes. Would local government be willing to fund township tourism associations so that entrepreneurs can receive all they need to thrive?

The individualistic business environment

Vilakazi Street, Soweto – Gauteng Province

Vilakazi Street is a successful tourism hub in Soweto. As the home of Nelson Mandela and Archbishop Emeritus Desmond Mpilo Tutu. Local businessmen bought houses on Vilakazi Street and created restaurants, event venues, art galleries, boutiques and shops to serve the local and international tourists attracted by Mandela House and the Hector Pieterson Memorial. Thabo Modise, owner of Shova Lifestyle Origin on Vilakazi Street, is proud to be part of the modern, vibrant lifestyle experience that is Vilakazi Street, still thriving 10 years later and driven by passionate artisans and businesspeople who want to see a return on their investments. The government created a favourable environment by refurbishing Vilakazi Street, Mandela House, and the Hector Pieterson Memorial as part of countrywide preparations for the 2010 Soccer World Cup. The businesses work hard on their offerings to keep the Vilakazi experience exciting, but there are many other notable locations around Soweto such as the Credo Mutwa Village. Some heritage and history sites form part of short tours, but they also need to become tourist precincts like Vilakazi Street so that more entrepreneurs can benefit from tourism. Thabo hopes that the newly created Soweto Tourism Association will drive the development of more tourism zones.

One fantastic product can attract local and international tourists into a township. It then depends on the vigour and liquidity of individual entrepreneurs to further develop more tourist attractions and facilities around the available hub. This was the case in Vilakazi Street, but Mzoli's Place in Gugulethu, Cape Town and Red Location Museum in New Brighton failed.

Mzoli's Place, Gugulethu – Western Cape

I remember the days I used to enjoy Saturday afternoons at Mzoli's Place in Gugulethu, Cape Town. A multi-racial group of friends alongside tourists and residents, we could have a tasty meal and dance freely as top DJs entertained the crowd. We always felt safe but returned less frequently because there were only so many DJs that made the trip from Tokai to Gugulethu worthwhile. The experience along the rest of NY115 could have been better. There was no parking and the few who traded outside the famous shisanyama[4] did not have the necessary, nice-enough kind of facilities to create an air of modernity similar to Vilakazi Street. Art galleries, various eateries, and playhouses would have made us regular patrons of NY115. Could an organised association have

---

4 Shisanyama is an urban South African term meaning barbecue. The word originates from the Nguni language group and means to 'burn the meat'.

developed an ecosystem for more local entrepreneurs to create a better experience and a tourism quarter along NY115?

Red Location Museum, New Brighton – Eastern Cape

A great mishap in the tourism landscape of Port Elizabeth in Nelson Mandela Bay is the Red Location Museum that was ruined by the community of the Red Location township before reaching its full potential. The Red Location Museum opened in 2006 as a memory bank and celebration of New Brighton's oldest neighbourhood and the part it played in the Liberation Struggle. With conferencing venues, a large restaurant, art gallery and world-class library, the award-winning, R22-million building was going to be a great asset to the community that shut it down in 2013 as part of a massive service delivery protest for housing. The museum, library and gallery are still closed and have been vandalised over seven years. According to Nelson Mandela Bay Tourism the damage amounts to R12 million.

Local artists and entrepreneurs hope that Red Location Museum will be revived and say that the city's development agency has plans to create an economic hub near the Red Location precinct. The agency may successfully implement a plan, but who will ensure that the community is ready to use the market stalls, galleries and other facilities that may be set up in this hub?

Mhleli Hallom is a member of the local business forum and hopes that the mistakes of the past will not be repeated. "Community buy-in is a pretentious concept that makes it appear like the community was involved, when really, people were shown a plan, promised many benefits, and asked to agree to it. People need to be taken by the hand, on a journey of education. It is dangerous for officials to assume that tourism is naturally understood as something good for the community. Our immediate concerns are food for our families, education for our children and roofs over our heads. Projects like the Red Location Museum can fulfil these needs over time; our community needs to be taught about the realistic implications of that timeline."

An organisation similar to the Greater Alexander Heritage & Tourism Association could play a vital role in the consultation between such development agencies, local government, businesspeople, and community leaders. An organisation with an unbiased objective for the good of the destination, mentored by experts, funded by government and authorised as an advisory body to local decision-makers.

Township Entrepreneurs: Architects of change, voices of vision

The three millennial township entrepreneurs I have spoken to advocate for collaboration, inclusion and fair representation. Their passions go beyond their unique talents and ventures. They are working towards positive changes for their communities. They are multi-talented and artistic, and I have found their viewpoints refreshing and useful for the future of South African tourism.

> *"I am an artist, and I think the ability to link art and tourism is what makes me unique. I tell stories that affect our life's today unlike focusing on historic stories and I believe it resonates well with the new market that want to know more about the current nuances." – Thabo Modise*

As the South African Tourism Industry grapples with the questions about what will come next. It would do itself a great service to seek out and listen to SMMEs, in particular, those who have built businesses in the townships of South Africa. Their businesses have been the target market for public–private partnerships. As beneficiaries, their experiences of these vary from successful mentorship programmes such as Explore Hidden Gems supported by T-Cubed, to victims of failed government aid which is tripped up by unrealistic regulations.

We need to start from the premise that our people will be innovative and know what to do if government performs its task of creating infrastructure and policies which support and underpin true inclusivity through opportunities for all South Africans who want to work hard towards a positive future.

Part 3

The Future of Aviation and the Traveller: Ensuring Safety & Peace of Mind and Tourism Crisis Recovery Checklist

Chapter 9

COVID-19: A catalyst for change in African Aviation

Derek Nseko

That aviation lives at the heart of the global economy has been highlighted by the coronavirus crisis.

With the widening of travel restrictions and the grounding of much of the global airline fleet sparking a near-shutdown of the global economy, it's in the same fashion that kick-starting our recovery will require the re-emergence of air transport operations at the frontline.

April 23, 2020: The International Air Transport Association (IATA) renewed its call for government relief measures as the impacts of the COVID-19 crisis in African deepen. The region's airlines could lose $6 billion of passenger revenue compared to 2019, i.e. $2 billion more than was expected at the beginning of the month.[1]

Industry response

This crisis threatens the very existence of the industry. Airlines are locked into various financial commitments. With leasing, maintenance and salaries adding to mounting fixed costs and coupled with an environment of little to no incoming revenue, airlines have taken to the most draconian of measures in a desperate bid to survive.

Employees have been the easy target and have had to face the full force of the effects of the COVID-19 crisis. Salary cuts and lay-offs have become the norm as companies look to cut costs. The African aviation industry supports about 6 million jobs and IATA projects that up to 3 million of these jobs are likely to be lost this year.

What can we do?

Going forward, airlines and airports have a huge responsibility to inspire confidence in the travelling public. For air traffic to pick up post-COVID-19, passengers will need to feel safe. Safety protocols by industry, individual companies and airports will be crucial with screening done by both airports and airline likely to be the norm.

---

[1] IATA *Airlines* Magazine. (2020). Aviation Relief for African Airlines Critical as COVID-19 Impacts Deepen. Retrieved from: https://www.iata.org/en/pressroom/pr/2020-04-23-02/

Before our airlines can take-off, governments are called upon to play a key role in creating and enabling an environment for a complete reboot and growth within the industry.

Aviation companies need financial support in the form of direct aid and loans to help mitigate the mounting losses. Tax breaks and waiving of various aviation-related fees has also been suggested as a way to help the airlines in the short to medium term

Tough lessons to learn

In life, you learn lessons. A lot of them the hard way. This rings true for the current state of aviation.
One of the great lessons learnt during this past year and across all industries has been the value of diversification. For example, clothing retailers have diversified their core product offering, clothes, to selling food and essential items. They have managed to pivot their business, thus avoiding closing their doors and opening another door during this crisis.

In the same vein, we have seen airlines with strong cargo operations maintain some level of existence. The likes of Ethiopian airlines who have been delivering essential medical supplies across the continent from overseas.

In order to adapt to a changing world, airlines and airports will have to think critically, carefully and out of the box about diversifying their revenue streams.

Long-term

Significant changes are required to drive the African aviation industry to a more sustainable future. The African aviation industry is very fragmented and as such our airlines do not enjoy the benefits of scale that are evident in Europe, the United States and recently Latin America. Indeed 80% of traffic that arrives on the African continent is carried by non-African airlines, this largely due to their competitive advantage. How can we bridge that gap?

Liberalisation

The narrative on deregulation in Africa spans decades. From the Yamoussoukro declaration in 1988, the Yamoussoukro decision of 1999 to its latest reincarnation, the Single African Air Transport Market. A continent of 54 countries with national airlines regarded as a trophy and aviation as a government cash cow, the airline sector in

Africa is characterised by a nationalist and protectionist mindset. It is easy to see why integration and consequently deregulation is akin to an extreme sport.

But something's has to give. One of the big lessons of the corona crisis has been that business as usual has got its limitations and vulnerabilities. There is no doubt that even more liberal markets across the world have been badly hit by the effects of the coronavirus, but it is also true that a bigger and stronger market is a more resilient market. We will encounter bigger threats in the future and we have to be ready.

Deregulation in the United States in 1978 and Europe gradually in the 90s sparked an evolution that inspired growth and the emergence of new business models which continue to thrive today. Flying became more accessible and affordable to so many people. By comparison, airline travel remains a huge privilege in Africa, with high operational costs and low profit margins keeping the cost of flying at a premium and chocking innovation. It is no coincidence that the low-fare market has failed to find a place in Africa. While quickly harmonising the air transport market in Africa is almost impossible, a process of gradual liberalisation at a regional level is within our means. The time is now.

Consolidation

2020 has already claimed its "business" casualties. And we are yet to see more as weaker and struggling airlines that cannot acquire government aid are consumed by extremely tough times. In the past, such periods of economic difficulty have been a catalyst for consolidation among airlines across the world.

Today Europe and the United States are both dominated by five large airlines/groups in terms of revenue, market share and profit. Indeed airline consolidation has become a global reality with strategic alignment a key to survival. But what are the prospects for Africa? Could addressing the issue of fragmentation with the creation of world-class airline groups give us the market position and scale to fly through the turbulence and see better profits?

Ethiopian Airlines, Africa's largest airline group has pioneered a model which has brought great success and today commands the largest share of Africa's aviation profit.

While African governments and their airlines might naturally be resistant to consolidation, multi-AOC integration is still possible for a continent as diverse as ours. With the most challenging points of integration being corporate culture, labour structure and customer experience, all added to national pride. Latin America is a shining example of how to extract synergies to streamline business process. Inspired by the merger between Avianca and TACA, LAN and TAM subsequently merged to continue a strong consolidation of the Latin American market. Airlines groups could still operate distinct airlines with separate brands and in the case of Latin America, ownership rules were satisfied by keeping voting stock in the hands of the nationals.

With a more consolidated and liberal market, Africa could have better connectivity and seamless passenger and cargo services across the continent with jointly owned maintenance and repair organisations ensuring revenue and cost synergies. Crucially, African aviation will then be stronger for the future.

Chapter 10

The rise of sanitised travel: A day in the life of an airline passenger

Simplyflying

Welcome to the age of sanitised travel

Air travel will never be the same after the advent of the COVID-19 outbreak. Just as how travellers would not have stepped on-board an aeroplane after 9/11 unless they were assured that there were no weapons on-board, they will not travel unless assurance is provided that there are no viruses on board.

SimpliFlying mapped out over 70 areas on the day of travel that would change due to new demands of the travellers. This chapter summarises the key stages of travel and how each stage will change. Welcome to the age of post-corona travel. The age of sanitised travel.

1. **Online check-in**

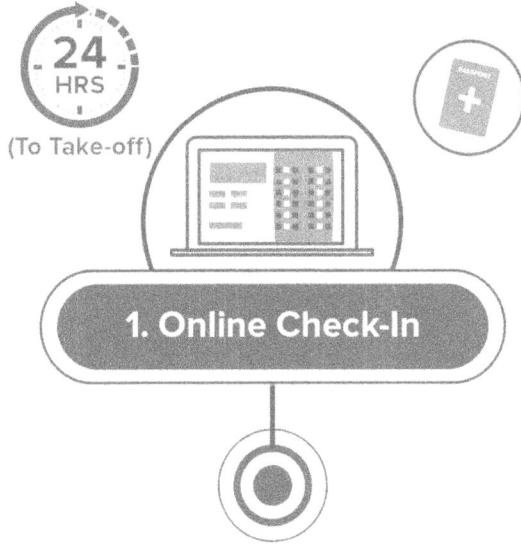

Figure 10.1: Stage 1 Online check-in[1]

---

1 Box.com. (n.d.). Online check-in. Retrieved from:
https://app.box.com/s/ers6i2r4udwux9rwkhu9hsbax6y8sop9

Previously, during online check-in, travellers only had to upload their passport details, choose seats and pay for optional services like checked bags.

In the age of sanitised travel, they will be required to upload an **immunity passport** confirming the presence of antibodies for COVID-19. This would be similar to the Yellow Fever card we need to carry when travelling from some humid regions.

> **New ancillary opportunities**
>
> There will be new opportunities for airlines to drive **ancillary revenues** as travellers would pay for **all-inclusive insurance** products that would issue full refunds in case they are denied boarding. They will also be able to buy **masks**, **gloves** and even pay more for **an empty seat next to them**.

2. **Airport curbside**

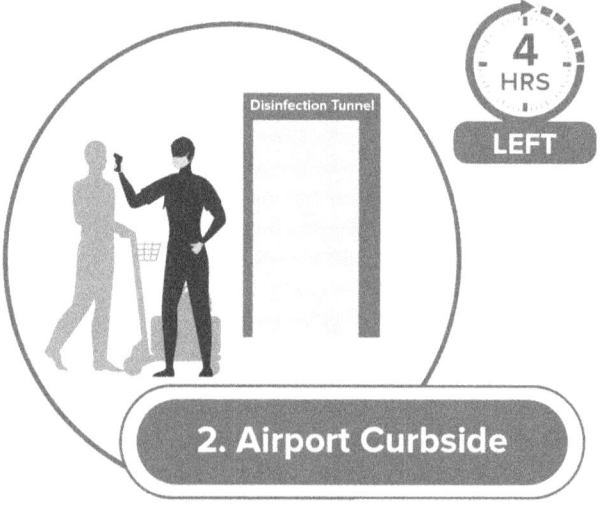

Figure 10.2: Stage 2 Airport curbside[2]

Previously, passengers and those dropping them off could arrive 1-3 hours prior to departure.

In the age of sanitised travel, only those travelling will be allowed to enter the airport, at least 4 hours prior to departure. Before they can be allowed in the departure area, they will either need to show their immunity passport or go through a **disinfection**

---

2   Box.com. (n.d.). Airport curbside. Retrieved from:
    https://app.box.com/s/fcl8jhuyek6pyj6ugsj7v34uqsns1xna

tunnel and **thermal scanners**. Only if they are deemed "**fit to fly**" will they be allowed in.

THA: Transport Health Authority

Just like 9/11 led to the creation of the TSA, we expect post-COVID-19 travel to be guided by a **Transport Health Authority (THA)**. Ideally, the THA would be led by WHO, ACI and IATA to define **health screening and sanitation standards** throughout travel, especially outside the airport perimeter.

Having consistency across countries for international travellers will prevent confusion and help boost confidence in travel.

---

3. **Check-in, Bag Drop**

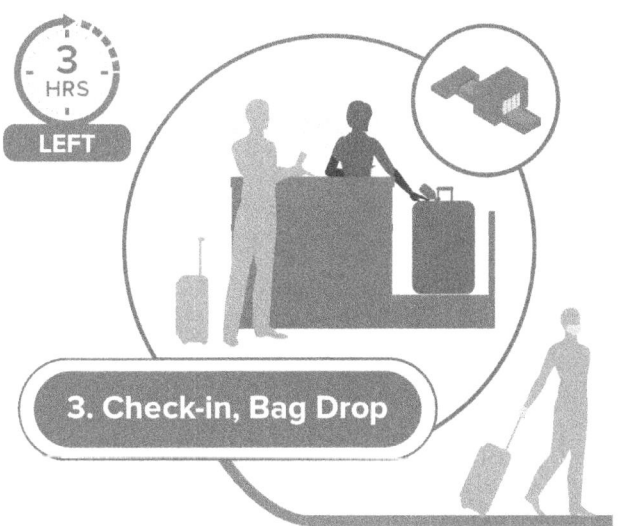

Figure 10.3: Stage 3 Check-in, bag drop[3]

Previously, passengers would have chosen their seats online and may walk straight through to Security. No longer. In the future:

- All passengers will need to head to the check-in counter to have an **instant assessment** of their health (like Biomind CT scan);

---

3 Box.com. (n.d.) Check-in, bag drop. Retrieved from: https://app.box.com/s/y346wk48dtqi74swq1kimaoc2p9zhcni

- Some airlines may administer **blood tests** as well. Check-in agents will be behind **protective barriers**, like those found in pharmacies;
- Bags will go through fogging or a UV disinfection process to be "**Sanitagged**";
- **Seats** will be **assigned by agents** to optimise in-flight distancing;
- Passengers will be handed **gloves and masks** to be worn through the rest of the journey.

> **The new check-in process**
>
> The check-in process may no longer be swift. From manually being assigned seats to a health scan being done, travellers will need to adapt to new realities.
>
> People may be required to show up at least four hours prior to departure, depending on the specific airline's and airport's procedures. This may inconvenience families with kids and the elderly the most. Business travellers may prefer to take the train or drive if possible, to avoid the hassles.

4. **Security**

Figure 10.4: Stage 4 Security[4]

Previously, passengers went through priority security or normal security. In the age of sanitised travel:

---

4   Box.com. (n.d.). Security. Retrieved from:
    https://app.box.com/s/h7haeg0341ku922izm720ou7ejq00ety

- All passengers will need to go through **hygiene-enhanced security** at least 2 hours prior to departure;
- Each carry-on bag and each tray will be **disinfected** upon entering the X-ray machine. This will be done through fogging, UV-ray disinfection or other "quick" techniques;
- All carry-on bags will then be "**Sanitagged**" as well;
- Passengers must keep their masks and gloves on and avoid touching anyone else's items;
- Security cameras will need to be updated as they will not be able to see through masks.

5. **Boarding area**

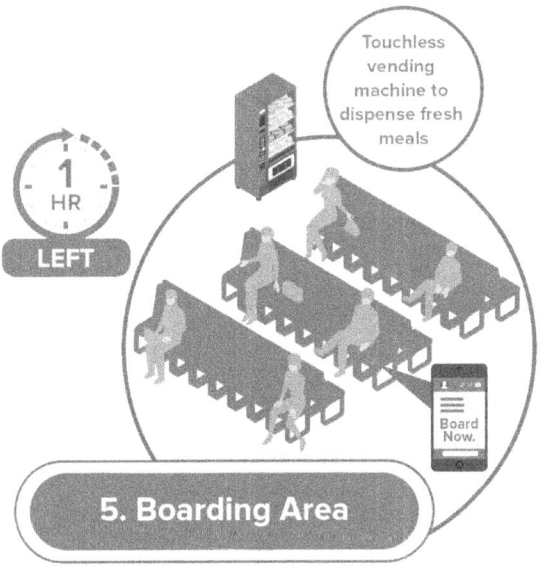

Figure 10.5: Stage 5 Boarding Area[5]

In the age of sanitised travel, the boarding process is set to be overhauled:

- Passengers will need to be present in the boarding area at least **an hour before departure**;
- They will need to maintain **social distancing in the seating area;**
- **Touchless vending machines** in the boarding area will encourage purchase of meals that can be consumed in-flight or pre-departure;

---

5 Box.com. (n.d.). Boarding area. Retrieved from:
https://app.box.com/s/5lb8fihv6drd0nqhe0h30uu6fu7w2psm

- Passengers will only board when they receive **individual notifications on their mobile phones** to proceed;
- Priority boarding will be offered to **"essential workers"**;
- Those with positive scan results (taken at the check-in) will be **denied** boarding.

6. **Jetbridge**

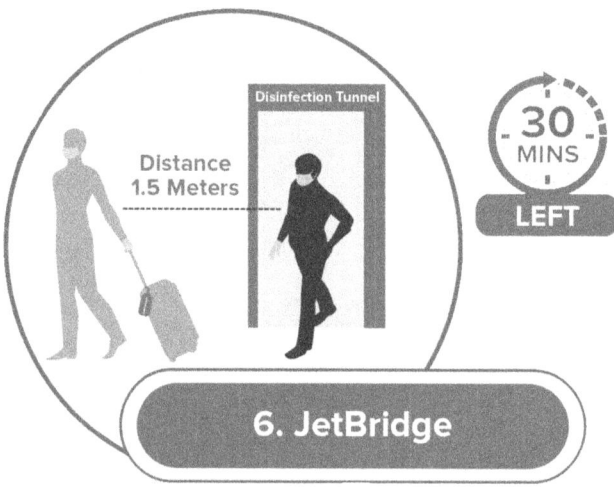

Figure 10.6: Stage 6 Jetbridge[6]

The JetBridge is currently a tightly packed space, with passengers standing close together, just waiting to get on board.

In the age of sanitised travel, the JetBridge will be less crowded, with social distancing in place. It will serve as the perfect space for a **disinfection tunnel**, ensuring that every single passenger stepping on board has been properly disinfected and is **not carrying anything other than their luggage on the flight**.

---

6   Box.com. (n.d.). Jetbridge. Retrieved from:
    https://app.box.com/s/h2d1moe3el4c9yv5do8icdvio1pcks2v

7. In-flight experience

Figure 10.7: Stage 7 In-flight experience[7]

Before take-off, in the age of sanitised travel, the in-flight experience is set to change dramatically.

- All cabin crew will be wearing **protective gear**;
- Upon boarding, the crew will **verify** all passengers have their own **gloves and masks on**;
- We will see passengers **wiping down** their own seats before being seated with wipes handed out by the cabin crew;
- The **safety video** will include a "sanitation" section;
- Any passengers displaying signs of being unwell may be **off-loaded before take-off**;
- There will be visible fogging of the cabin;
- A **hand-sanitiser service** may be provided by the crew every 30 minutes.

---

7   Box.com. (n.d.). In-flight experience. Retrieved from:
    https://app.box.com/s/kwz8zpflhjnbp8k0xaksyqca2ml8gk6o

A Touchless Cabin

Figure 10.8: The end of the in-flight magazine[8]

Gone will be the days when the crew came by to serve multi-course fresh meals in premium cabins. Now, all passengers will get a **pre-packed, sealed meal** to prevent any viruses from getting in the food.

We expect **personal device use** to significantly grow as passengers avoid touching seat-back screens. Cash transactions will no longer exist. Seatback pockets will be left empty and the safety card will be stuck at the back of the tray table. This will also mean **the end of the printed in-flight magazines**. *Welcome to the touchless cabin!*

The in-flight janitor

Such will be the need for visible efforts towards cleaning that some airlines may hire **dedicated in-flight janitors** to keep lavatories and high-touch areas clean regularly.

We have seen airlines like Emirates employ crew who specifically keep their in-flight showers aboard the First Class sparkling clean. Passengers also need to book a time upon take off for their shower.

Similar measures may be taken across all classes, especially by legacy airlines, such that the in-flight janitor can **clean surfaces and lavatories at regular intervals**. A **realtime cleaning log** can be made available to passengers via an app to boost confidence. Don't be surprised if you are asked to **rate the cleanliness of the cabin** a few times during the flight.

---

8   Box.com. (n.d.). The end of the in-flight magazine. Retrieved from: https://app.box.com/s/tqmqbyxyxf37qmfnn6fk9rhc7wjnyeen

8. Upon landing

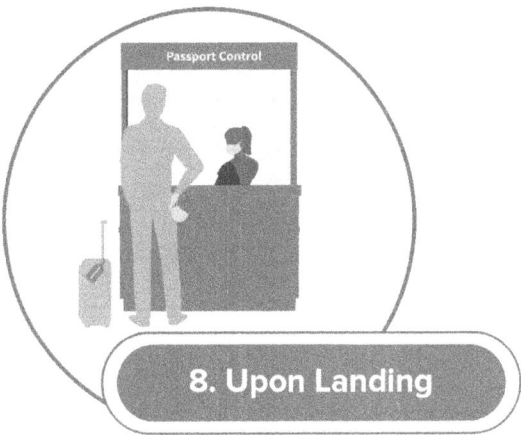

Figure 10.9: Stage 8 Upon landing[9]

In the age of sanitised travel, things will also change when arriving at the destination:

- Upon landing, bags will be "Sanitagged" **before** they are placed on the conveyor belt;
- **Thermal scanners** will be used to identify passenger with a potential fever or developing temperature;
- At the border control, **counters will be screened off** to protect the officers;
- An **immunity passport** will also have to be verified before entering the country.

Airlines will **no longer** be able to turnaround their aircraft and get them ready for their next flight **in just half an hour or less**, as deep cleaning will have to take place after every flight, and not just overnight.

> **The end of the 30-minute turnaround**
>
> The rapid 30-minute turnaround times that airlines have been diligently trying to shorten, even more, especially LCCs, will become a thing of the past.
>
> In the age of sanitised travel, every aircraft, after every flight will have to be deep cleaned, fogged and perhaps even sterilised with UV lights or other new technologies. Doing it overnight only will no longer be sufficient.

---

9   Box.com. (n.d.). Upon landing. Retrieved from:
    https://app.box.com/s/krzar5spljewcmoz20gu50hf147n21yr

In total, over 70 different areas in the passenger journey are expected to either change or to be introduced from scratch to restore confidence in flying after COVID-19.

Before the flight

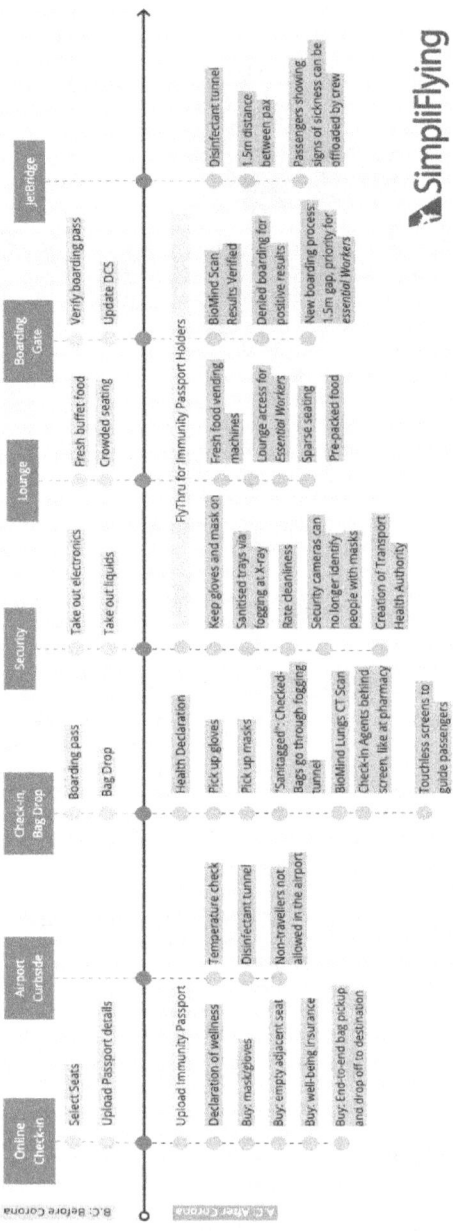

Figure 10.10: Timeline before a flight[10]

---

10 Box.com. (n.d.). Timeline before flight. Retrieved from:
    https://app.box.com/s/0lax3x0und13pqrfz0rksb9hpbt7qbnn

During and after the flight

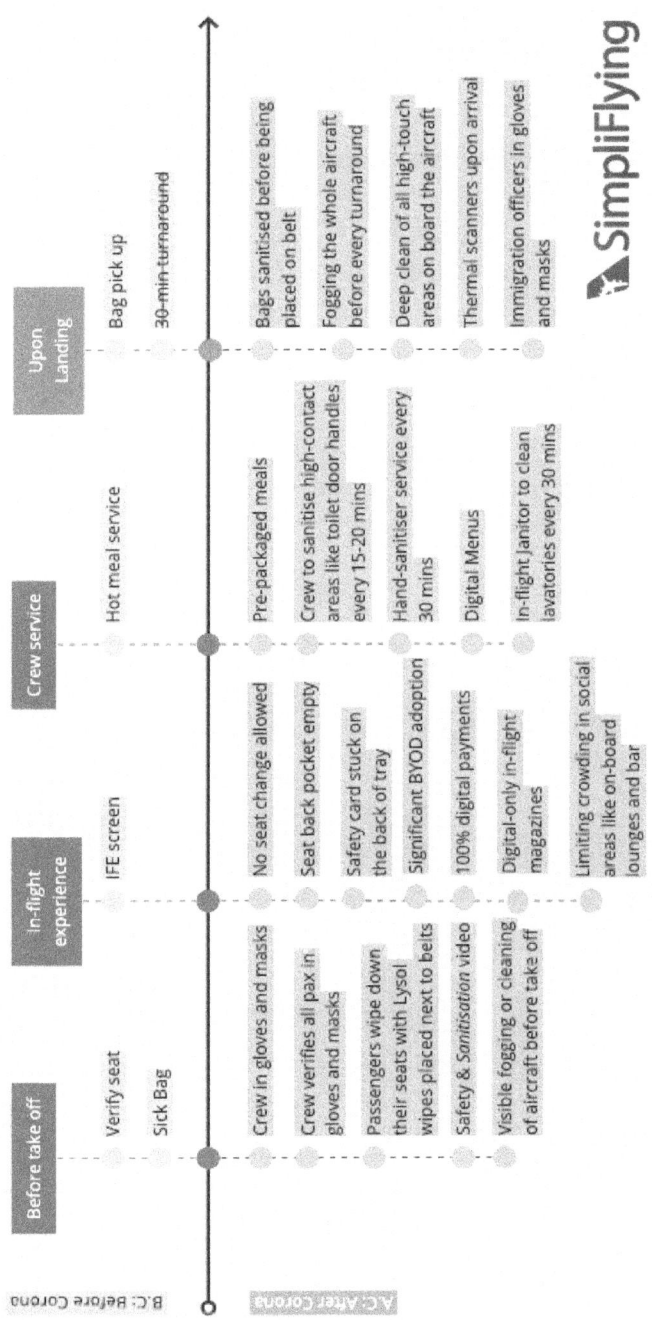

Figure 10.11: Timeline during a flight[11]

---

11 Box.com. (n.d.). Timeline during flight. Retrieved from:
    https://app.box.com/s/egkqursgq0i5btwo1xpmlvk4tfcqm6v3

We can help you navigate and adapt to the realities of sanitised travel.

Our Rapid Response Team can run through the customer journey map with over 70 areas set to be affected due to coronavirus.

Get in touch rapidresponse@simpliflying.com

Chapter 11

The sky has limits for the African Aviation Industry

Joan Vilardell

COVID-19 Outbreak. A global aviation recession[1]

45% Global cut-off on seat offers (Week 30-03)

The COVID-19 outbreak is having a major impact on national and international aviation, and air traffic is expected to further decline in the coming weeks. **No region of the globe will escape the depression.**

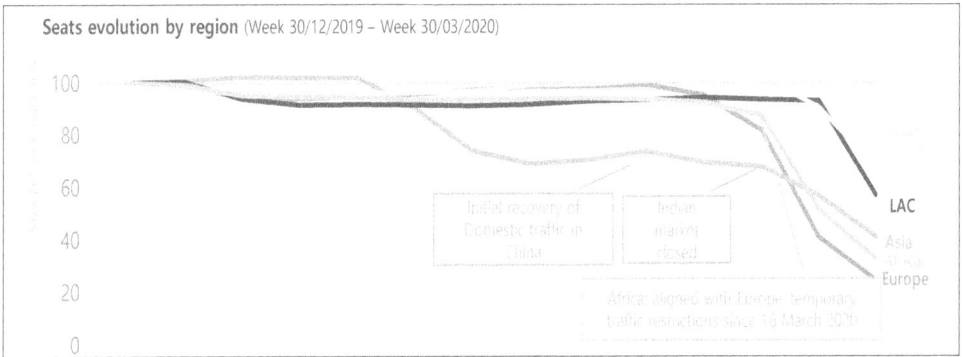

98% of the global air market is under severe confinement and flight restrictions

According to *IATA COVID Financial Impact Assessment*, dated March 24, in 2020 Africa will experience one of the starkest declines in traffic. At present, many airlines in the region have completely ceased operations as most African countries have closed their borders in order to combat the spread of COVID-19.

---

1 ALG Transport & Infrastructure Newsletter. (2020). *Covid-19 aviation briefing. African Aviation Industry.* Retrieved from: https://algnewsletter.com/

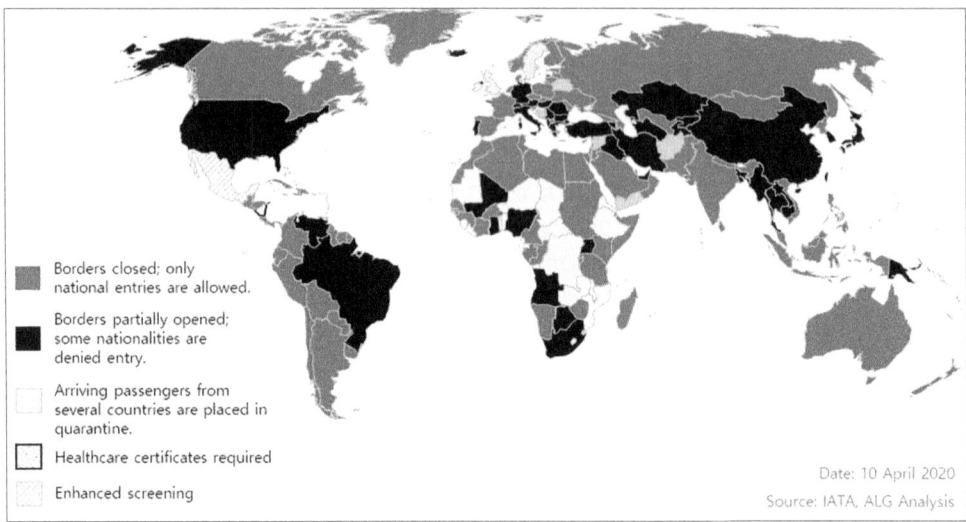

Unprecedented crisis for the air transport sector

Health crisis + global economic sudden stop

For the first time since 2008, the global GDP growth for 2020 is expected to be negative. Research from the World Travel & Tourism Council shows that, globally, up to 75 million jobs are at immediate risk.

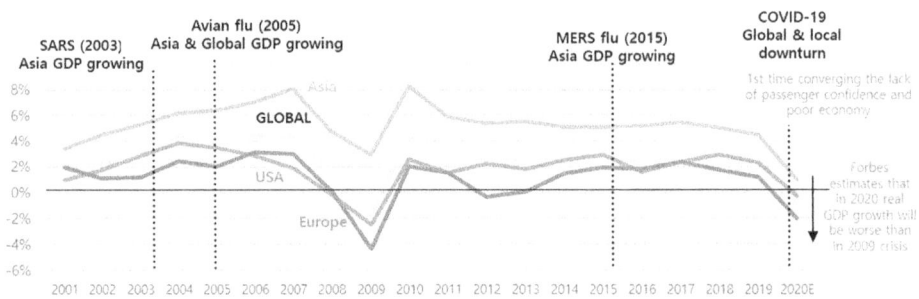

Global outbreak and uneven timing

While some parts of the world will be able to control and minimise the outbreak in a few months, in other countries it could take longer. As a result, air services from/to some regions will resume sooner than others in which restrictions may still apply.

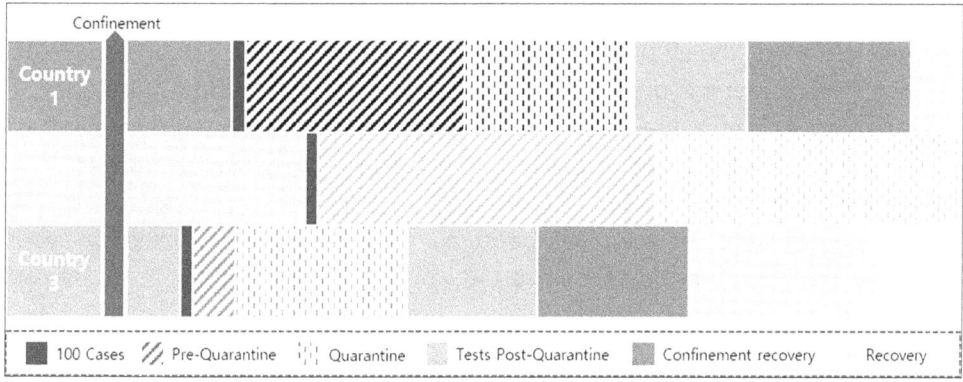

The recovery scheme works as **plates sliding** at different speeds. The slowest plate (country), due to friction (trade, trade relationship) slows down the system as a whole. As a result, the **recovery rate** is defined by the country with the **worst strategy** against COVID-19 (longer duration of the pandemic stages).

It is expected that **domestic/enclosed markets with proper policies against COVID-19** (i.e. US domestic or Intra-EU traffics), will **recover faster than international segments**. The international traffic rebound will be harder as it will also depend on each country pair. The agreement in the measures applied between regions will define the future of Africa-Europe/Intra-African connectivity.

Dramatic drop in demand will impact all sectors of the aviation industry

Commercial air transport has direct and indirect impacts in many business activities including manufacturers, lessors, infrastructure providers, regulators, service providers, airlines, distribution channels based on the demand foundation, etc.

The COVID-19 outbreak has triggered a cascade effect. The fall in demand has had a direct impact on airlines, which are simultaneously spreading their financial crisis to the whole industry. This includes aircraft returns and requests of lease relief to lessors, cancellations of aircraft orders to manufacturers, airports deprived of flights, passengers, and retail, generating lack of revenues, with supporting services (handling, maintenance, cleaning) costs still to be covered.

The sustainability of the aviation sector in Africa will depend, to a large extent, on the adequacy of the stimulation packages implemented by each of the regional governments.

- In the short term, the liquidity of airlines should be guaranteed, as they from the weakest link in the chain. Several countries in Africa are announcing support for the aviation sector in order to reduce the impact of the COVID-19.
- Subsequently, measures should be implemented to reactivate the demand so that the sector's liquidity problems do not result in insolvency problems and bankruptcies.
- Airports will also require relief measures. Governments will have to consider additional measures to rebalance the concession contracts of many airport operators.

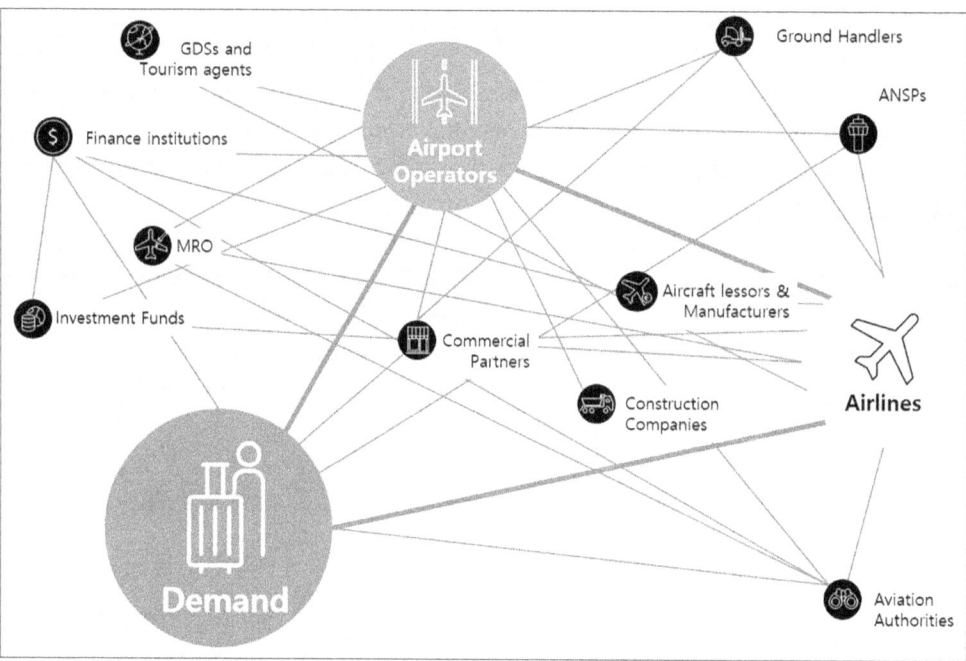

Africa has been hit as hard as other affected regions

Airports capacity cut-off by market (updated 06/04)

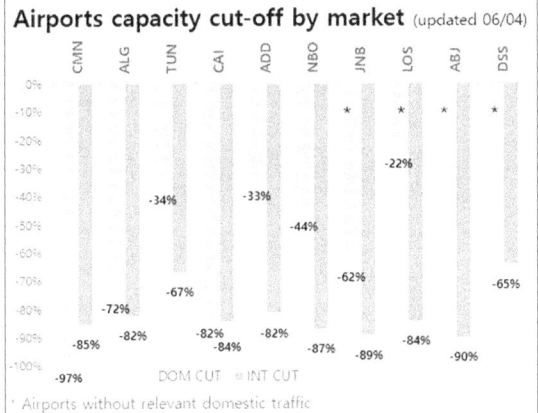

MORE AIRCRAFTS ON THE GROUND THAN EVER

Airports are currently operating some domestic traffic and other minor international flights under strict disinfection measures. Specific measures have already been adopted, such as temporary slot waiver in EU airports, recalibration of cargo operations and charter flights for evacuations.

Airlines capacity cut-off by market
(updated 06/04)

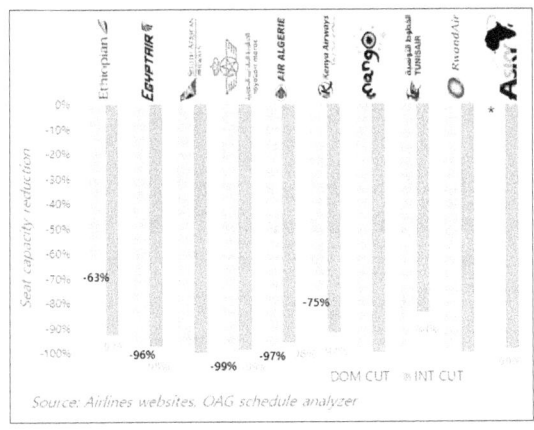

The vast majority of airlines' fleet are on the ground, keeping operations to a minimum. Airlines plan to resume their services and achieve relative normality at the beginning of July.

African air market is highly exposed to international resolutions and decisions

Air transport market supply's segmentation by region (Jan 2019-Feb 2020)

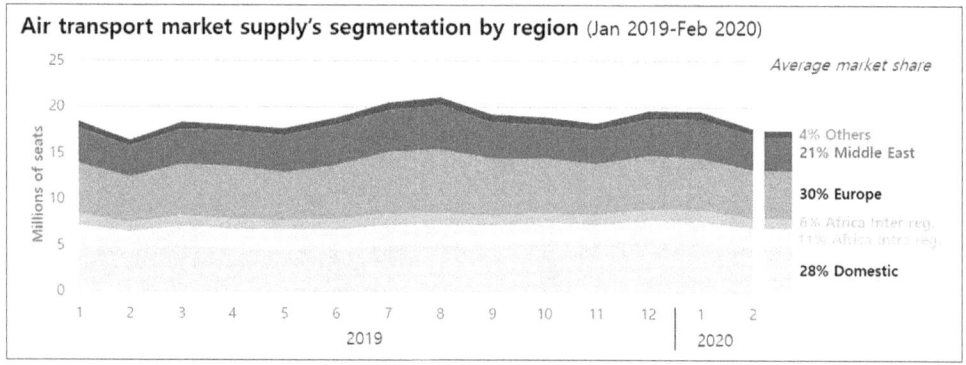

Unlike the European and US markets, where internal flights represent more than 85% of the seats, the **African market is more exposed to the international segment,** where the recovery of passengers' willingness to fly is expected to be slower.

Within the African market, **domestic flights represent 28%** of the seats and, as previously discussed, **recovery paths will mainly depend on each country's responses against COVID-19**.

On the other hand, the **regional market represents 17%** of the commercial seats. The Single African Air Transport Market (**SAATM**) is implemented differently depending on the region and, although there have been improvements, it is still at an early stage. At present, the inter-regional traffic accounts only for 6% of commercial seats.

The **intercontinental segment represents 55%** of market share, having even a higher economic impact on airports. This market is **severely threatened in the short/mid-term.** From an airline perspective, this market is dominated mainly by international carriers and therefore, its opening will be determined by European/Middle-East countries. If these countries were to be under lockdown, their recovery could be delayed.

Chapter 11: The sky has limits for the African Aviation Industry

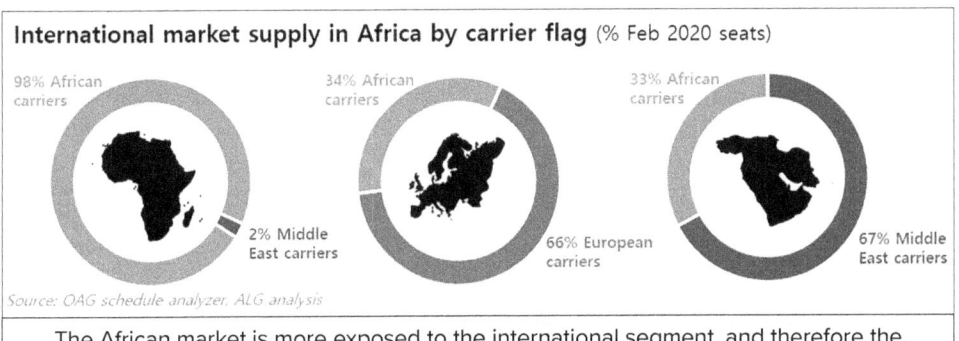

Source: OAG schedule analyzer, ALG analysis

The African market is more exposed to the international segment, and therefore the international carriers' strategy will affect its development.

Main African airlines will face viability risks due to liquidity issues

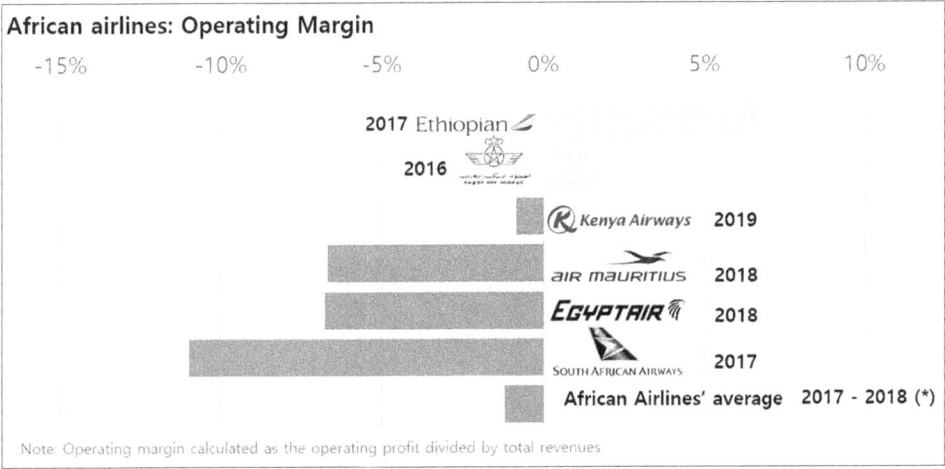

Note: Operating margin calculated as the operating profit divided by total revenues

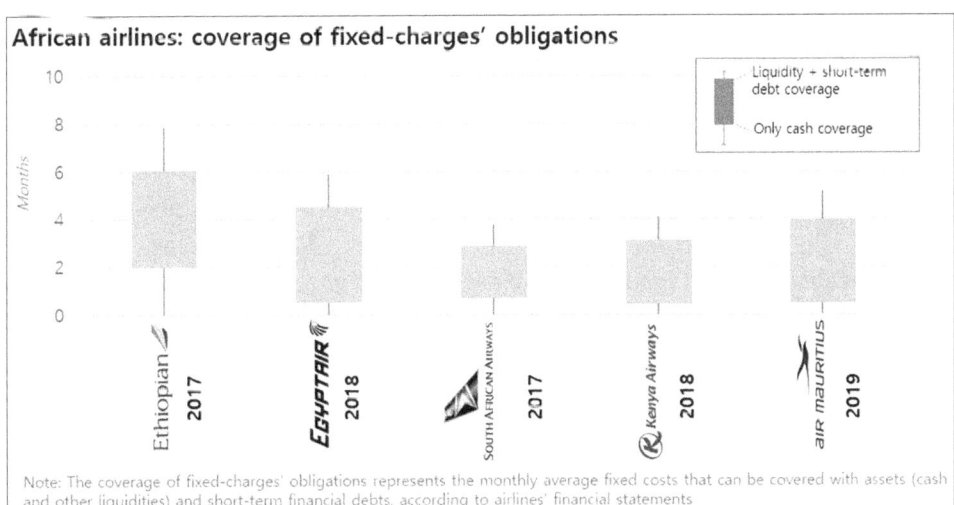

Note: The coverage of fixed-charges' obligations represents the monthly average fixed costs that can be covered with assets (cash and other liquidities) and short-term financial debts, according to airlines' financial statements

Some airlines will not have enough cash reserves to manage their financials and they will be driven to technical bankruptcy states or breached debt covenants. Governments should consider providing financial support/aid to guarantee the survival of their local airlines.

> African airlines can only guarantee their survival under a commercial lockdown for a period of 1 to 5 months, if no additional aviation business support measures are implemented.

Looking forward: different recovery scenarios

Aviation has never faced a similar global crisis. The COVID-19 outbreak will deeply change the air transport demand's scheme and patterns. The depths of the change will depend on how long it takes to overcome the pandemic. Even when the health crisis ends, the recovery of the economic downturn and passengers' willingness to fly will continue to impact the aviation sector.

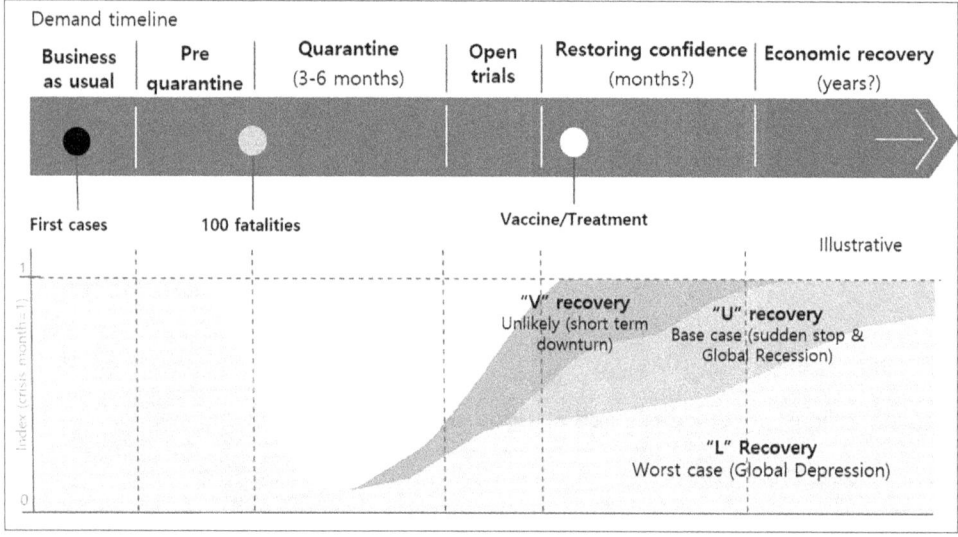

Different recovery shapes depending on Markets & Travel Purposes

- **Domestic/enclosed markets.** They are expected to recover first if governments implement effective social distancing initiatives.
- **International markets.** Different recovery rates depending on each country pair, and affected by many unmanageable factors: policies against COVID-19, duration of the quarantine period, availability of treatments, macroeconomic impacts, etc. We expect some countries to be affected for longer than others.
- **Travel purposes**

- Business: A fast recovery is expected for businesses where mobility is a must. However, passengers who can carry their activities via teleworking may no longer need aviation services.
- Visiting friends and relatives: The recovery will take longer, especially for populations that have low-income and are exposed to massive layoffs.
- Tourism: The sector has been heavily hit and its recovery is expected to be delayed. The change in passengers' leisure trends and the effect of the economic recovery are likely to penalise this passenger segment.

Africa's capacity expected to decrease ~32% in 2020 (base case scenario)

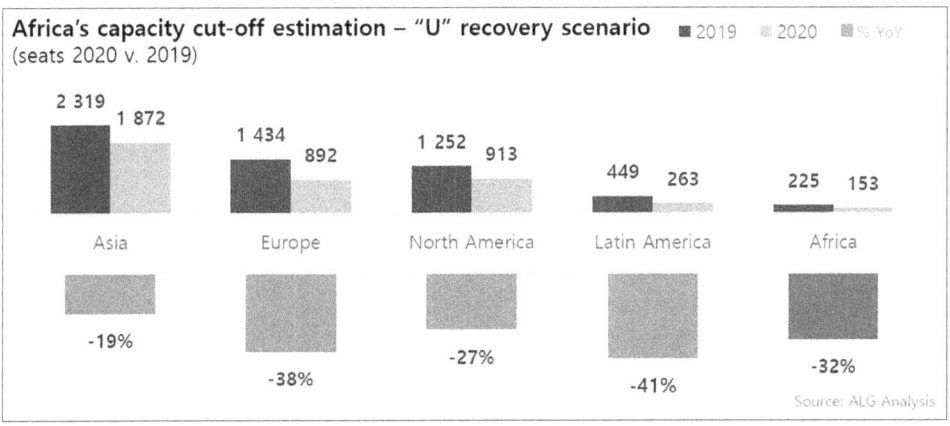

Airlines may have to implement social distancing policies. In this sense, non-African carriers operating long-haul flights will be the most affected, whereas African carriers with lower load factors will be less impacted.

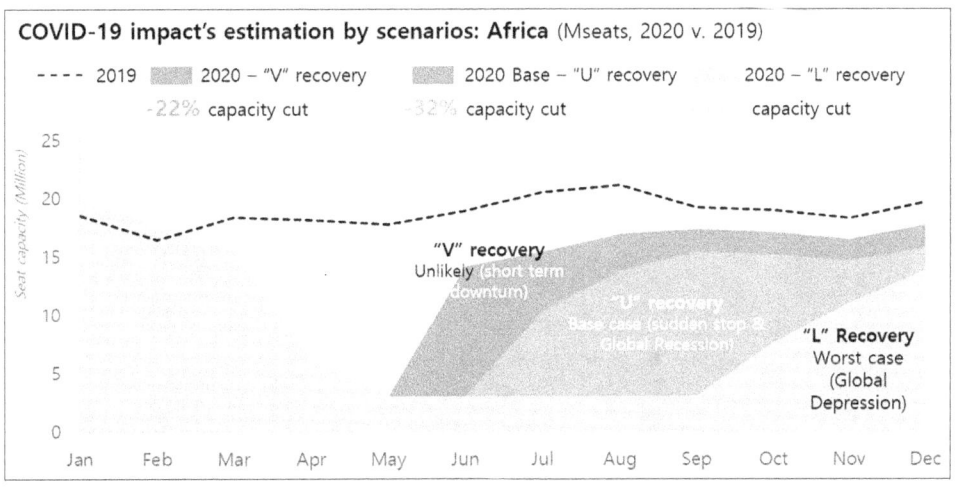

Seat **capacity is expected to decrease between -22% and -53% in 2020** in African aviation market.

The base scenario ("U" recovery) considers that the **African market will require more than 1 year to recover the pre-crisis demand levels.**

Expected recovery rate segmented by African regions

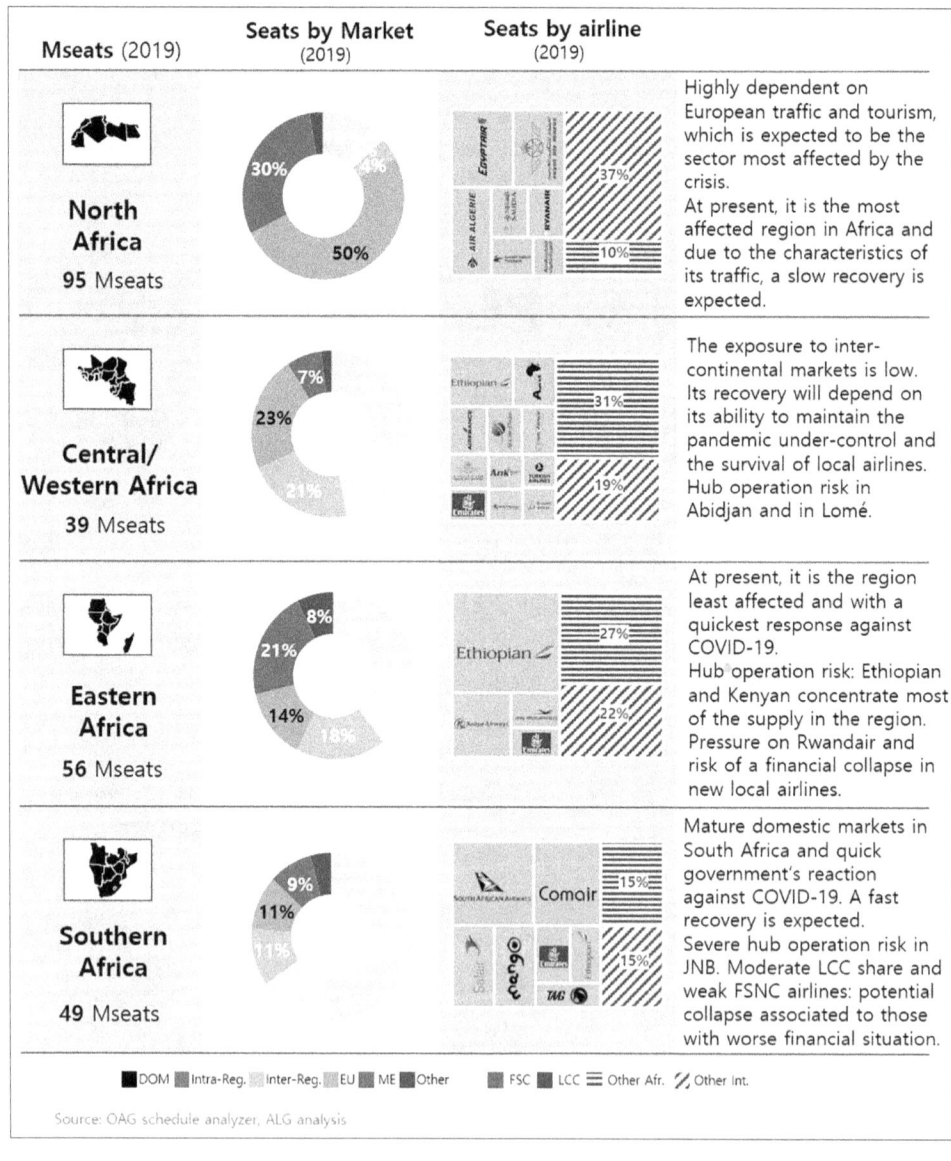

Source: OAG schedule analyzer, ALG analysis

Expected recovery rate in selected Aviation Nations

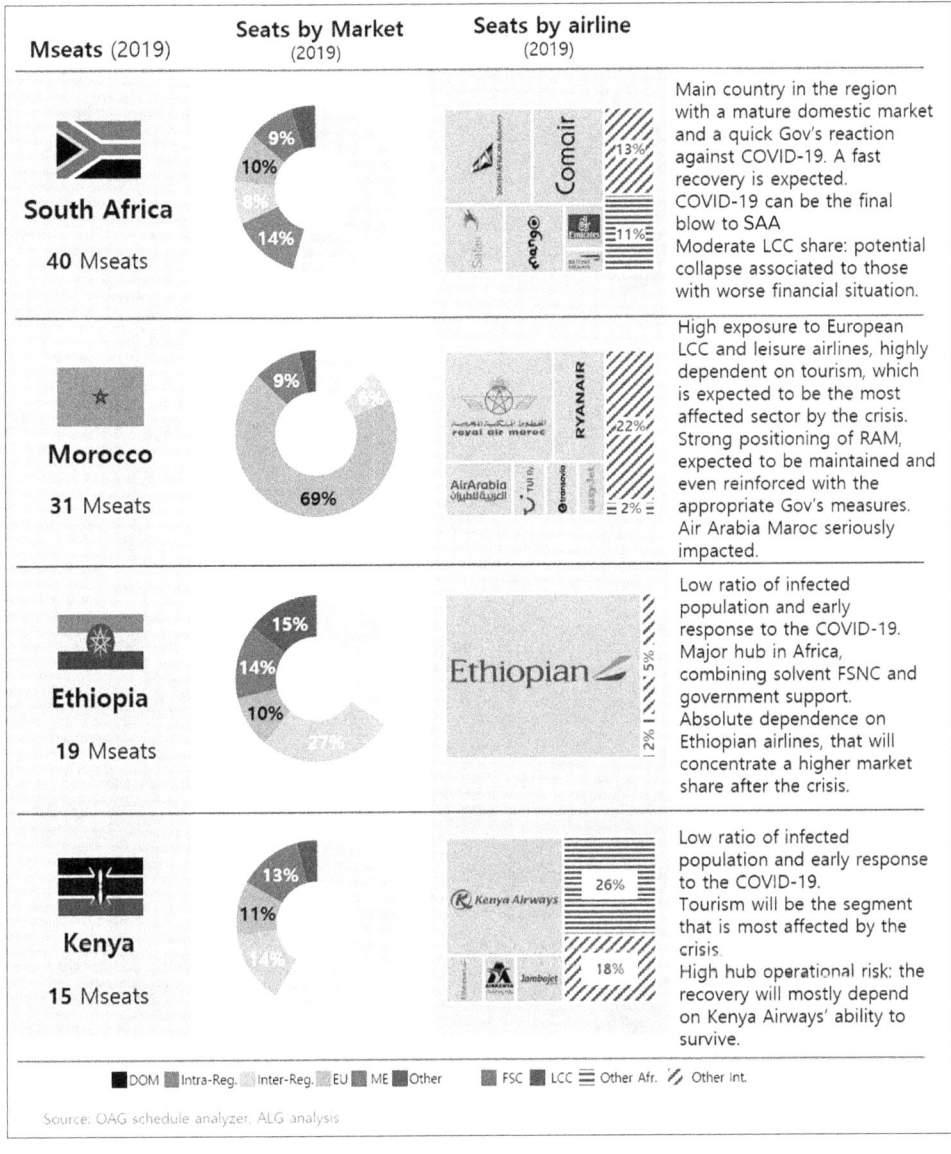

Mseats (2019)	Seats by Market (2019)	Seats by airline (2019)	
South Africa 40 Mseats	9% / 10% / 8% / 14%	Comair 13%, South African Airways, Mango, Safair, Emirates, British Airways 11%	Main country in the region with a mature domestic market and a quick Gov's reaction against COVID-19. A fast recovery is expected. COVID-19 can be the final blow to SAA. Moderate LCC share: potential collapse associated to those with worse financial situation.
Morocco 31 Mseats	9% / 69%	Royal Air Maroc, Ryanair 22%, Air Arabia, TUI fly, transavia, easyJet 2%	High exposure to European LCC and leisure airlines, highly dependent on tourism, which is expected to be the most affected sector by the crisis. Strong positioning of RAM, expected to be maintained and even reinforced with the appropriate Gov's measures. Air Arabia Maroc seriously impacted.
Ethiopia 19 Mseats	15% / 14% / 10% / 27%	Ethiopian, 5%, 2%, 1%	Low ratio of infected population and early response to the COVID-19. Major hub in Africa, combining solvent FSNC and government support. Absolute dependence on Ethiopian airlines, that will concentrate a higher market share after the crisis.
Kenya 15 Mseats	13% / 11% / 14%	Kenya Airways 26%, Jambojet 18%	Low ratio of infected population and early response to the COVID-19. Tourism will be the segment that is most affected by the crisis. High hub operational risk: the recovery will mostly depend on Kenya Airways' ability to survive.

■ DOM ■ Intra-Reg. ■ Inter-Reg. ■ EU ■ ME ■ Other   ■ FSC ■ LCC ≡ Other Afr. ⁄ Other Int.

Source: OAG schedule analyzer, ALG analysis

Expected recovery rate in selected African markets

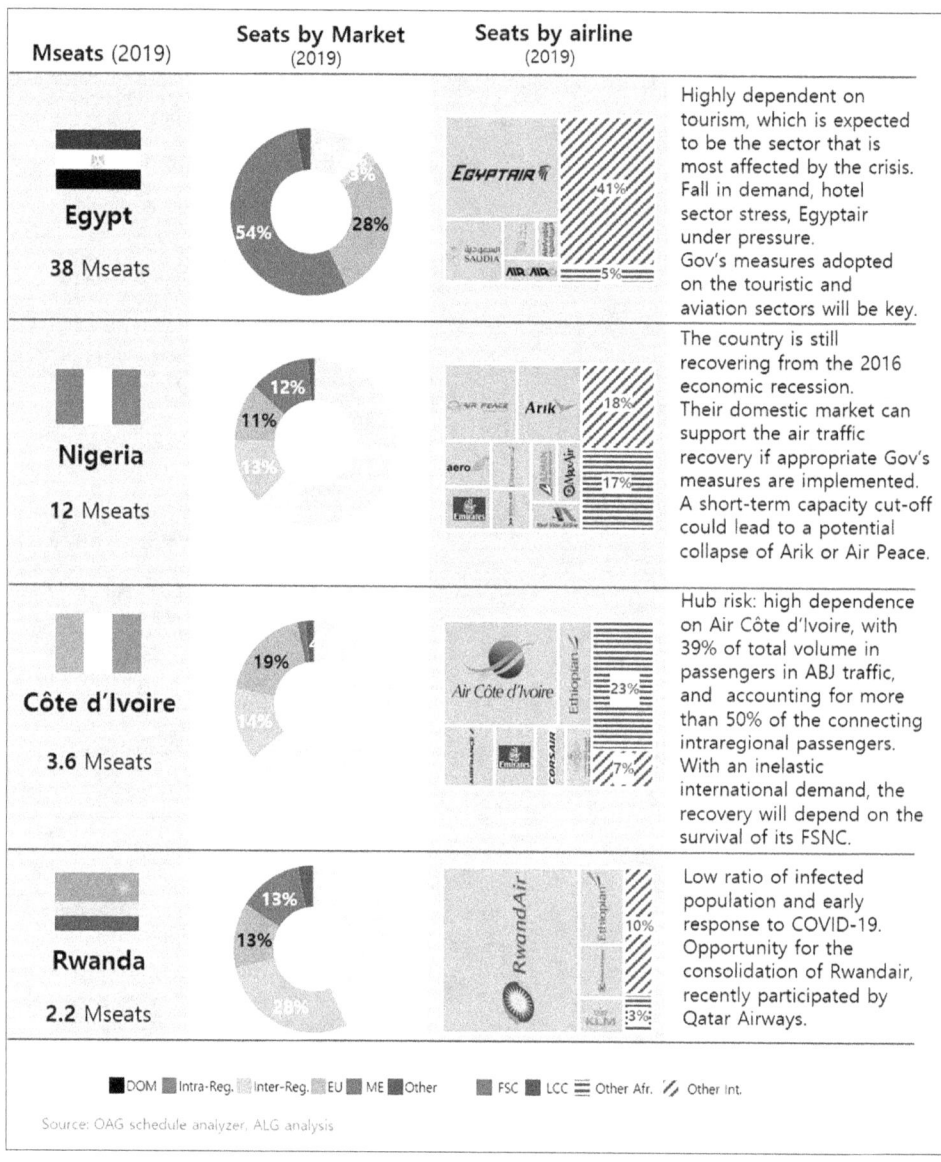

Source: OAG schedule analyzer, ALG analysis

Different airport recovery profiles: will the investment plans be impacted?

Airport recovery profile (dependent on each country's policies against the pandemic)

"U" recovery

- Major hubs combining solvent FSNC that will tend to concentrate a higher number of operations and are likely to receive governmental support.
- Regional hubs with a balanced fleet to provide international services and that are likely to receive governmental support.
- Country gateways with an inelastic demand and with an international economic interest.
- International hubs and airports without a solvent FSNC will depend on the governmental support received.
- Major/medium touristic airports, especially those with a high long haul services share.

"L" recovery

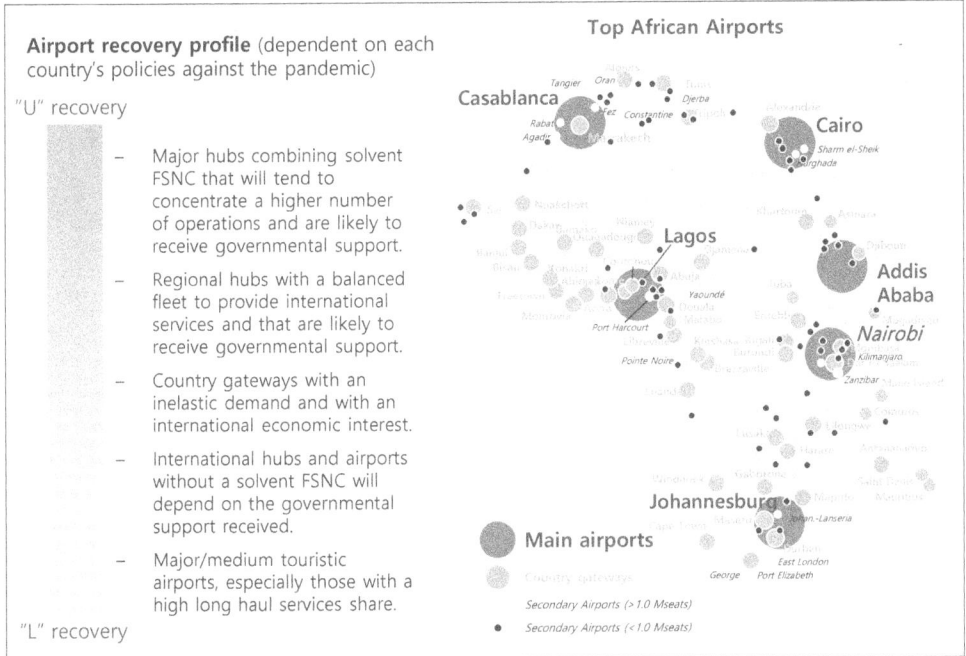

Top African Airports

Main airports
Country gateways
Secondary Airports (> 1.0 Mseats)
• Secondary Airports (< 1.0 Mseats)

Will investment plans remain necessary for major African airports/cities?

Addis Ababa — New International Airport
Cairo Airport — General airport/terminals expansion
Johannesburg / Cape Town Airports — General airport/terminals expansion
Luanda Airport — New International Airport
Dodoma Airport — New International Airport
Khartoum Airport — New International Airport

Airports require public support to make the recovery process viable

Revised IATA revenue forecast (31 March 2020) estimates that impact of the pandemic now stands at -41% fall in RPKs and minus USD15B versus the 2019's levels for the region.

It is pivotal for Governments to start the implementation of several initiatives needed to ensure the sustainability of the African air transport sector.

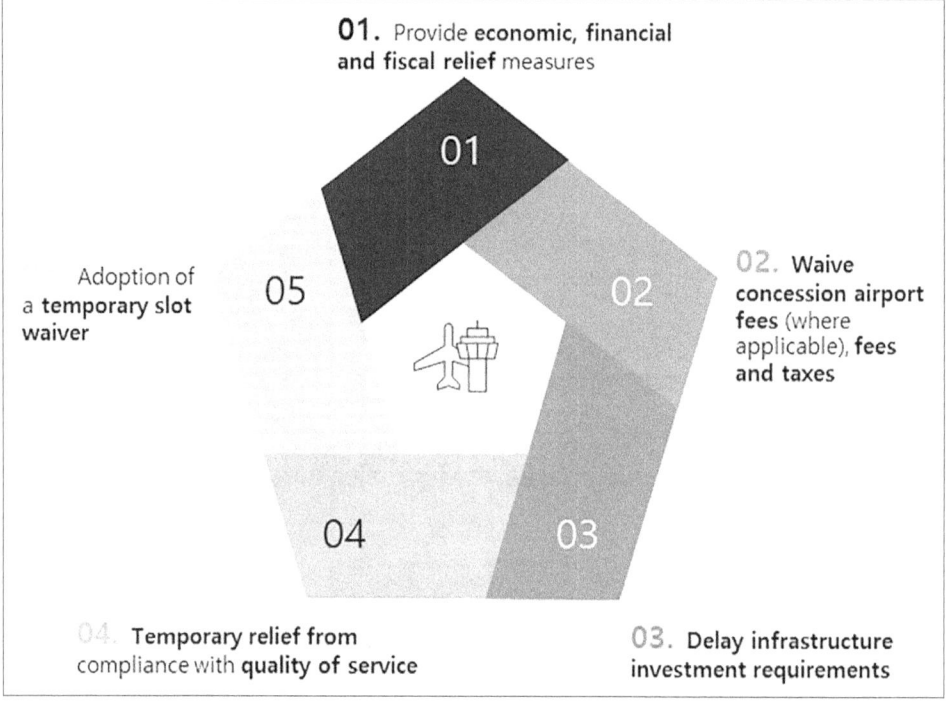

01. Provide **economic, financial and fiscal relief** measures

Adoption of a **temporary slot waiver**

02. Waive concession airport fees (where applicable), **fees and taxes**

04. Temporary relief from compliance with **quality of service**

03. Delay infrastructure investment requirements

The **multilateral development banks** are key in the recovery of this sector in Africa:

They need to reinforce their presence in the region with a triple objective:

1. **Mobilise finance**
2. **Support public procurement**
3. **Increase technical assistance and advisory services for knowledge creation and knowledge transfer**

Airport Operator responsiveness

Pre quarantine

Business Continuity Plan

In order **to deal with the health, social and economic crisis linked to COVID-19**, most of airport operators **are implementing their Business Continuity Plan**. According to the *Business Continuity Management Framework for Health-related disruptions at airports* issued by ACI in 2012, a Business Continuity Plan needs to **outline how the essential operations and services are maintained** and achieved, **either by establishing deeper layers of resiliency to essential operations and services, or through alternative arrangements.**

Quarantine (3-6 months)

Open trials

Smart operating models

COVID-19 can act as a catalyst to speed up the development of smart operating models; resilient, sustainable and innovative. **Biometric IT solutions** (facial/iris recognition), **smart H&S** and **paperless resilient, collaborative, connected and flexible processes** should be adopted to minimize contact.

Refinancing Operations

Additionally, airport's **operator companies will require refinancing packages and loan modification programs** to manage the outbreak by cutting the financing costs.

Restoring confidence (months?)

Concession Agreement & Scheme Review

Most of **airport's operators will require financial support/aid from governments**. Airports under PPP scheme will apply their Force Majeure Event clause considering the Concession Agreement Review. **A review of the economic concession model will be imperative** to ensure the financial viability of the concessionaire.

Economic recovery (years?)

It will also be necessary to **review the PPP Concession Agreement Schemes** used by some of Governments, incorporating the best practices and lessons learned from this crisis **in order to make the agreements more self-adjusting**. The revision of the contractual frameworks should focus on single/dual till schemes **to improve flexibility with respect to the demand's behavior** and allowing to minimize rebalancing in the event of demand outbreaks.

*Based on our experience, the minimum adjustment measures that need to be considered when rebalancing a concession are: **reviewing the concession term, the revenue share (%) and the capital project plan** (size and term of the investments).*

Chapter 12

A tourism crisis recovery checklist during and post COVID-19

TRINET

Initial TRINET Responses to COVID-19 Tourism[1]

The unprecedented societal changes brought on by the COVID-19 pandemic are dramatically affecting tourism. It is too early to know the full nature and impact of these changes, but it is clear that they will be transformative for the entire planet, and every destination will need to re-create its tourism from the ground up. TRINET, which is an electronic discussion forum of over 3 000 tourism researchers and educators worldwide, is seeking to assist with knowledge in this crisis. Its initial response is taking two forms.

First, the immense opportunity to re-define post-COVID-19 travel and tourism to be based more on regenerative principles is starting to be realised. This re-birthing of tourism will require new sets of values, new paradigms, and a dramatic shift from the over-tourism, overconsumption and excessive greed that defined much of pre-COVID-19 tourism. These discussions are fledgling and will continue. Professor Alan Lew, with other TRINET members, has started to put structure around this initiative to further these discussions through the "Travel and Tourism Transformed" platform.[2] TRINETTERS are invited to contribute their knowledge, intellect, compassion and vision for a new tourism future on this platform. Please contact Alan Lew through the TourismTranformed.com website.

The second initiative, spearheaded by Professor Bob McKercher, member of the TRINET International Advisory Board, is "A Tourism Crisis Recovery Checklist" (below). This document presents our current knowledge on how to deal with tourism crises. It distils ideas, actions and strategies that destinations and enterprises can consider when responding to and recovering from a range of crises. While the genesis of this initiative is the COVID-19 outbreak, it has broader applicability. The materials presented here were gathered from various sources, including industry reports,

---

1 Travel and Tourism Research Association (TTRA). (2020). Initial TRINET Responses to COVID-19 Tourism (v. April 2, 2020). Retrieved from: https://ttra.com/wp-content/uploads/2020/04/TRINET-COVID-19-Recovery.pdf

2 Travel & Tourism Transformed. (n.d.). Travel, Tourism & Hospitality in a COVID-19 World. Retrieved from: https://www.tourismtransformed.com/

academic publications and the collective knowledge of the global academic TRINET tourism community. The document focuses on tourism issues only, even though it is recognised that crises affect all aspects of a community and society. If you have further contributions to this checklist, please contact Bob McKercher through email: bob.mckercher@polyu.edu.hk.

Tourism Crisis Recovery Checklist

Crises have phases

Every crisis situation is context-specific, including scale (global to national to local to sector to individual business), nature (natural, war, medical, etc.), extent (severity vs. ability to keep the event fairly localised), time frame (short to long term duration and impact), affected sectors (markets, destination or both) and stage of the event (incipient, rapid growth, peaking, getting better, second wave, recovery, post-event, etc.).

All crises have predictable phases:

- Pre-event and predictive— No indication as yet of the impending crisis, but time to be prepared and have a crisis management plan in place in the eventuality that an incident occurs.
- Prodromal (early symptoms) – In most cases, early warning signs are evident, but are ignored or misinterpreted. Screening of media outlets can identify early warning signs. Now is the time to prepare/update plans and activate them, update training, prepare to respond.
- Emergency – The key rule of thumb is do not make it worse. Safety of guests and staff is critical. Accurate and effective communications are important. Strategies and actions to protect the business need to be implemented. Its employees and the community it operates in must be considered.
- Crisis continuity – The crisis is ongoing. What are short-term solutions that can be implemented? Care for staff and clients is essential. Monitor the situation to see what the longer-term implications and/or predicted duration will be. Prepare resilience plans.
- Recovery – Establish recovery objectives and timelines. Stratify and prioritise target markets. Work with intermediaries and the public. Be positive and honest in communication. Implement plans. Treat media, including social media as an ally. Demonstrate appreciation to others.
- Resolution – What actions to take to recover as quickly as possible? What lessons have been learned? Are you prepared for the next crisis? Rapid recovery often occurs after an event.

During the Event

A range of actions can be undertaken during the event. Importantly, it must be appreciated that consumer confidence has been damaged and will not return until the event passes.

Strategic actions

- Step back and plan for the relaunch. Evaluate the position and develop plans at a destination, corporate or property level.
- Sharpen market research to identify strong segments likely to recover first, new markets or new segments in existing markets that can be actualised.
- Develop a new branding strategy as the old one may be tarnished by the crisis.
- Look at ways of diversifying the market post-recovery if overly reliant on one source.
- Work closely with industry to develop a series of packages that can be launched at short notice. Packages can include special rates for airfare, accommodation, food and beverage, etc.
- Forward book through vouchers and coupons to keep some cash flowing into businesses.
- Arrange mutually beneficial terms and conditions with suppliers. Make them part of the problem and the solution. Work out smart solutions and make real-time rearrangements.
- Take this opportunity to restructure and open new avenues for business.
- While price cuts can deliver a brief spike in volume, they can also result in long-term pain for any business that pursues this strategy.
- Renegotiate contracts with intermediaries and OTAs.

Operational Issues

Finance

- Secure additional funding to launch the recovery when the time is right.
- Set up a fund to support re-training, short-term job search skills, support groups, etc.
- Manage costs as much as possible. Work with suppliers to arrange suitable terms, cut non-essential services, etc.
- Work with financial institutions for finance, credit and loan restructuring.
- Try to minimise fixed costs.
- Instil short-term cash flow monitoring discipline that allows cash flow predictions and intervene in a timely manner.

- Stress test any tier one and tier two suppliers that may be impacted.
- Extend credit or postpone payments.

Marketing

- Severely restrict all marketing activities – consumer confidence has been damaged and will not return until the event passes. Advertising and heavy discounts do not work if consumers are unwilling to travel.
- Maintain channel promotions if costs are minimal as it will maintain a good relationship with suppliers.
- Utilise social media effectively.
- Focus on the most cost-effective booking channels. Ensure that book-direct perks are prominently displayed throughout websites and on social media outlets.
- Focus on increasing revenue from every booking. Consider launching length of stay offers.
- Reduce and restructure advertising budgets.
- Refocus budget on domestic and nearby markets.
- Aim for the local market and promote staycations.
- Promote safety to international tourists.

Staffing

- Keep tourism staff in their jobs and develop mutual solutions as much as possible. Empower them to make decisions and make mutually beneficial arrangements.
- Try no paid leave or send people on leave, rather than letting them go. Once staff leave it will be hard to replace them when things get better. You risk losing good people.
- Release casual and part-time staff first and essential staff last.
- Support staff development especially for people who have free time and can work from home.
- Monitor the mental health of staff and intervene if needed.
- Implement flexible working patterns, work remotely, staff self-isolation, reduced workdays, etc.
- Support equipment to facilitate effective work-from-home solutions.
- Support teleconferencing and video conferencing technology.
- Retrain staff to multi-task.
- Reassure and involve staff as essential stakeholders.
- Ensure protection of workers from unemployment and loss of income (short-time work schemes, upskilling and reskilling programs) and support for self-employed tourism stakeholders.

- Freeze pay rates.
- As an emergency action – replace highly paid employees with new low paid employees, but be careful, for short-term fixes may cause long-term problems.
- Increase outsourcing if cost-effective.

Operations

- Facilitate re-bookings to avoid, where possible, cancellations. Everyone is hurting. Do not add insult to injury. Reconsider cancellation policies.
- Close non-essential operations or scale back operations. For example, hotels with multiple food outlets can close one or more of the outlets. Close floors. Reduce services.
- Offer 'Corona Vouchers', whereby travellers and tourists who had to cancel their trip will be reimbursed with this voucher instead of giving them their money back. This voucher can be used for any other trip and is valid for one year after issuing. This should be optional.
- For meetings and events, hoteliers should liaise with the event organisers to postpone the event instead of accepting outright cancellations.
- Postpone non-essential building maintenance.
- Postpone non-essential systems maintenance.
- Utilise staff skills in tasks outside their normal role.
- Have action plans ready in case guests/clients become ill. Implement appropriate screening measures on check-in. Enhance cleaning and sanitation.
- From buffet to plated food. From shared food to individual.
- Implement technological solutions to address fears (contactless and robotised access, information) and reduce unnecessarily close human contacts.

Consumer Confidence

- Wait and watch consumer sentiment to see when it changes.
- Reassure consumers that you are doing all you can to make the destination/business safe.

Community

- Develop public relations strategies and implement them at a community level to talk about the benefits of tourism and to remind people to welcome tourists when the time is right.
- Look after affected people as much as possible.
- Work closely with health authorities to minimise the spread of disease.

- Offer support to the elderly and most affected stakeholders through the delivery of food or shopping or undertaking critical tasks that require available equipment. Offer training and development training for people to develop skills and work closely with you in the future.
- Deliver food and offer hospitality to front-line workers.
- Launch public welfare activities, whereby front-line workers can gain free or heavily discounted entry to tourism attractions or scenic spots.
- Promote, shape and implement closer cooperation and trust between and with industry and non-industry partners at large, including NGOs.

Communications

- Have a single point of contact and a single voice to communicate about the issue.
- Accurate and timely information is critical for everyone as is an analysis of the trends.
- Tell the truth and be transparent.
- Stay on message and do not speculate.
- Challenge untrue statements.
- Do not impose a media blackout.
- Respond in the same medium.
- Develop holding statements – release information that you do have.
- Respond quickly.
- Use social media and continually monitor the online conversation. They are ideal to provide up- to-date information.
- Maintain regular contact with suppliers regarding their capability to deliver goods and services.

Government Relations

- Promote policy solutions for recovery and avoidance/mitigation in the future.
- Promote solidarity.
- Look for big picture policy initiatives that can be considered, such as visa waiver changes.
- Lobby government for a grace period on local taxes.
- Fast and easy access to short- and medium-term loans to overcome liquidity shortages.
- Fiscal relief (both at source market and destination level), starting with SMEs and extending to operators of all sizes.
- Immediate passing of temporary airport slots waiver.
- Organize civil action to convey a unified voice to government.

- Lobby for longer-term actions such as simplification of visa rules, reducing or waiving travellers' taxes and supporting economically hit destinations with promotion and marketing to attract tourists.
- Lobby government for financial help to protect the incomes of workers who will be temporarily laid off.
- Seek cash flow assistance to support large and small tourism stakeholders.
- Consider initiating the formation of a public–private partnership crisis management team to manage crises and develop recovery strategies.
- Government interventionism to stimulate local demand for tourism through the provision of a voucher for each worker and this voucher can be used only for domestic tourism consumption
- Try to encourage grants and forgivable loans and try to discourage non-forgivable loans. They only delay the problem but do not resolve it.

Post-event

Recovery plans can begin during the event but must be implemented effectively post-event.

What can we as academics do?

- Volunteer your services as money is very limited.
- Work collaboratively with others. Now is the time to cooperate.
- Provide targeted research backup, including to inform policy changes.
- Share our collective research with DMOs and industry.
- Promote a different way to conduct tourism.

Policy

- Rebuild trust in a concerted and cooperative effort involving government, DMOs and industry.
- Reconsider the balance between volume and quality of target markets for tourists.
- Develop system-wide recovery strategies.
- Develop system-wide crisis strategies.
- Identify and focus on sustainable competitive advantages.
- Communicate the benefits of tourism to the local community.
- Mitigate any tendency to tourist phobia and racism involving tourists from certain regions.

Sustainability

- Promote more sustainable actions.
- Be humble and appreciate that the commercial tourism sector is the facilitator of experiences and not the experience itself.
- Tourism can be a regenerative industry locally, nationally and internationally. Encourage relevant policy development.

Marketing

- Relaunch the destination/product.
- Launch packages and promotional specials that have been developed during the event.
- Progressive market expansion aiming at cured markets first and then expanding to more markets.
- Target loyal markets.
- Work on local MICE sector.
- Focus initially on domestic and nearby international markets. There may be country boundary issues to deal with.
- Social networking – Instagram, Facebook, etc. – with good news stories.
- Focus on business travel – it is far less discretionary.
- Follow PATA's nine step marketing and Communication process:
    - **Step 1:** Get prime message out: We are open for business; tourists are welcome and wanted;
    - **Step 2:** Setting out the facts: Our destinations/hotel/tour/ attraction/flights are operating; outline restrictions and limitations;
    - **Step 3:** Complementary alliances with principals: Joint arrangements with hoteliers, resorts, restaurants, attractions, land tours and air links; value-added arrangements between complementing principals;
    - **Step 4:** Restoring confidence in source markets: Travel agents and travel writers' familiarisation trips – choose opinion leaders;
    - **Step 5:** Protecting profitability during marketing recovery: Offer incentives which will enable the business to sustain profitability – value add rather than discount;
    - **Step 6:** Re-image the business and the destination: Re-theme advertising and promotion;
    - **Step 7:** Incentives which attract tourists – value-added products;
    - **Step 8:** Publicize the positives – positive news of resurgence of tourist arrivals, rebuilding and enhancements of infrastructure;
    - **Step 9:** Reporting and monitoring progress – publicise the changes and enhancements made.

Integration

- Work with transport providers to reduce barriers to entry.
- Coordination by governments at all levels (national, state, regional, local) to deliver a consistent message to the consumer.
- Reassure the local community.

Community

- Buy goods from local producers.
- Build an online platform to connect local food producers and the industry.
- Altruism and solidarity.
- Encourage VFR to build traffic and link with resident needs to visit family following any lock-down.
- Encourage local residents to visit the local attractions or spots first. People are more aware of the real situation of the local epidemic, so they are more confident to have some tourism-related activities with family in local areas.

Consumers

- Allow people with antibodies against the coronavirus to travel freely if the issue is still unresolved. Have them bring a certificate issued by their home country.
- Assure consumers the destination is safe.
- Remind them of any actions the destination may still be implementing (such as virus checks, other security measures, etc.).
- Explain sanitisation processes.
- Build on trust and relationship. Promote sustainability, respect nature.
- Educate tourists not to damage the physical and social environment.
- Emphasis on service quality by offering the true meaning of hospitality.
- Be prepared for a strong rebound in demand. Like a coiled spring, the harder it is depressed, the stronger it bounces back.

Longer-term

Rationalisation and opportunity:

- There will be a shakeout in the industry with many businesses ceasing operations. This will create new opportunities for businesses to fill the void.
- Forced rationalisation of non-profitable operations.

Crisis Management Plans

- Develop a crisis strategy and review it regularly. Most crisis strategies are written once and then put on a shelf.
- Identify a leader, voice of the crisis and establish a chain of command to follow.
- Have regular training for staff, given the high staff turnover.
- Train at regular intervals.

A crisis matrix can help identify the type of events that are likely to occur and their impact.

	Low probability	High probability
Low impact	Rare, non-critical problem • Prepare standard operating procedures • Retain the risk	Routine, non-critical problem • Prepare standard operating procedures • Reduce the likelihood of consequences • Reduce the consequences of occurrence • Transfer the risk (i.e. insurance)
High impact	Crisis that is difficult to predict and prepare for • Prepare crisis and disaster plan • Set contingency plans	Critical event that is easier to predict and prepare for • Prepare standard operating procedures • Prepare crisis and disaster plan • Avoid the risk • Transfer the risk (i.e. insurance)

Prepare and update crisis management plans. All crisis management plans should include:

- People involved and their tasks;
- Key external stakeholders;
- Updated and current contact list;
- Methods for identifying crises;
- Methods for involving management;
- Lines of communication;
- Mechanisms for reporting;
- Process for decision making;
- Equipment, facilities and occupation of crisis management centre;
- Levels of control and authority limits.

Tourism crisis management strategies should:

- Describe activation procedures – what needs to be done first and by whom;
- Means of alerting personnel and activating the tourism crisis management system;
- Allocate tourism crisis management roles and responsibilities;
- Identify control and coordination arrangements;
- Include standard procedures for the response to and recovery from crises;
- Assess the effects of the crisis upon facilities;
- Describe public relations and media management arrangements, including social media;
- Identify critical business activities to be recovered and the time frame and level of recovery needed;
- Identify options for offsite backup IT materials;
- Identify alternative suppliers.
- Develop standard operating procedures.
- Develop a social media strategy.

TRINET, the Tourism Research Information Network, connects members of the international tourism research and education community. Its purpose is to promote an open exchange of ideas, information, and opinions that are relevant to tourism scholarship, including theory, research, education, policy development, and operational matters.

Part 4

Crisis Leadership Excellence

Chapter 13

Crisis leadership excellence: Navigating in, beyond and through a crisis[1]

Theo H. Veldsman

Leadership is about imagining possible futures proactively, and realising a chosen, shared, desired future with followers making up a team, organisation, community or society. True leadership is proactively being the architect of a chosen, desired future, not the reactive victim of an imposed or reacted-to future. Formally described, leadership encompasses the exercise of persuasive influence by one or more persons (=leaders), engaging a set of stakeholders (=followers) in an enabling and empowering way with regard to a joint course of action (=dream), intended to bring about a collective, ensured future outcome with a desired effect (=legacy) within a specific context.

But how must leadership respond when a crisis arises? A crisis is an unexpected, threatening event, which as a significant interruption endangers the likelihood of a team, organisation, community or society realising its chosen, shared, desired future, contained and expressed in their shared dream with its intended legacy. A crisis threatens either to derail the journey undertaken to realise the chosen, shared desired future; and/or to destroy the chosen, shared, desired future by rendering it highly undesirable as an outcome. More specifically, a crisis can threaten to disrupt a system, structure, a way of doing/living, accepted values and/or people. A crisis is the unholy, wicked confluence of unexpectedness, threat, uncertainty and urgency. In short, a crisis is an emergency that detrimentally disrupts the expected status quo, resulting in dire consequences.

Often, a crisis is not so much a crisis in an objective, factual sense, but becomes such in the eyes of those who have to deal with and are impacted by the event, given their perceptions of the threat, as well as their stake in, the impact of, and the consequences of, the event. These perceptions give a certain rhythm or pulse to a crisis: fast/slow; positive/negative; trust/suspicion; good/bad; important/unimportant; contained/widespread; winners/losers. Although the word 'crisis' as a dangerous threat invokes all of the foresaid, it also simultaneously triggers the opportunity to make things differently and/or better.

---

1   This chapter originally appeared in Crous, W. (2020). *Managing Organisations During the COVID-19 Vortex: Comprehensive guidelines for leading your organisation through the vortex*. Bryanston: KR Publishing.

A crisis is always accompanied by a pressure cooker-like stress for a number of reasons: important decisions have to be taken under conditions of typically quite severe time pressure; there is often insufficient information, especially because of time pressure; the event is not static but evolving in its knock-on consequences and impact – frequently rapidly; choices and trade-offs have to be made between often unattractive alternatives; additional resources have to be found quickly to deal with the crisis; and the close, ongoing public scrutiny by stakeholders of every move made, even bringing to bear the history of past moves on other/related matters, strongly fuelled and given momentum by the social media in a uncontainable, runaway fashion.

The purpose of this chapter is to elucidate what an appropriate leadership response is for leaders to a crisis who are aspiring to remain proactive architects of a chosen, desired future. The chapter only focuses on organisational leadership. It proceeds by addressing, *first,* the make-up of an appropriate crisis leadership response: 'In-Beyond-Through'; *second,* the critical success factors for an effective 'In-Beyond-Through' crisis leadership response; *third,* core crisis leadership capabilities; and, *fourth*, the ten commandments of crisis leadership excellence.

Make-up of an appropriate crisis leadership response

As a departure point, leadership needs to respond in an integrated, comprehensive and balanced manner to a crisis. The essence of such a response can be summed up in a single phrase: *Leadership has to navigate concurrently In, Beyond and Through a crisis.*

In engaging with a crisis, leadership has to concurrently demonstrate the following responses:

- **'Navigate'**: leadership has to respond in a juggling, iterative, adaptive and systemic manner to a crisis, because a crisis cannot be managed in a programmatic, linear fashion due to its unexpectedness, uncertainty, ambiguity, evolving nature and unpredictable impact.
- **'In'**: leadership has to recognise that the organisation faces a crisis, and *Frame* the crisis correctly in order for leadership to engage appropriately with it.
- **'Beyond'**: leadership has to *Anchor* the crisis by using the identity of the organisation as a secure reference point and fixed compass setting during the chaos of engaging with the crisis.
- **'Through'**: leadership has to *Resolve* the crisis by crafting and rolling out a fit-for-purpose solution – the intervention – to recover from the crisis.

Whilst *Framing-Anchoring-Resolving* a crisis, leadership must ensure, grow and maintain adequate levels of Organisation and People Capitals (explicated later) within their organisation in order to address the crisis successfully. On the one hand, leadership must protect the running down of these Capitals during the crisis, while on the other, they must leverage these Capitals to deal with the crisis effectively.

Figure **13.**1 depicts the above discussion in the form of a Crisis Leadership Response Triangle. The lines linking the three responses illustrates the navigating nature of addressing a crisis. Each ingredient of the Triangle is discussed below.

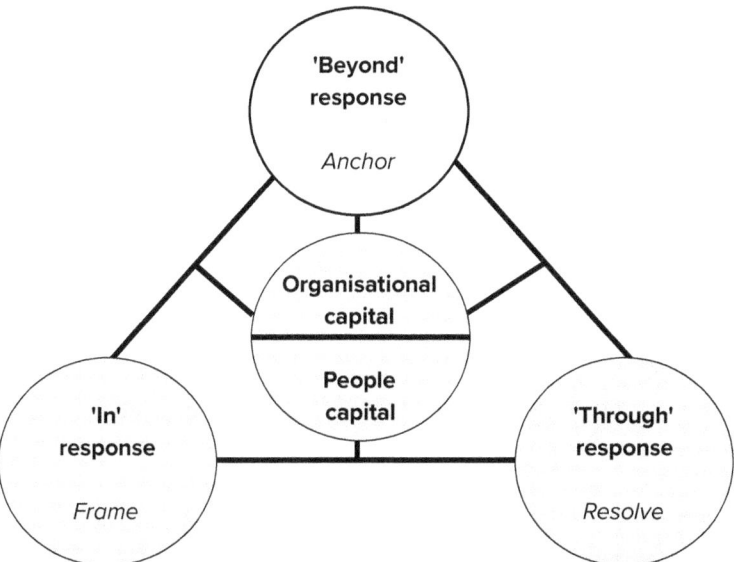

Figure 13.1: Crisis Leadership Response Triangle

'In' Leadership Response: *Frame*

The unexpected, threatening event has occurred; leadership is 'In' the crisis. As the initial triggering response to put the wheels in motion, leadership must put on the right set of glasses to ensure that they have a 2020 vision of the crisis. This set of glasses enables them to take stock of and position the crisis right if they are to have any chance of dealing with it appropriately.

At least three factors must be considered in framing the crisis right: territory, dynamics and engagement mode.

Factor 1: Territory

The territory of (or 'space' occupied by) the crisis has to be demarcated correctly by considering at least the following factors in order to accurately profile the threat faced:

- *Magnitude* – the variables/stakeholders implicated with the numbers per variable/stakeholder affected: uni-dimensional vs. multi-dimensional in a contained, extrapolative progression vs. unbounded, exponential progression.
- *Interdependency* – the interconnectedness of variables/stakeholders affected: independent vs. serially or reciprocally interdependent.
- *Urgency* – the timeframe required to deal with the crisis: sudden, acute, here-and-now threat vs. smouldering, creeping threat.
- *Uncertainty* – 'knownness' of crisis: unknown vs. known.
- *Severity* – degree of impact: temporarily (=deviation from normal) vs. permanent (=new normal.)
- *Timeframe* – single, once-off event vs. unfolding series of evolving events.

A high level static and/or dynamic model can be built based on the above to map the crisis in terms of different probable scenarios as the crisis unfolds, allowing predictions and thus enabling the proactive identification of recovery actions. The greater the scope, complexity, urgency, uncertainty, severity and timeframe of a crisis, the greater the threat it poses and the more difficult its manageability.

For example, in the case of COVID-19, scientifically derived, epidemiological projections based on a static model, with a large amount of uncertainty, during the 2nd/3rd week of March 2020 for South Africa showed that a slow and inadequate response by the South African government to the outbreak of the virus could result in anywhere between 87,900 (10% infection of population) and 351,000 (40% infection of population) deaths, and cause the health system to be totally overwhelmed and collapse.

Apart from the medical impact and personal emotional trauma, the knock-on economic impact (e.g. employees unable to be at work and hence not being paid, and organisations earning no/little revenue with the resultant retrenchment of employees and reduced tax income to the state) and socio-cultural impact (e.g. restrictions on social and religious events, shopping and entertainment) have to be modelled.

Factor 2: Dynamics

Demarcating the territory of a crisis provides a relatively static picture of it. A more dynamic picture must therefore be built of the crisis based on the accurate recognition of the nature of the situational dynamics represented by the crisis that has to be addressed. A crisis can represent one of four types of possible situational dynamics, indicative of the complexity of the crisis faced. Table **13**.1 provides an overview of the different types of situational crisis dynamics.

Table 13.1: Types of Crisis Dynamics

TYPES OF SITUATIONAL CRISIS DYNAMICS	LEVEL OF KNOWNNESS	SITUATIONAL CHARACTERISTICS	EXAMPLE
Simple Crisis	Known knowns	Clear cause and effect relationships/repeating, stable patterns, apparent to everyone. One, self-evident, right answer exists.	• IT system crash • Mine fire • Volcanic disruption • Oil spill • Tylenol capsule poisoning
Complicated Crisis	Known unknowns	Cause-and-effect relationships discoverable but not immediately apparent to everyone. Multiple right answers possible, of which at least one is the best fit at a given time.	• Pandemic like COVID-19 • 2008/9 world economic crisis • Nuclear disaster
Complex Crisis	Unknown unknowns	Flux and unpredictability. No right answers exist. The search is to uncover emergent, instructive patterns, with understanding emerging only after things have already happened.	• Global warming • Cyber attack
Chaotic Crisis	Unknowables	High turbulence and fluidity with no clear causal relationships. Futile to search for the 'right' answer as it changes all the time.	• 9/11

Factor 3: Engagement Mode

With accurate recognition of the type of situational crisis dynamics faced within the demarcated crisis territory, leadership next has to choose the best overall mode to engage constructively with the crisis concerned. Table **13**.2 gives different leadership engagement modes with their associated actions relative to the different situational crisis dynamics.

Table 13.2: Crisis Engagement Domains with Leadership Modes and Actions

TYPES OF SITUATIONAL CRISIS DYNAMICS	ENGAGEMENT DOMAIN	LEADERSHIP ENGAGEMENT MODE	LEADERSHIP ACTIONS
Simple Crisis	Domain of best practice	Consultative, fact-based leadership • *Individual* • *Top down* • *Long term* • *Plan*	• Sense, categorise, respond • Ensure formalised, standardised, expert-referenced processes are in place • Communicate in clear, direct and inclusive ways
Complicated Crisis	Domain of experts	Co-determination, ideas-based leadership • *Shared* • *Top down* • *Long term* • *Plan*	• Sense, analyse, respond • Investigate several options related to good practice • Enable and listen to conflicting, diverse advice from multiple sources
Complex Crisis	Domain of emergence	High involvement, pattern-recognition leadership • *Shared* • *Top down/ Bottom up* • *Medium term* • *Improvisation*	• Explore/discover, reflect, respond • Creating situations and probing "safe-to-fail" experiments to allow innovative ideas to germinate and emerge in safe situations, and patterns to surface • Intense, inclusive interaction and communication
Chaotic Crisis	Domain of rapid response	Directive, pattern-discovery leadership • *Individual* • *Top down/ Bottom up* • *Short term* • *Improvisation*	• Act, discover/understand, and transform context • Immediate action to re-establish order and staunch bleeding instead of finding the right answer • Clear, direct, top-down communication

The basic thrust of the 'Through' response (to be discussed below) is to move the level of the manageability of the situational crisis dynamics as rapidly as possible from a Chaotic Crisis to a Complex Crisis and then to a Complicated Crisis (see Table **13**.2.)

In summary, the 'In' leadership response enables leaders to *Frame* the crisis right by demarcating the crisis territory appropriately; accurately recognising the situational crisis dynamics; and choosing the appropriate mode of engaging constructively with the crisis. It must be stressed that *Framing* is an iterative, ongoing process, where an initially adopted *Frame* may change over time as the crisis unfolds, as a different/deeper understanding of the crisis emerges, and as the 'manageability' of the crisis is improved by leadership.

'Beyond' Leadership Response: *Anchor*

As an unexpected, threatening event, a crisis creates turbulence, fluidity, uncertainty and ambiguity. In countering these crisis qualities, leadership has to *Anchor* the organisation 'Beyond' the here-and-now existential threat of the crisis. They can do this by using the identity of the organisation as a secure reference point and fixed compass setting. Organisational Identity must inform – in real time, all the time, in all places – leadership's thinking, decisions and actions during the unfolding, and seemingly overwhelming, snowballing chaos of dealing with the crisis effectively.

Organisational Identity (we, us and them) relates to organisational members' understanding of who and what their organisation is; what it stands for and does; who it belongs to; and what it aspires to. *How do we see ourselves? What do we stand for? How are we seen?* The constituent elements of the organisation's Identity are depicted in Figure **13**.2.

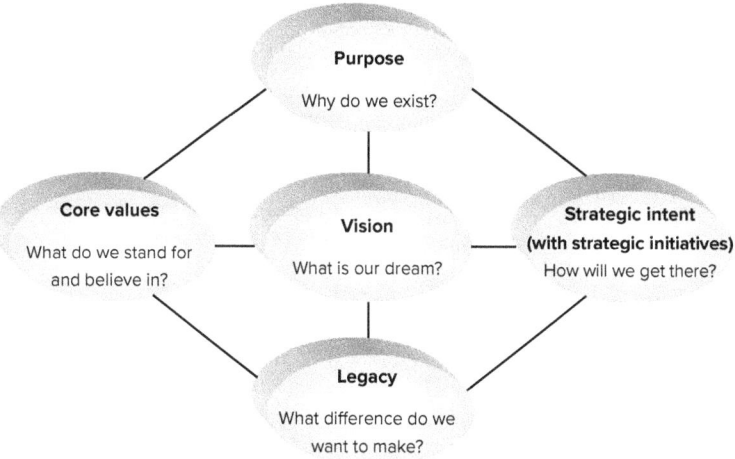

Figure 13.2: Constituent Elements of Organisation's Identity

A strongly entrenched Organisational Identity empowers everyone at their level in an organisation to take the right decisions and actions because Organisational Identity serves as a common comparison base. In this way, everyone in the organisation and beyond can be turned into a leader in his/her sphere of action, and hence take on the burden jointly to deal effectively and successfully with the crisis. A leadership miracle can happen: everyone becomes an amazing leader. A strongly entrenched Organisational Identity also reduces the likelihood of short- term, reactive, destructive thinking, decisions and actions compromising the future performance, success and sustainability of the organisation.

'Through' Leadership Response: *Resolve*

Relative to and in-between the 'In' response: *Frame* – the right set of glasses to profile the crisis accurately, and the 'Beyond' response: *Anchor* – Organisational Identity as secure reference point and fixed compass setting in the sea of chaos, the 'Through' response has to occur. Leadership has to *Resolve* the crisis by crafting and rolling out a fit-for-purpose solution as an intervention to the crisis. The solution must enable leadership to work 'Through' the crisis by *Resolving* it in order to recover sustainably.

Resolving the crisis with the aim of ensuring an effective recovery entails a number of steps that are depicted in Figure **13**.3. Important to note from this figure is the interdependency amongst the steps, as well as the embeddedness of the 'Through' response steps in the 'In' and 'Beyond' responses in an iterative, integrated, complete and balanced manner. Given space constraints, only highlights of each step is briefly discussed.

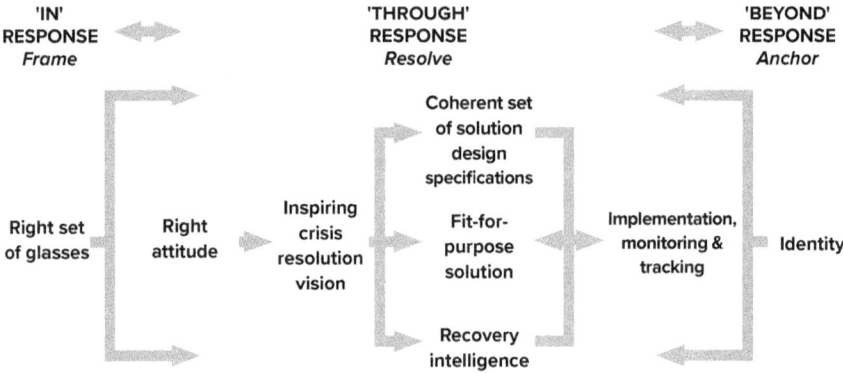

Figure 13.3: Steps making up the 'Through' Response: Resolve

Right Attitude

As a departure point to the 'Through' response, the right attitude must be adopted and shared by all organisational members, modelled by leadership: *"The crisis can and must be resolved whatever it takes. Our very future is at stake."* This 'can do', barrier-busting attitude must be infused by, and leveraged from, the right People Capital (see below.)

Inspiring a Crisis Resolution Vision

Next, a clear, inspiring Crisis Resolution Vision must be crafted relative to the Organisation Identity: *"When we have resolved the crisis, what will our team, organisation, community or society look like in having successfully addressed the crisis with all of its impacts, consequences and knock-on effects?"*

If the crisis is radical and fundamental in its impact, the Crisis Resolution Vision may have to describe a new normal. For example, the successful relocation of people displaced by rising sea levels; a healthy population immune to the COVID-19 virus; or a different mode of working, e.g. working from home.

Coherent set of Solution Design Specifications

Given the right attitude and a clear, inspiring Crisis Resolution Vision, a coherent set of Solution Design Specifications for a fit-for-purpose crisis solution must be generated, which is able to resolve the crisis. Examples of such specifications are: core value coherence; contextual-fit; requisite complexity; outside-in; stakeholder inclusivity; solution delivery anywhere, anytime, anyway, anyhow, to anyone; and the solution improves after every use (=minimum viable design.)

Fit-for-Purpose Solution

Relative to the inspiring Crisis Resolution Vision and Solution Design Specifications, a fit-for-purpose Solution must be crafted to resolve the crisis in terms of its triggers, evolution, impact and consequences. The Solution must include a clear, robust Recovery Strategy with priorities and a Recovery Plan, detailing the why, what, how, who, where and when.

Recovery Intelligence

The Solution must be accompanied by the formulation of an Intelligence Measurement Model to monitor and track the full range of possible Solution outcomes impact, in this way providing real time, in time intelligence with respect to the effectiveness of the Solution, i.e. a 'smart' Solution has to be crafted, enabling the monitoring and tracking of the crisis recovery.

The Intelligence Measurement Model's 'radar screen' and 'bandwidth' must be broad enough to pick up the full dimensionality of the Solution outcome impact: intended and unintended; positive and negative; tangible and intangible.

Implementation, Monitoring and Tracking

Finally, the Recovery Solution is implemented, monitored and tracked in terms of the Intelligence Measurement Model, and course adjustments made.

Navigation

Crisis implies change by its very nature; the unexpected has occurred, causing a threatening disruption which needs to be minimised or eliminated. From the moment a crisis has occurred and an 'In-Beyond-Through' response is triggered, a sound change navigation strategy and plan must be crafted and rolled out in support of the response.

It is outside of the scope of this chapter, given space constraints, to address change navigation in any great detail. Suffice to say that the same change navigation principles apply in the case of dealing with a crisis as with any large scale organisation intervention. The only difference being the features of a crisis – outlined in the introduction of this chapter as a threatening emergency which detrimentally disrupts the expected status quo with dire consequences, infused by unexpectedness, threat, uncertainty and urgency – impose a different flavour and rhythm on the application of these principles.

Protection and leverage of People and Organisation Capitals

Navigating the 'In-Beyond-Through' response through *Framing-Anchoring-Resolving* requires the protection and leverage of two critical Capitals: People and Organisation. These Capitals must infuse the 'In-Beyond-Through' response into their very being.

People Capital

The occurrence of a crisis implies an event outside of the normal range of expectations, duties and functioning of organisational members, invoking a real and perceived sense of losing control over their destiny. The typical people responses are *Freeze*, *Flight*, *Fight* or *Face*. *Face* as constructive response will capacitate organisational members to regain and maintain a sense of coping and being in charge.

To *Face* a crisis effectively, the People Capital of the organisation must be grown, nurtured and maintained by leadership in order to generate the required people energy to address the crisis. By implication, negative People Capital must be detected and countered.

The critical, major People Capital ingredients are: *Efficacy* (instead of Helplessness); *Hope* (instead of Despair); *Optimism* (instead of Pessimism); *Confidence* (instead of Self-doubt); *Courage* (instead of Cowardice); *Passion* (instead of Disinterestedness), *Perseverance* (instead of Half-heartedness) and *Resilience* (instead of Overwhelmed.)

Organisational Capital

During the 'In-Beyond-Through' response, leadership must protect and leverage core organisational capabilities to deal with the crisis. Core organisational capabilities are the 'crown jewels' of the organisation, which refers to what the organisation must be able to do exceedingly well in order to gain and retain an ongoing, competitive edge. These capabilities must not be compromised, thereby putting the sustainability of an organisation at risk.

The crown jewels to be protected and leveraged during the crisis must therefore be identified early on. At least the following core organisational capabilities are critical: Organisational Reputation; Stakeholder Goodwill; Leadership Reputation; Client Delivery (especially to strategic clients); and Supply Chain (particularly strategic suppliers within the chain.)

Critical success factors for an effective 'In-Beyond-Through' leadership response to a crisis

At least the following critical success factors are essential:

Navigating Response

- Know and communicate at any given time which *crisis life cycle stage* is active, and properly close out each stage: crisis acknowledgement, crisis assessment, crisis handling/containment/recovery, and crisis close-out.
- *Model the way* as leader by setting the example in all ways and in everything.

'In' Response: Frame

- *Acknowledge the presence of the crisis* with unconditional honesty, warts and all, in a realistic way from the start, and throughout.
- Set up clear, robust crisis *governance structures and processes* that work effectively and efficiently.
- Deal with the *true crisis* by accurately mapping the territory of the crisis with its situational crisis dynamics and associated mode of engagement.
- Show and express *concern for the people* of the organisation in tangible ways at all times, in all places. Demonstrate that their troubles matter more than those of the organisation.
- Reach out to, mobilise and engage all *stakeholders*, in this way engendering their trust and full support throughout the crisis.
- Be at all times *physically visible and accessible* as leadership at the front line – in the 'moments of truth' where and when things happen that matter genuinely, in resolving the crisis, and where reactions to the crisis are manifested. Do not delegate and/or disappear.
- Ensure *substantive, quality communication*. Say what you mean, and mean what you say. No waffling, posturing, dithering, and mixed messages.
- *Communicate, communicate, communicate*. Keep all stakeholders informed at all times, in real time, accurately and timeously. Plan intended communication frequency, and then multiply it by a factor of 10 to arrive at the actual frequency.
- *Learn, relearn and unlearn* from a crisis in order to enhance the future leadership's 'In-Beyond-Through' response capability.

'Beyond' Response: Anchor

- Ensure a distinct, widely shared, and deeply entrenched and understood Organisational Identity to serve as a secure reference point and fixed compass setting. Reinforce the Organisation Identity constantly in all communication, thinking, decisions and actions.
- Relative to the Organisational Identity, *enable and empower* as many organisational members as possible within their action domains to deal with the localised roll-out of the Crisis Resolution Solution, as well as dealing with knock-on effects, fall-outs and blow-backs of the crisis within their domains. Everyone must become a leader.

'Through' Response: Resolve

- Give *credible assurances;* no pipedreams or unrealistic expectations.
- Courageously stand up and be *accountable and responsible* for events, decisions, actions, consequences and outcomes. No ducking and diving; the blaming of circumstances beyond own control; and/or seeking scapegoats.
- Generate real time, in time, all the time, accurate, timeous *crisis intelligence*.
- Apply *big picture, innovative, out-of-the box thinking* with no holy cows, using *cross-functional, multi-disciplinary teams* (especially critical in the case of Complex and Chaotic Crises.)
- Craft a *real solution* whatever the cost, and not a make-believe, public relations solution aimed at smoothing one's own conscience and/or appeasing stakeholders.
- Prepare for unexpected *contingencies* to rapidly counter unexpected blowbacks from the recovery actions.

Core crisis leadership capabilities for an effective 'In-Beyond-Through' leadership response to a crisis

Figure 13.4 depicts the minimum core 'In-Beyond-Through' Crisis Leadership Capabilities necessary to deal with a crisis successfully.

LEAD SELF	LEAD OTHERS
• Authenticity: unwavering honesty • Integrity: stick to core values regardless • Perseverance • Stamina • Pacing to prevent poor decisions because of fatigue and burn out	• Credibility and legitimacy: licence to lead • Caring, compassion and support • Communication • Active listening • Sense- and meaning-making and -giving storytelling
LEAD ORGANISATION	**LEAD IN WORLD**
• Vision-driven and value-referenced • Requisite complexity of thinking and acting • Disciplined execution • Sound, consistent judgement and decisiveness • Confident calmness	• Agility • Resilience • Transparency • Courage • Responsiveness • Creativity

Figure 13.4: Portfolio of the minimum core 'In-Beyond-Through' Crisis Leadership Capabilities

The chances of finding all of these core Crisis Leadership Capabilities in a single leader is indeed slim: the futile search for the superperson leader. Instead, an organisation will have to switch to distributed (i.e. shared) leadership, where the total portfolio of Crisis Leadership Capabilities is distributed in its sum total throughout the leadership community of an organisation on an as-needs basis.

Another approach could be to categorise the portfolio of Capabilities by crisis – given the nature of each crisis – into 'Essential', 'Desirable' and 'Nice to'. Those leaders who have the essential Capabilities would take the lead in a specific crisis. This implies a pro-active audit of Crisis Leadership Capabilities needed by an organisation, their development, and the rapid deployment of leaders according to the Capabilities needed as shown by the audit, as and when a crisis occurs. This Capability Inventory will form part of the Crisis Handling strategy and plan of the organisation.

Ten commandments of crisis leadership excellence through an 'In-Beyond-Through' leadership response to a crisis

The shaded box contains the suggested Ten Commandments for Crisis Leadership Excellence.

Thou shall…

1. always have an up-to-date crisis handling strategy plan, and process handy;
2. have a competent crisis handling team, who have distinct roles with clearly spelt out accountabilities, responsibilities (including consistently used, trained spokespersons, including persons from the front line) and a general mode of working;
3. have regular simulations to rehearse, practice and train in leading and managing crises;
4. face the unwavering, true reality of the crisis faced without any denial, rationalisation or projections, and not a make-believe reality;
5. tell it all, tell it fast, and tell it honestly when a crisis has occurred, including how it is being dealt with and the expected outcomes;
6. keep all stakeholders fully informed at all times about all things, and use the media as fully fledged partners, not as enemies;
7. refuse the temptation to blame, speculate, muddy matters and obfuscate;
8. demonstrate compassion and care;

9. learn from each crisis in order to enhance the organisation's crisis leadership capability; and

10. celebrate when progressive milestones and successes are achieved in resolving a crisis and its consequences.

Conclusion

Crises will occur. This certainty is woven into the very fibre of life. Yet in the current VICCAS of increasing **V**ariety, **I**nterdependency, **C**omplexity, **C**hange, **A**mbiguity and **S**eamlessness, the likelihood of crises has increased significantly. Organisations that excel at Crisis Leadership will win the race to the future they desire.

This chapter set out to explore and elucidate what I believe to be the appropriate leadership response to dealing with a crisis: navigating through an 'In' (=*Frame*) - 'Beyond' (=*Anchor*) -'Through' (=*Resolve*) response. The chapter covered the make-up of this response; its critical success factors; the core Crisis Leadership Capabilities required by this response; and lastly, the Ten Commandments of Crisis Leadership Excellence through this response.

Chapter 14

Managing uncertainty, complexity and chaos in a crisis vortex[1]

Sonja Blignaut

"This is not just an era of change; it is increasingly a change of era."
—General Sir Nick Carter, head of the British Army

"Overall, you must assume that the past you believed you understood will not return."
—António Guterres, UN Secretary-General

I have been working in the field of Complexity for two decades. In that time, I have seen it move from the far edges of decision-makers' peripheral vision into sharper focus. There has been a growing awareness that our old ways of managing and organising are no longer serving us, but the call of the familiar was often too seductive to overcome. We could choose to ignore the Complexity and pretend that we were still in a nicely linear world, where we can manage change and create multi-year strategies, until now.

As we enter a new decade, the world has become entirely bewildering. Australia experienced extreme drought, wildfires and floods in a single season. We see a rise in nationalism, populism and racism in virtually every nation around the globe. And now, COVID-19, the global pandemic that experts have been warning us about for years, is quite literally on our doorstep. We are in uncharted territory, yet we are expected to make decisions that might impact not only our short-term survival, but also result in long-term implications for the families and businesses for which we are responsible. All of this leads to a sense of being "unmoored"; of losing our bearings and having no solid ground to anchor us. It also forces us to continually confront and navigate the boundary between competence and incompetence. We live in a world governed by narratives that equate our worth to knowing, having answers and being confident, but the knowledge and skills that brought us past success are now becoming irrelevant at a mind-bending pace.

---

[1] This chapter originally appeared in Crous, W. (2020). *Managing Organisations During the COVID-19 Vortex: Comprehensive guidelines for leading your organisation through the vortex.* Bryanston: KR Publishing.

In the "here-and-now" experience of everyday life, situations emerge and evolve from moment to moment. What will happen next is inherently uncertain and unpredictable. For us not to become paralysed, we need to be able to make sense of what we are facing, and then have the courage to maintain momentum and not get stuck when we don't know.

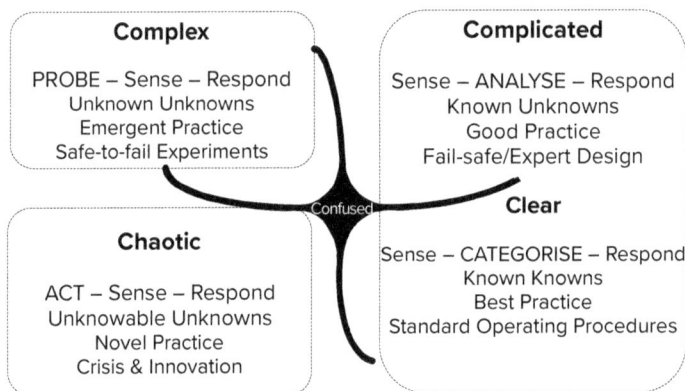

Figure 14.1: Cynefin sense-making framework

Dave Snowden's Cynefin™ sense-making framework[2] distinguishes between five different contexts. Mostly we are familiar with the two ordered domains on the right. Our existing tools and practices equip us well to function in ordered systems; we are comfortable there as we are dealing with known unknowns. We are less equipped to operate in the other three domains, and unfortunately, this is where we find ourselves now.

In the Complex and Chaotic domains on the left we are dealing with unknown, and even unknowable, unknowns. We cannot discern cause-and-effect relationships, we need to navigate a non-linear world where things are interconnected in ways we cannot understand, and small, seemingly insignificant, events can trigger disproportionate system-wide unintended consequences. In Complexity we need to interact, or dance, with the system to gain an understanding of the patterns and dynamics at play. We act experimentally; small, local safe-to-fail experiments help us find our way forwards. Here analysis leads to paralysis and checklists, and best practices are dangerous. With the current pandemic we are dipping more often into Chaos, a temporary domain of crisis where there are no effective constraints and no discernible patterns. When we experience a so-called black swan event[3], we often find ourselves in Chaos. Here we need to act to impose constraint and enable patterns to form and stabilise. The final domain, one that is often ignored, but which I believe is of extreme importance in

---

2   Snowden, D., & Boone, M. (2007.) A leader's framework for decision making. *Harvard Business Review, 85*(11): 68-76

3   Taleb, N. N. (2007.) *The Black Swan.* New York: Random House. Retrieved from: http://citeseerx.ist.psu.edu/viewdoc/download?doi=10.1.1.695.4305&rep=rep1&type=pdf

this time, is the central domain of disorder or Confusion. We find ourselves here when we do not have enough information to make sense of where we are.

While most people feel that COVID-19 has dumped the world into Chaos, I believe we are more often in the central domain of Confusion or disorder. The danger is that we get stuck there, which may lead to a descent into Chaos.

How, then, do we navigate the extreme uncertainty of the Confused middle domain? There is no simple answer to that question, but here are a few practical guideposts:

1. **Change your vantage point**. If you are caught up in what feels like operational Chaos, get off the dance floor and get a balcony view.[4] It is easy to become myopic about details and operational crises, for example focusing on individual patients, safety incidents or even dysfunctional teams, and missing the systemic patterns that are the real problems. Or, sometimes we can focus so much on operational necessities like cash flow and productivity that we miss a key shift in the market that may be a big risk or opportunity. Alternatively, if you think you are stuck in analysis paralysis, get closer to the system. Join the dance for a while to gain an "on-the-ground" perspective.
2. **Ensure requisite diversity**. Surround yourself with people who have diverse perspectives and dare to challenge your assumptions.
3. **Put fast feedback loops in place**. Leverage informal networks.
4. **Eliminate unnecessary noise**. Communicate only what is most important and be careful what you pay attention to.
5. **Make sense of where you are and what kind of problems you are dealing with**, then:
    a. delegate the Clear problems;
    b. assign the Complicated ones to appropriate experts;
    c. adopt an experimental approach in Complexity. Try many different things at once; monitor for unintended consequences; and adapt fast. In Complexity, the available evidence will support various, and even competing, hypotheses. Let go of the need for consensus and agree to test any coherent hypothesis with a small experiment. Critical here is understanding that the context is dynamic – something that didn't work yesterday, may work today. We can shape but we cannot control; we must learn to "dance" with the system; and
    d. if you find yourself in Chaos, the key thing is to act fast. Doing the wrong thing and adapting fast is better than doing nothing at all. Action should be focused on containment and imposing constraints so that patterns can emerge and hopefully stabilise into Complexity. As in Complexity, pursuing consensus in Chaos is dangerous. Time and decisiveness are of the essence.

---

4   Heifetz, R., Grashow, A., & Linsky, M. (2009.) The Practice of Adaptive Leadership: Tools and Tactics for Changing Your Organisation and the World. *Journal of Applied Christian Leadership*, 4(1): 16.

6. **Remember that the situation is dynamic.** Don't assume that what was true yesterday is true today; adopt a stance of continuous situational awareness.
7. **Work in crews, not teams.** In crews, members are trained to step into particular roles when the need arises. In a crew, someone with higher status in the formal hierarchy can relinquish authority to someone who is their junior if the context requires that person to step into the role. In a crisis, status and rigid roles are unhelpful.

The crisis vortex we are in is forcing us to continually confront the tension between knowing and not knowing; between competence and incompetence. This can create tremendous anxiety and some very unhelpful responses that can become blind spots. It is wise to watch out for these responses in ourselves, and also to ask our trusted advisors to alert us when they observe them playing out in our behaviour:

- **Rigidity:** Sometimes the anxiety of not knowing is so high that it compels us to ignore facts that are right in front of us. We end up clinging to beliefs, knowledge and ideas that served us in contexts that no longer exist.
- **Overwhelmed and confused:** Dealing with information overload and at the same time paradoxically not having enough information to inform our decisions can be exhausting. Often I find myself unable to make simple decisions such as what to cook for dinner, never mind having to make decisions about how to protect my staff and keep my business afloat in the middle of a raging pandemic.
- **Becoming dependent:** When we don't have answers and cannot guarantee that our decisions will be sound, it is very seductive to seek out experts or place our hope in a leader who will be our "saviour". When we do this, we abdicate our responsibility and betray our competence.

> "Our personal relationship with uncertainty is fundamental to being human, yet over the last 30 years, we've begun outsourcing it to other people. You have a relationship with those big questions."
> –Diego Espinosa[4]

- **Withdrawal:** Sometimes the only option that seems safe is to withdraw; to "check out". An even more dangerous manifestation of this is abject denial. Stories abound of people in Italy and South Korea ignoring warnings, breaking the rules and worsening the pandemic because they simply couldn't accept their new reality. We need to actively resist the temptation to put our heads in the sand and pretend that we will not be affected.

---

5 Diego Espinosa, Founder, Sistema Research, Prof. Finance at the University of San Diego

- **Running:** Speed and busyness can be very effective ways of hiding. If we keep moving, even in circles, we can avoid facing our anxiety and feelings of incompetence. We can continue pretending that we have answers and that we know where we are going. We believe that as long as we are moving, we don't have to acknowledge that we are lost.
- **Paralysis:** This can show up in different ways. There is the so-called "deer in the headlights" response, where anxiety leads to complete inaction, then there is procrastination, where we keep putting things off, waiting for the right time or enough information. Sometimes it shows up as avoidance – keeping ourselves busy with other inconsequential tasks and not engaging with the real issue, or we refuse to make choices and try to do everything, or be everything to everyone. All of these responses have the same effect: profound stuck-ness.

All of the above responses make it virtually impossible to learn, and it also causes us to miss windows of opportunity where our actions could have made a difference.

While we need to avoid the responses listed above, we can focus on cultivating the below:

- **Humility:** We need to admit the limits of our competence, and instead of withdrawing, giving into dependence or becoming overwhelmed, resolve to stay present. To "sit in the fire" as Arnold Mindell advocates. One of my clients reflected that when she truly understood that she was dealing with a complex system it was as if a weight lifted off her shoulders. She realised that it was "ok not to know". No-one can know everything and we are all learning and evolving together. Humility enables us to journey with, and learn from, others who bring different wisdom and perspectives, but also conflict. This takes courage and a willingness to confront some uncomfortable truths about ourselves.
- **The courage to be vulnerable:** Brené Brown[6] defines vulnerability as: "The emotion we all experience during times of **uncertainty, risk** and **emotional exposure.** Vulnerability is not about winning or losing; it's about the **courage** to show up when you **can't predict or control the outcome.**" Showing up is the opposite of withdrawing; it means feeling incompetent and afraid, but speaking up and trying anyway.
- **Being open to necessary endings[7] and saying NO:** When confronted with the limits of our knowledge and competence in the face of a volatile and even chaotic situation, making decisions can be tough. It is tempting to hedge our bets and try to cover too many bases. If we spread ourselves too thin, we may end up getting nothing done.

---

6   Brown, B. (2018.) *Dare to lead.* New York: Random House.

7   Cloud, H. (2010.) *Necessary Endings.* London: Ebury Publishing.

One final point on Chaos. While Chaos is a domain of crisis, it is also the domain of innovation. While many believe that innovation flows from creativity, the truth is that innovation and creativity often emerge in the presence of an urgent need. Dave Snowden has identified three pre-conditions for innovation: resource starvation, time pressure and perspective shift. Currently we have all three in abundance. As we navigate this crisis, let us keep in mind that this is also a Kairos moment – an opportune time where large-scale systemic change is possible. Let us not allow the post-pandemic world to emerge haphazardly; instead, let us find ways to work together to shape this world into a better one.

Chapter 15

Promoting personal and workplace mental health in the age of COVID-19[1]

Navlika Ratangee

Infectious disease outbreaks, such as COVID-19, can be scary and affect our mental health. According to the World Health Organization (WHO)[2], one in four people will struggle with a mental illness at some point in their lives, however global megatrends show that this will soon change to one in every two people.[3] This is why it is important for us to look after our mental health in the context of the COVID-19 pandemic.

There is a lot in the media around what we can do to take the necessary precautions to look after ourselves physically, but not much is said about how we look after our mental health during this time. There are so many things to feel anxious about. With the increasing levels of fear around dealing with the COVID-19 crisis, the risk of exposure and the fear of loved ones being exposed or sick, there is an increase in panic, which results in an overall increase in anxiety levels. It is only natural to feel overwhelmed, vulnerable, stressed and anxious. This can be further complicated if you have experienced a trauma or a mental health problem in the past, or if you have a long-term physical health condition that makes you more vulnerable to the effects of COVID-19.

It may be helpful to anticipate an increase in your levels of discomfort and feelings of distress. Acknowledge how you are feeling and remind yourself and each other to take care of your mental health.

This chapter is split up to address possible areas people may feel anxious and stressed about, and highlights what they can practically do to look after their mental health. The chapter ends with some specific guidelines for organisations to implement to ensure that they are promoting mental health in the workplace in the age of COVID-19.

---

1 This chapter originally appeared in Crous, W. (2020). *Managing Organisations During the COVID-19 Vortex: Comprehensive guidelines for leading your organisation through the vortex.* Bryanston: KR Publishing.

2 World Health Organization. (2001.) *Mental disorders affect one in four people.* Retrieved from: https://www.who.int/whr/2001/media_centre/press_release/en/

3 Watson, R. (2017.) *What's Next: Top Trends.* Retrieved from: https://toptrends.nowandnext.com/2017/05/08/map/

Dealing with the overflow of information

The sudden and near-constant stream of news reports about an outbreak can cause anyone to feel worried.[4] While it is important to keep abreast of the most up-to-date information relating to the status of COVID-19 and the measures put in place by the government, the overflow of information needs to be controlled to support and manage our well-being. Check in with yourself and assess how you are doing – physically and mentally. If you find that the news is causing anxiety and stress for you, focus on how you filter this information and find a balance. Give yourself permission to take a break and unplug from the constant flow of information.

Ensure that you are empowering yourself and those around you with the right information. Avoid listening to or following rumours or sensationalising things; fake news and speculation can fuel anxiety. Before reacting to any concerning messages, be sure to check these on reliable websites or news platforms. If you are sharing content, do this from trusted sources only, and remember that your friends and family may be worried too.

Balance the information you engage in. Find the positive stories, for example focus on the recovery rate as being a good news story. It might make it easier if you temporarily unfollow social media accounts that only focus on the negative, and decide which accounts you will follow so that you don't feel overwhelmed.

Concerns about being exposed

The risk of exposure to COVID-19 is a real one, and feeling constantly anxious and even paranoid about touching things, washing our hands, and being around others when it cannot be avoided becomes a constant preoccupation. The message may sometimes feel like a confusing one – be obsessive in our hygiene habits but maintain routine and normality as far as possible. It is important to consider that these are unprecedented times and we are presented with having to deal with our responses to such crises in a rather novel way.

Be kind to yourself. It is normal to worry about the risks related to COVID-19. Whether it is about you or your family being exposed, finding out that you or a family member tested positive, considering whether you will be part of the population that recovers without complications, etc., the truth is that we will never know what course it will take until it happens. We have to continuously remind ourselves to take a balanced view of all that concerns us. We must remain focused on what we can proactively do to take

---

4　Organizacion Mundial de la Salud. (2020.) *Mental Health and Psychosocial Considerations During COVID-19 Outbreak.* Retrieved from: https://www.who.int/docs/default-source/coronaviruse/mental-health-considerations.pdf?sfvrsn=6d3578af_8

care of ourselves such as hand washing, staying at home, sneezing or coughing into the crook of the elbow or into a tissue that is then discarded, etc. However, we also need to plan for the unexpected. Just like your workplaces are frantically executing business continuity plans, you can also spend some time proactively working through what your plan of action would be if you were impacted. The reality is that despite your best efforts you may still be exposed or may catch it. Planning for this eventuality could help you and your family to feel more prepared. Know who to phone and where to go. Have basic medication on hand, consider childcare arrangements, understand what isolation would require of you practically, create communication strategies and know what you would need to do to get through this possibly life-changing time.

This is not meant to create more anxiety for you, but rather to provide a plan of the eventuality that you may be impacted and allow the whole family to be on board with what is required. Going through this process may reduce the time spent worrying about all the different scenarios and feeling fearful of them. It allows you to feel more in control of possible scenarios that you may actually not be able to control.

Dealing with being in self-isolation or in quarantine

If there is a chance that you have been exposed or you are practicing social distancing, you are trying to avoid mixing with other people and chances are you are not even leaving your house. This may feel daunting as you may be watching carefully for possible symptoms, concerned about how you will go about getting items you may run out of at home, and what to do within your four walls to keep busy.

Research suggests that quarantines are often associated with negative mental health effects including post-traumatic stress symptoms, confusion and anger.[5] Stressors are related to longer quarantine duration, infection fears, frustration, boredom, inadequate supplies, inadequate information, financial loss and stigma.

It is important to note that this is not a normal way of life and thus it may result in increased anxiety levels. In order to reduce the negative mental health effects and cope better during this time, it may help to try and see this as a different period of time in your life, and not necessarily a bad one, even if you didn't choose it. In this time it is important to keep things in perspective, and not wait to feel symptoms that may or may not appear. Try to keep your daily routine where possible, but be mindful that the way in which you get through your day may look very different. Create a daily routine that prioritises looking after yourself. See it as an opportunity to try new skills, practice relaxation techniques, bed down an exercise routine, experiment in the kitchen or

---

5   Brooks, S. K., Webster, R. K., Smith, L. E., Woodland, L., Wessely, S., Greenberg, N., & Rubin, G. J. (2020.) The psychological impact of quarantine and how to reduce it: rapid review of the evidence. *Lancet, 395:* 912–20.

catch up that series that you never had a chance to watch or the book you didn't get a chance to read!

Eat well and ensure you are taking care of your wider health needs, such as general supplementation or access to prescription medication where needed. Stay hydrated and stay active. Keep focused on your personal health goals during this time. These are all linked to staying on track in looking after our mental health.

Stay connected to loved ones. Technology today allows us to stay in touch using digital platforms such as video calling, instant chat, emailing, etc. Also recognise if the constant messaging is contributing to an increase in your anxiety levels. If so, keep your messages on mute and check in when you have the energy to sift through them, as it is also important to stay updated during this time.

This is also an opportune time to rest and reflect. Taking the time to understand what our personal triggers are that elevate our stress levels is critical to building our personal stress management toolkit. Use the time to understand yourself better. There are a number of tools available online that can assist with an appropriate line of questioning. Journaling can also be a useful tool to reflect on and make visible our own patterns of behaviour that we may want to address.

Talk to your children

It is important to include your children in discussions around the COVID-19 outbreak. Children can present with anxiety and confusion with everything going on around them, and they need the opportunity to talk through this. One way of doing this is to start by understanding what they have already heard about the outbreak and use that as an opportunity to provide factual information – on what they can do to protect themselves and reduce the risk, and teaching them to practice hygiene rituals.

It is important for you to stay calm so that it does not cause everyone alarm. If your child is at home on an early school holiday or they are having to experience home-schooling, talk to them about how they feel about these changes. How can you work together as a family to overcome some of the challenges this presents and how can you use this as an opportunity to create new family experiences?

Every child expresses emotion in their own way. Monitor the reactions of your children so you can assist in supporting them timeously. Talking to your child about how they feel helps to put words to their feelings, like scared, fear, sadness and worry. It is also a gift to help your child unpack what makes them feel this way, for example, fearing a positive COVID-19 result and what self-isolation means for a child. It can be quite a relief for them to express what they are really feeling.

Minimise the negative impact that over-exposure can cause for children by ensuring that they also follow as normal a routine as possible. Sometimes distraction can be useful, like engaging in a creative activity, playing or drawing. It is also important to engage with this 'scary topic' in an age-appropriate way. Be truthful about the facts. There are many great video clips and infographics available to assist in explaining COVID-19 in very practical ways. Talk about the loss they may also experience with the change in their schedule, the sudden cessation of all their extra mural activities, etc. Continuing to stay active in their own way, for example by playing outside, is also important for their own mental health.

If you are all practicing social distancing together, you might be spending more time together as a family. This connectedness and being kept close to family may feel very containing for children, and it can automatically create a safe environment if used for open communication. If you are not living with your children, try to maintain regular contact with them to minimise the fear and concern they might feel, for example schedule twice-daily phone calls or video calls.

Be mindful that children model adults' behaviours. They watch your reactions, behaviours and emotions, and they also follow your cues regarding how to manage one's emotions. Be aware that your children may be more demanding and seek more attachment during times that feel scary to them. This is common in times of stress and crises. Reassure your child that you are there for them and seek help when it feels overwhelming for you or your child.

Working from home

An effective working from home arrangement requires effort and intention; it is not as simple as one may imagine. The advent of the COVID-19 pandemic has resulted in many people being sent to work from home who never did so in the past.

Working from home requires one to adapt to a different way of working almost instantly. With meetings being held using teleconference or video conferencing facilities, it changes the nature of engagement altogether. Ensure that expectations have been discussed with you and that you have discussed your expectations with your team so that performance outcomes are clear. Over communication is required in a period like this to ensure that work colleagues and team members are all aligned, that expectations are clear, and that some level of productivity can still be maintained. Stay in touch with your manager for any questions and support, and log technological challenges speedily to minimise disruption to your productivity.

Working from home can be quite challenging: we need to maintain a professional environment as far as possible; we need to be mindful of background noise when we are speaking to clients or colleagues; and even our backdrop needs to portray a professional image. This can be particularly hard if your children are also home. What is sometimes useful is creating a special space in your home where you can work free from distraction. Have a discussion with your children where necessary about some of the ground rules regarding what it means for mom and/or dad to be working from home – this is new for them too! This discussion may also need to extend to others living in your home. Communication is needed to ensure that everyone can respect meetings that might need to take place and when quiet time needs to be implemented.

Working from home also requires flexibility in your schedule; you may have to try different things to see what works best for you. Perhaps you prefer to get meetings out of the way earlier in the day and then focus on individual work in the latter part of the day, or vice versa. Get creative and explore the changes that are required of you to practice a new kind of productivity.

Check in with yourself regularly… what is working and what is not? Look for the positive in the situation – it may be an opportunity to show your value in a completely different way in the company, or allow you to be more productive. If harnessed positively, it may provide further opportunity for new ways of working once the crisis is over.

Being the healthcare worker

First of all, thank you for putting the needs of others and your community above your own. It is normal for a healthcare worker to feel pressurised during a time like this. It may feel overwhelming for you with the constant risks you face and managing the feeling of doing your best and not single-handedly being able to save the world. Focusing on doing the best that you can and reminding yourself that the stress you feel is not related to not being able to do your job adequately.

It is more important now than ever to look after your own mental well-being: rest when you can, eat healthy foods for sustained energy, exercise where possible, and stay in contact with your own support systems. Even though much of what you are experiencing is unchartered territory, it can be helpful to rely on coping strategies that have helped you through difficult times in the past.

Some healthcare workers may experience distancing of their support systems due to fears around being exposed to risk, which may cause unnecessary challenges and related stigma. Lean on those who understand the nature of your work, even if it is by digital means only. Your colleagues may be going through the same and may be a great source of support during this time.

It is important for the general population to acknowledge the efforts of our healthcare workers during this time; particularly for the sacrifices they are making to keep ourselves and our loved ones safe.

The key focus for all of us is to contribute to flattening the curve. We need to do this for the following reasons:

- To reduce the impact on the health care system.
- To give the health care system time and space to learn more about the virus, and to develop the necessary treatment.
- To reduce the mortality rate.

The truth is that there is a high likelihood that we will all get COVID-19 eventually. It is estimated that 40-70% of the world population will get it within the next year. The majority of the population will have had it by year 2, but hopefully by then we will have the necessary care and treatment. We have to do what we can do to look after ourselves and manage these figures down. Understanding the role we each play in this crisis can be very meaningful when it comes to anticipating the distress and anxiety it will cause, as is recognising how we contribute to the whole. If you are feeling increasingly stressed or overwhelmed, you are not alone and are encouraged to reach out for support to friends and family, and/or helplines that exist for emotional support. Employee assistance programmes may be very useful for those who have access to such support. Try to reassure people you know who may be worried about you, and check in with people who are living alone and not coping.

Workplace considerations

The well-being of the workforce has never been more important than now, in the midst of this coronavirus outbreak. Employee well-being will become even more important in managing the crisis, as will containing the anxieties discussed above related to COVID-19, and managing the aftermath of the trauma with the impact on self and organisation. Thus the mental health of the entire organisation is at the heart of the organisation's ability to recover from this crisis.

At this stage, organisations are activating business continuity plans in all ways and forms. This has already had both positive and negative impacts on individual employees' ability to feel calm about what is to come. Open, ongoing and transparent communication is key to employee well-being and productivity within the organisation.

The impact of COVID-19 on organisations has far-reaching consequences for individuals, families and employers. Whilst organisations continue to troubleshoot regarding next steps to take to ensure business continuity, they also need to remain cognisant of the impact on their individual employees, including their mental health. Part of delivering this message is to ensure that leaders always communicate important business continuity-related information with care and concern for employee well-being. Showing your genuine concern consistently will ensure improved productivity and engagement from employees.

Communicate often and share with honesty. Open up channels for dialogue, enable concerns to be raised, and provide an opportunity for supporting one another in these difficult times. The organisation will also need to create a space to mourn the losses experienced, both literally and figuratively, in the time spent apart – even when employees are reintegrated into the workplace post the traumatic incident.

Business targets will need to be readjusted, and communicating this clearly will be useful to alleviate employee anxiety. There is no doubt that the advent of COVID-19 may have a devastating impact on your business, financially and otherwise. It will take time to rebuild the business and to re-strategise on the way forward. You will need a healthy workforce to realise the new opportunities and deal with the new challenges this brings.

An important consideration upon reintegration into the workspace is whether there may be any residual stigma or discrimination that might exist in your employee population. This will need to be addressed proactively to communicate that such negative behaviours will not be tolerated. It is a time to show empathy and support to those who have suffered directly or indirectly, not to judge or jump to conclusions about those affected by COVID-19. Ignoring the impact of the stigma and discrimination linked to COVID-19 may reinforce the stigma related to mental illness as well, as these individuals may hide their struggles and may be reluctant to seek support for both COVID-19 and mental health conditions.

Dealing with the impact of COVID-19 on business is bringing about new ways of working. Balance this with being flexible about the challenges your employees may be facing in this time, such as home schooling, taking care of the sick and vulnerable, childcare, and the like. The above factors will go a long way in promoting personal and workplace mental health and well-being in the age of COVID-19.

Chapter 16

Positive mental mind-set versus COVID-19 upset – winner takes it all

Kobus Scholtz

Contextual Introduction

Multiple scientific studies have highlighted the impact that a positive mind-set has on an individual. Ranging from having a more optimistic life view, to effective stress and anxiety management, to mood swing control, to being more confident and even being a catalyst for positivity and hope for those you interact with – family, friends, colleagues and people you meet in a queue at a shopping mall. Even the American psychologist Abraham Maslow was fascinated with this concept. Whilst psychology in his era had a single-minded focus on mental illness, neurosis and psychosis as the central themes in attempts to seek to understand and potentially heal mental afflictions, Maslow took a different approach. Instead of studying mental illness, he asked a different question; **"What does positive mental health look like?"** Despite all the studies and literature available advocating the essential need for more positive thinking, mature psychological development is incredibly rare. The statistic you'll often find in the literature is less than 2%. That is, more than 98% of people not reaching close to their potential as mature adults, and the main culprit – lack of a positive mental health mind-set.

What is the main cause for something like positive thinking to be under such pressure, and as the statistics show, seldom achieved? There could be a number of reasons, from societal programming, cultural programming to traumatic events stored in the recesses of our grey matter to psychological programming which includes those already mentioned as well as poor eating and drinking habits. Unless understood and controlled, these factors make us all prone to be controlled by our external environment. Uncertainty combined with fear creates a toxic mental condition exacerbated by bombardment of negative media information, conspiracy theories, doomsday prophecies and an insidious feeling of hopelessness. Just consider the devastating effect the Covid-19 pandemic is having on everything we considered as normal. It is the same thing every day, thinking the same thought, performing the same actions, creating the same experiences and emotions, same life, over and over again. You start to think equal to your environment and before you know it your whole focus is based on the psychological wounds of feeling unsafe, unloved and unworthy. Combine these thoughts with negative emotions, and you have a recipe for disaster.

Unless you are able to control the threat of your outer environment, the sub-branch of your Autonomic Nervous System, the Sympathetic Nervous System kicks in. Its job is for protection from threats and dangers. This system is switched on automatically and once turned on a host of physiological functions begin to happen automatically. When you are feeling constant fear, anger, aggression, panic etc. you are living by the hormones of stress because of the release of adrenal hormones. The three main stress hormones being adrenaline, cortisol and norepinephrine and because stress is knocking your brain your body is also out of balance; no energy for growth, repair, lack of energy for long term projects to name a view. Once life view also takes a knock, the hell with positive thinking, I am too busy focusing on my psychological wounds. The results: stress not just seriously impacting your immune system, but you become a victim of your environment. The brakes must be applied and the starting point is to access the second branch of the Autonomic Nervous System, the Parasympathetic Nervous System. This is where the body conserves energy, utilises nutrients and transport chemicals to the cells. Our metabolism goes up, growth, repair and restoration occur and above all, it allows us to access the prefrontal cortex of the brain more frequently. This part of the brain is involved with emotional regulation and decision-making, where we store the sense of self, our value system, our self-control, to suppress emotions and access higher order thinking and executive functions.

How does the brain work?

The brain has many parts; it is highly complex but has revealed many of its secrets due to the advancement of technology and neuro-scientific research. To appreciate why positive thinking as a mind-set is in furlough despite these advancements, a closer look at certain parts of the brain may explain this age old dilemma.

Brain Stem	Most basic part of your brain yet highly complex. Responsible for the basic and vital functions of breathing, heart rate, hunger, sex, sleep and wake cycles.
Neo-cortex	This is the part of the brain that you think with. It is creative and involved in basic and sophisticated problem solving. It covers about 40% of the frontal lobe, but it is not the part of the brain that makes decisions for you.
Limbic System	This is the emotional brain. It processes information approximately 50 000 times faster than your neo-cortex. This means that long before you make a decision, the limbic system has already made it for you. The purpose of the limbic system is to keep you safe and saves your life.

However, there is an unspeakable primordial calculator, deep within you at the very foundation of your brain, far below your thoughts and feelings. It monitors exactly where you are positioned in society and to what extent your external environment impacts on the quality of the results you're experiencing – professionally and personally. It is referred to as the **Reticular Activating System (RAS).**

This system is a most powerful system – it is your lightning-fast personal search engine that connects only with the neurological connections in your brain. Literally every sensory impulse received will go through it first, where it decides whether the information received is important to you or not. The limbic system assigns value to sensory inputs received from the Reticular Activating System.

- The RAS is a filter system that allows certain information into your brain and it blocks out other information.
- For example: If you were brought-up to believe that life is hard, money is evil, you are unlovable etc. your RAS is going through the day and it is going to point out every single piece of evidence that confirms the negative belief that you have.
- If you think that people don't like you at work, the RAS will literally look for evidence to confirm that belief all day long.
- Can you imagine being subconsciously driven by a belief that life is hard during this pandemic? Having a positive mind-set will be a mere pipe dream.

Key functions of the Reticular Activating System (RAS).

Deletion – Selects and filters according to our moods, interests, pre-occupation and general alertness. Deletes information and forms our ideas from what we notice.

Distortion – Changes our experience, amplifying some and diminishing others. When we distort events, we give more weight to some experiences than others (confirmation bias).

Generalisation – We take one experience and make it represent a group. A child sees how their parents treat each other and makes a mental model of how men and women treat each other.

Having a positive mind-set is therefore not a conscious intervention alone but a re-programming of the subconscious mind. This is often why personal development books or motivational seminars with all due respect seldom produce a positive mind-set. The secret lies in the subconscious mind – the neurological connections in the brain that wire together when stimulated. Only through neural science, neuro-linguistic programming and several energy psychology modalities can the subconscious mind be re-programmed. It is this programming that then produces a natural positive mental mind set.

In the interim, the following practical steps can help you to start creating a process of positive mental mind setting. By doing this on a regular daily basis, one is starting to suggest alternatives to the RAS.

Creating Positive Mental Health – A Practical Guide

Flush the Mind

Our five senses are always on. We gather information continuously through conversations, watching television, reading newspapers, listening to music, etc. We are bombarding ourselves daily with images of violence, death, fear, worries, negativity and victimhood. We are conditioned, hardwired by this information. Most people live through their senses – what they see, hear, smell, taste and feel. This causes most people to be subservient to their outside world. We become conditioned to respond to this information.

> **Operate on a low information diet**
> What are you watching and listening to on the radio/television/movies/shows?
> What newspapers or magazines are you reading?
> Are you participating in gossip, backbiting and/or bullying?

To protect your mind with a vengeance, what are you prepared to "flush out" in terms of	
Radio/television/movies/shows?	**Flush Out Options**
Newspapers/magazines?	**Flush Out Options**

Stimulate the Mind

Read 10 pages of a good book a day or read for 30 minutes a day. Set your iPhone, CD player or any device per day and listen to educational, inspirational audios.

5 – 3 – 1 Stimulate the Mind Program (90 days)	
5 top inspirational books to read (10 pages minimum or 30 minutes per day):	
3 top motivational audio programmes to listen to:	
1 webinar/learning programme I can access on the web:	

The Importance of Feeling Good

It is important to know what you are feeling. It is very important to stop negative emotions **immediately**. Negative emotions **at that moment** literally invites something you don't want. Your goal must be to **"feel good"**. The more you stay in the "feel good" mode, the more you will access the Parasympathetic Nervous System. Always have as a goal to "feel good now" – not later, tomorrow or this evening – **NOW**. Feel good means a feeling of happiness, being content, feeling secure, feeling confident, blessed, bliss, joy, exhilarating, loved, exuberant, etc. and then keep feeling better ... These feelings might change from day to day and hour to hour. There is no right or wrong good feeling.

Gratitude

The emotional significance of gratitude means you're getting something. If you are in an emotional state of gratitude, every thought is going to make it right down into your body. If you elevate your state, there are about 1 200 different chemical reactions that go in your body that begin to restore and repair the body to be in a state of gratitude. If a person changes fear, worry, anxiety to gratitude, and they really start training the heart (heart is beating, gets regulated more coherently, starts to release energy to the brain, starts creating an ambient field around the body) the heart is starting to work for you. If you are in state of gratitude, you are in a state of receiving then the thoughts that you think will make it to the body and ignite the parasympathetic nervous system.

Create your own **Personal Gratitude Journal**.

Every day, and as often as you can, record events, thoughts, circumstances, people, etc. that provoke an emotion of gratitude within you. Keep the journal handy. Endeavour to enter at least 5 aspects of gratitude's per day. Continue the process as often as you can. Eventually you will end up with a comprehensive journal detailing your perspective of gratitude

Repeat these as often as possible especially as you awake from sleep.

Personal Gratitude Journal

I am so grateful for..

I am so grateful for..

I am so grateful for..

I am so grateful for..

I am so grateful for..

I am so grateful for..

I am so grateful for..

I am so grateful for..

I am so grateful for..

I am so grateful for..

I am so grateful for..

The above are basic and relatively easy steps to maintain some degree of positivity and sanity amidst a world that no one really knows how it will look in future. The world of Psychoanalysis and Positive Psychology offers us, as humans, a deeper understanding of our being, behaviours and the results that we experience, giving us this reality we call life. To this end, we offer training solutions that delve to the core of human behaviour, human authenticity and human growth. It is a practical, no nonsense approach leaving the individual with a clear roadmap, not only to realise their full potential but also experience results personally and professionally that are fulfilling, peaceable with self and others, and appreciating and celebrating our authentic self. Please contact us for more information at kscholtz@xsinet.co.za or by cellular 082 372 5800.

Part 5

Embracing the challenge and finding solutions to do our part for humanity, conservation and tourism

Chapter 17

How Rhino Africa is navigating COVID 19 through Thought Leadership[1,2]

David Ryan and Grant Rapaport

Thought Leadership

Over the past few days, a number of people have been asking us for our view, in addition to how we at Rhino Africa are planning to navigate this Covid-19 Crisis. Cognisant of the fact while much has been written about Covid-19, the virus and the economic and human consequences, there has been very little written with specific reference to our Safaris based Tourism Industry. The intention of this collaboration is to articulate the complexity of our Tourism ecosystem, and how that ecosystem will need to work collaboratively as we scenario plan through this uncertainty.

These are indeed unprecedented times, and we are conscious of the fact that we are all doing this for the first time. We are reminded how every business strategy became outdated and irrelevant in just a few weeks, and where we stand today, that "old box" has been well and truly shattered and we can now only think outside of it.

At the heart of this crisis lies uncertainty, and engaging with our mentors, industry peers, partners and associations have all been key to our scenario planning. As we write today, our primary source markets continue to see exponential growth in infections, increasing our belief that a recovery from the effects of Covid-19 will be longer than initially anticipated just a few weeks ago.

In all instances, the recovery of our industry is entirely dependent on the reopening of borders and the resumption of international flights, which will allow for mobility on scale.

Despite what for many may seem like insurmountable challenges related to the impact of Covid-19 on our industry, we need to continue to rise to this generational challenge. We continue to look to tourism as the game-changing force that uplifts communities and protects our wildlife. Tourism enriches so many lives, we need to

---

1 **Note:** All information in this chapter was retrieved from https://blog.rhinoafrica.com/2020/04/08/how-rhino-africa-is-navigating-covid-19/

2 Ryan, D. & Rapaport, G. (2020). Thought Leadership. Retrieved from: https://blog.rhinoafrica.com/2020/04/08/how-rhino-africa-is-navigating-covid-19/

redouble our efforts and consider every option and plan for all eventualities as we work as an industry to do our part to maintain decades of brand equity and livelihoods built on the foundation of bringing guests to African soil.

In order to ensure economies throughout Sub-Saharan Africa are able to recover in the wake of Covid-19, there is no getting around the fact that tourism must be at the forefront of our recovery, a pillar for economic growth and employment. For that to happen as quickly as possible we need to ensure that the businesses that make up the backbone of our industry, from lead generation to logistics and accommodation, are able to survive, in order to meet and entice the return of world demand for African travel.

As a first step to understanding this complex impact this pandemic will have on our interconnected industry we need to identify and understand a number of key factors and beliefs as the basis for our forward planning:

- Treatment and Vaccine horizon
- Ability to Travel from Key Source Markets
- Destination Markets' Ability to Reopen and Host
- Structural Differences between Flights, Beds and Activities and Tour Operations
- Recovery Tailwinds

Treatment and Vaccine horizon

We start with a recognition that there are no existing treatments for Covid-19, despite trials that are underway to test the efficacy of existing drugs, along with the timelines to produce a vaccine. These timelines include the required safety and efficacy through clinical trial results and scaling manufacturing required which are estimated to take 12-18 months. As data continues to come in to support high transmission (R0 of 2-2.5) and high hospitalisation (~19%) rates worldwide, the current approach, which focuses on containment, is unlikely to be short-lived with extended disruption to international travel.

SEASONAL FLU VS COVID-19 STATISTICS

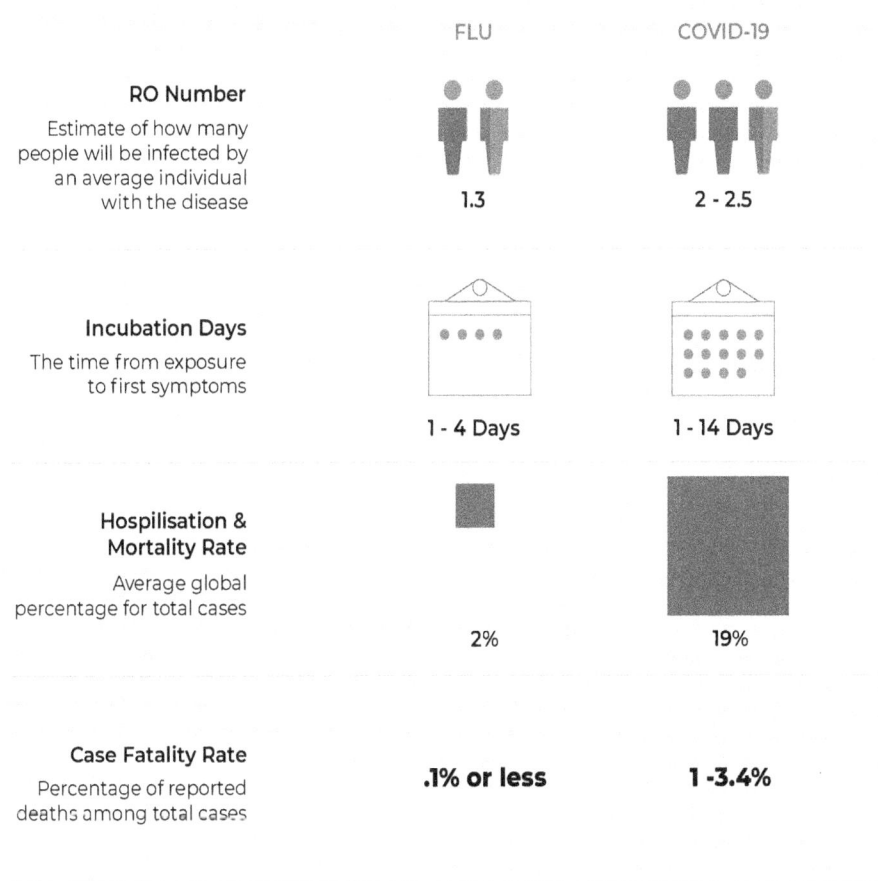

Sources: CDC, WHO, NCBI, VOX

Ability to Travel from Key Source Markets

Three major factors are required for our key source markets to recover. Simply put there needs to be healthy guests with the disposable income to afford travel and a flight network servicing long-haul destinations in Africa.

Firstly, in general, our primary source markets continue to see exponential growth in infections with slow or late government responses with a few exceptions, like that of Germany's low mortality rates. Overall experience to date demonstrates a much lower level of containment in Europe, the UK and the United States than seen in China. Containment in the absence of treatment is a key consideration when considering how countries that are flattening the curve will regulate their borders and restart global mobility. That being said, with the US targeting lower than a 1% infection rate, there will still be a large pool of potential guests given the stabilisation of infection rates and appropriate testing.

Secondly, the money to travel. As we think forward to the restart of local then global economies we need to look beneath the economic turmoil and segment the impact it would have had on different parts of the population in our source markets and their disposable income. Setting aside the travel bans, the economic impact will likely not be borne equally across source markets or within them. In rich countries, the burden of this pandemic will sadly fall disproportionately on the working classes. We see a massive shift by knowledge workers to working remotely, shielding their income while physical, generally lower-paid labour cannot, and are therefore at higher risk of being laid off. Additionally, we have already seen in the majority of our source markets an unprecedented scale of governments stepping in to fill the gap left by constrained economic activity, further socialising the cost.

This is good news for many private and public companies and their owners and may, therefore, limit the worst impacts of the stock market as private wealth declines. Direct stimulus packages have also been adopted at a time when personal spending is physically constrained and there could well be further pent up demand accumulating, particularly in the luxury and experiential spaces. While this is mixed news, our belief is that our guests' disposable income may be less impacted than initially thought, driving our recovery in demand for travel post the crisis.

Lastly, flights and the massive infrastructure investment every global city has made to facilitate the movement of people and investment is a fundamental building block of our modern society. Governments have already moved to shore up airlines to ensure they are ready to be part of the global restart in trade and commerce. Like we saw in the aftermath of 9/11, there was a massive and sustained mobilisation of security measures effectively to underwrite the confidence in air travel. That is what we will see repeated as this crisis moves forward. Rapid passenger pre-flight testing will soon become part of the normal airport experience driven by the urgent need to underpin economic recovery with the normalisation of flight service. Asian countries have already employed these techniques to great effect and we can expect rapid iterative improvements as the airports shift their resources to roll out these measures for the dual purpose of containment and the critical return of confidence to the sector.

Destination Markets' Ability to Reopen and Host

While initially concerned that a lack of containment of the virus in the destination (Sub-Saharan Africa) would have a long-term adverse effect on our recovery due to an inability to host, we are encouraged by what we are witnessing locally and regionally, through decisive leadership necessary, given the vulnerability of our populations. These are early days still but cautious optimism is warranted. That said, in a best-case scenario where we are relatively successful in containing the outbreak of Covid-19 in Sub-Saharan Africa, there is still a high probability that our borders may have to remain closed to our primary source markets, not due to an inability to host, but rather the high risk of imported infections.

We take note of the stringent measures China has employed to safeguard its population from an imported resurgence of the virus. These would be harder to deploy in the African context although a combination of far lower inbound volumes and rapidly improving testing capacity as well as investments made at departure points may prove sufficient. We also note that countries like South Africa have deep infectious diseases know how which would support these efforts.

Current key source and Destination Full and Partial Lockdown status:

Structural differences between flights, tour operations and beds and activities

In order to understand how this crisis plays out in the local tourism market, we have broken the industry into three major components to understand the vastly different recovery scenario impacts. Flights, our industries' logistical backbone, Bed Operations and Tour Operators. Overall based on our assessment we note that current widespread travel bans have dried up revenue generation throughout the sector. For each major area, the operational requirements triggered by this disruption are first acutely felt by Tour Operators needing to shift significant resources into moving bookings while Flights and Beds are mothballed in the short term. Flights and new bookings for Tour Operations are then the next to see recovery followed lastly by Beds and Activities.

- **Flights**

As we have seen, the extent of travel bans has arguably had the most direct and immediate impact on airlines with an unprecedented number of long-haul flights no longer operating, and limited domestic and regional flights feeder connections continuing in all source markets. One benefit in this space is that flight bookings are highly automated and include real-time visibility which allows airlines to have the most scalable and agile responses to market changes in booking demand as it returns and plenty of capacity to be returned to service.

That being said, actual flight operations are far more complex and require a coordinated response with each airport, government and regulator to operate, especially as one could expect necessary controls on movement in this phase of the containment of the virus. Routes are likely to come back in a piecemeal fashion based on regional and international routings that show credible and sustained control over the virus as commerce returns. In Sub-Saharan Africa, this is too early to tell, but flights and in particular SA Airlink's domestic and regional network will be a critical backbone service for the return of any form of scaled, safari-focused tourism. We expect this to start with limited service in conjunction with robust rapid Covid-19 testing facilities at and around airports given the risks associated with travel and reigniting localised epidemics once we see containment measures lifted.

Chapter 17: How *Rhino Africa* is navigating COVID-19 through Thought Leadership

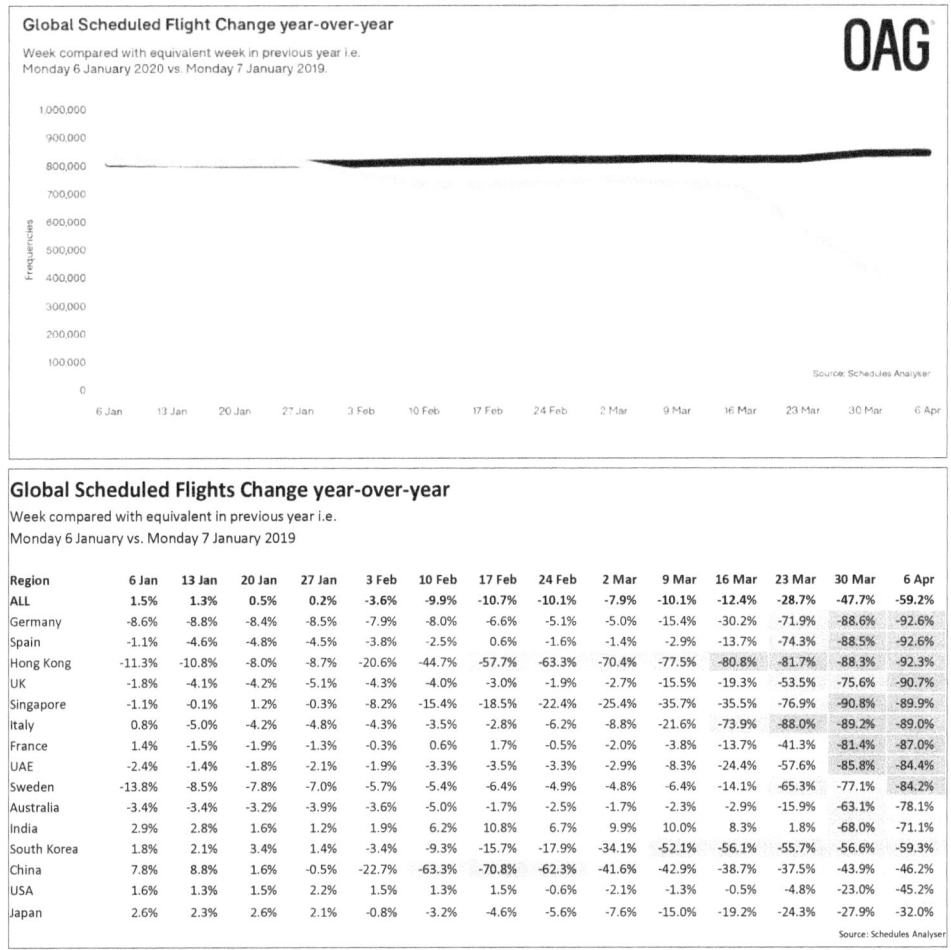

- **Tour Operations**

Existing bookings – unlike airlines with loaded, scheduled products in a largely homogeneous marketplace, Tour Operations involve the connection of guests, logistics, activities and accommodation in the curation of tailor-made holidays. Hence, in the first phase of this crisis, we have dealt with record volumes of guests scheduled to travel in March and into Q2 that had to either be postponed or in some cases cancelled, requiring our entire capacity to be directed at these tasks, all without any additional revenue to contribute these incremental costs. In ordinary times the full-service B2C model does necessitate multiple touchpoints that increase the workload but this is worth the investment in the long term as we see repeat and referral guests drive our growth. In times of crisis, this also allows us the clear benefit of having a primary voice in ensuring our guests can be presented and consider all options available to avoid cancellations. Through this relationship-centric approach we have seen positive results in maintaining a large proportion of the forward book which will aid the recovery of both flights and beds with a base load of guest arrivals in the future.

New bookings – we have seen a dramatic drop-off in online search interest in the last 45 days as the world is preoccupied with the immediate impact of Covid-19. This will change over time as we see search interest and enquiries slowly return as potential guests see more certainty in the future which currently looks too cloudy to facilitate commitment to future travel. As this interest returns, we expect to see average lead times (booking to travel) for high-end guests which are normally six months to potentially be even longer as we saw post other health scares like Ebola. The search interest return and the lead time we will see will be extended if governments and airlines don't set clear expectations regarding schedules and border control regulations which have the ability to reassure guests if done well. What we do not need is stories of flight cancellations or self-inflicted wounds through policies like we saw in the unabridged birth certificate saga.

Regardless of the facts on the ground Tour Operations will be at the forefront of disseminating accurate, reliable, real-time information related to the inevitable patchwork of additional travel restrictions, in addition to the ongoing need for guiding clients back to Africa in order to facilitate guest conversion. Industry associations like SATSA, TBCSA, ATTA and TSA will need to coordinate closely with regional and international governments to ensure certainty and clarity is the goal of all messaging.

- **Beds and Activities**

Accommodation and related activities are fundamentally driven by heads in beds. Therefore, the timing delay until we see guests arriving back into Sub-Saharan Africa at scale is the critical driver to bed operations recovery. As a long-haul international destination, this will be significantly impacted by the success of all the factors we have identified. While international markets remain closed, we can expect some short- to medium-term demand from our domestic and regional markets. These will require adjustments to operations and pricing in many cases. Given the small size of the local luxury market, this will be limited in volume and drive significant price flexibility and SADC rates.

For bed owners, one will need to weigh the financial and human costs of mothballing operations versus those related to adapting operations for local demand and the ability to generate domestic or regional demand in the short term. Added to these risks, if history from the 2010 Fifa World Cup reminds us of anything, it's during times of low occupancy, as experienced post the 2008/9 financial crisis, a gluttony of highly discounted 5- and 6-star beds is hugely detrimental to bed suppliers that are geared to servicing the 3- and 4-star markets.

As international arrivals start to scale, these arrivals will displace local demand. The sheer complexity of the international travel ecosystem, that we have taken for granted over the last 20 years, presents timing risks to be managed and monitored in order to transition pricing strategy while managing occupancies.

The lead times highlighted in the Tour Operator section then need to be considered in the recovery which adds additional time to the road to bed occupancy recovery. That is also why deferral, rather than cancellation of current future travel pipelines, is so critical as these international arrivals will provide support for bed owners as the buildup of new bookings ramps up in the 6 to 12 month timeframe. The recognition of these structural constraints is critical for bed operators to plan for ensuring sustainable operating cost levels are achieved rapidly post local lockdown periods or alternatively access to bridge funding is secured to ride out this layered demand recovery.

We are conscious that as the travel bans persist, there is a large amount of international travel still booked for travel through the next 6 months that may require postponement, creating great adversity and complexity to bed, flight and logistical services.

Recovery Tailwinds

- **Emerging Market Currency Weakness**

We have seen a perfect storm of credit downgrades in South Africa, flight to quality and upcoming necessary government fiscal and monetary policy interventions that have already significantly changed country and regional financial risk profiles of the developing world. We have seen this in 15-25% currency weakening in South Africa and its direct neighbours and closer to 40% in the Zambian Kwacha while East African destinations have been spared with 10-15% declines this year. This bodes well for destination competitiveness for an industry that still hasn't largely moved to dynamic pricing.

- **Availability and Lowered Operating Costs**

As we have seen significant demand-side shocks we have seen and expect further price reductions from suppliers especially in the short term and holding or reductions in 2020 rates. Weaker regional currencies mean African beds will be trading at 2014/2015 US dollar pricing levels, with little appetite from bed suppliers to increase rates due to lack of occupancy through the better part of 2020. With labour market disruptions and lower oil prices, for the first time, a depreciation in regional currencies will not mean a direct increase in inflation, further dampening the requirement for price increases. On the contrary, we predict that US $ priced bed rates will need to decline into 2021 if they want to compete with their Rand-based counterparts, as they brace for a recovery in occupancies. This bodes well for destinations like South Africa and Namibia but will require a competitiveness review for destinations like Botswana, Zambia, Zimbabwe and East Africa that largely follow US $ based pricing. Thus if bed operators were to work with a common purpose, our road to recovery could be further aided by ensuring highly competitive destination pricing. This extends to lower long-haul airfares which are also likely in the medium term as loads build and are aided by oil prices that look set to remain low.

- **Psychology**

While Covid-19 is deeply impacting all of us, we know that this moment will pass and travel will be back, because the desire to connect is in all of us. We are seeing people throughout the world find innovative ways to feed that need during this time of isolation and we expect the need to connect and embrace life and experiences will be stronger than ever once the forced isolation eases. Our belief is, therefore, that the psychology of mortality enhances a desire for connectedness that will drive an increased demand for experience. And with a developing consciousness, Africa has both experiences and connectedness in abundance. As we all know, there are few places in the world that families and loved ones can come to reconnect for long hours every day, away from the distractions of endless Zoom meetings and chat apps, like that of the back of a Land Rover.

- **Giving Back**

In addition to the incredible experiences Africa has to offer, the shared humanity of this crisis which is truly global has already seen millions of people and businesses stepping up to support those in need. The established indirect and direct connection between tourism and poverty alleviation, education and wildlife preservation should all be strong drivers of both our industry leaders in this time of crisis, as well as additional motivators for our guests to come back to Africa in support of these amazing causes. The reality is as destinations and source markets reopen, guests will have a plethora of options available for travel and few destinations have the impact story so closely linked to why travel to Africa should be at the top of the list of those guests with that consciousness to give back.

Pulling All This Together – What Is In Store?

Having identified the major trends and structural elements we are tracking, we have entered our scenario assessment as we plot the way forward for our business. With a strong conviction that this moment will pass and travel will be back, our immediate attention is focused on how we endure and see this Covid-19 crisis playing out. Here we have chosen to focus on two primary scenarios. The first being a 6-12 month time frame to rein in the pandemic and restart travel and the second looking at 12+ months as the pandemic continues.

As we examine the current situation we have already discounted a third scenario, that Covid-19 would last between 3 and 6 months. A best-case scenario where we are relatively successful in containing the outbreak of Covid-19 in Sub-Saharan Africa, given the developments in our source markets, there is a high probability that our borders may not be able to be opened to these high-risk countries for some time, leading to the discounting of the optimistic scenario.

Both our scenario plans for recovery start with the premise that capacity will be required as we anticipate all travel booked and scheduled to end July 2020 will need to be postponed to future dates and August to October travel should be considered at risk, based on the structural factors identified.

Scenario 1: A 6 to 12 Month Disruption Due to the Pandemic

Our best-case scenario for planning a recovery strategy for Rhino is based on the premise of virus containment within a 6 to 12 month period. What does this look like? In this scenario, the curve has largely been flattened globally (most critically in our key source and destination markets), which means the healthcare infrastructure is coping, and people and businesses are returning to their normal economic activities. Airlines have resumed consistent service between major airports though likely at a reduced frequency to start. Airports and governments have worked to implement procedures to ensure the safety of passengers and destination populations most likely utilising rapid testing capacity at airports pre-boarding meaning that all passengers are Covid-19 negative and facilitating the responsible relaxation of border controls.

Once the logistics are in place, confidence will be the most critical factor that will dictate the speed of recovery for travel at scale. In this scenario, governments in source and destination countries work closely to establish and roll out testing guidelines like those currently commonplace in the airport security sector. This will give guests the confidence to travel and not be denied entry on arrival, or on their return. The memories of forced quarantine post-arrival will be fresh in everyone's minds and this will need to be counterbalanced by clear, consistent guidelines. The more globally accepted, the better.

All governments will now be on high alert having paid a huge economic price for the required containment steps and the cost of moving too quickly will be well known. These containment efforts in Southern and Sub-Saharan Africa have been predominantly successful through a combination of aggressive lockdowns, testing improvements, and learning from the experience of the Northern Hemisphere countries. This will allow the easing of domestic and regional mobility by mid-year and as measures taken to prevent the spread of Covid-19 in this process show results this will give governments the confidence to fully re-open borders to key long-haul destinations. Inevitable health issues will come up but rapid response teams will efficiently deal with these in a private-public partnership to widespread praise, proving greater tangible confidence that tourism is back fuelling the recovery and bookings as a result.

During the initial phase, we expect to see some opportunistic local demand for high-end, experience-based leisure travel at lower yields and business travel as executives reconnect and realign their businesses post isolation. Specials targeted at local markets would support this first phase recovery and could be necessary to build confidence in the staying power of the destination's sustained containment efforts. This would send a strong signal internally and externally that "We are open for business" aiding our medium-term recovery and getting operations back on track. International arrivals will take some time to ramp up as distressed airlines would initially focus on short, profitable routes and avoid higher risk, load-dependent long-haul routes. This wait and see approach from both governments and airlines are likely to limit volumes throughout July to September and as demand picks up we expect to see long-haul flight schedules starting to return to regular schedules in Q4 2020. Coinciding with these confidence-building measures some of the existing forward book of guests will be able to travel in Q3 and will work through the system over the next 6 quarters through Q4 2021.

Lead generation will start to pick up as the acute shock of Covid-19 wanes but we expect these early signs of life in search interest and repeat guests to require significantly longer to convert to bookings as all guests will be waiting to see consistent signs of recovery. The return of travel insurers to the market and/or upfront flexibility from bed, flight and logistic providers on more flexible terms. As confidence returns, search interest will increase as well as improved conversion ratios to booking and shorter conversion and lead times. Destination longer-term macro trends will again start to emerge unless regional branding is improved to change this picture. In the two years pre Covid-19, destinations like South Africa were already witnessing annual declines in arrival numbers from our traditional markets, placing added pressure on many long-haul carriers' viability into Southern Africa. This was not the case in East Africa which had been witnessing year-on-year growth.

If in line with our scenario analysis, if we witness a containment of Covid-19 within a 6 to 12 month period and the associated certainties around international mobility, we would expect to see a recovery in Tour Operator bookings commencing in late Q2, steadily improving into early 2021. Travel dates would lag this with currently scheduled guests and some new bookings expected to start travelling in larger numbers from late Q3 2020 and into the middle of 2021.

One remains cognisant of the fact that, due to the postponement of current forward books into late 2020, 2021, new bookings potentially face availability challenges and hence the latter half of 2021 could be a bumper year for tourism as we see overflow into shoulder seasons as the postponements of March to September 2020 travel take up peak availability in late 2020 and 2021.

Scenario 2: A 12+ Months as the Pandemic Continues

Our second scenario in planning a recovery strategy for Rhino is based on the premise that virus containment efforts are less successful in one or both of our key source and destination markets. The premise of this scenario includes several rolling waves of travel bans and lockdowns that are necessary as stretched healthcare systems are unable to cope as Covid-19 persists through the northern summer with even possible resurgence in Northern Hemisphere's Autumn/Fall 2020.

That being said, as the initial shock turns to more coordinated action, increased surge hospital capacity, the advent of treatments, and newly galvanised world populations educated in the importance of basic precautions, a reduction in the R0 and mortality is possible, moving Covid closer to a serious, but manageable enemy as we forge an uneasy peace with the virus while waiting for widespread vaccine availabilities and increased recovered populations into 2021. These conditions, though not ideal, will mean increased economic hardship and longer travel restrictions. These elements will reduce the buying power of even high-end guests significantly and mean that the crucial element of confidence in travel will simply take longer to establish.

This delayed slower recovery means international tourism volumes would be expected to remain very low for the remainder of 2020, only increasing in 2021 and into 2022. Booking lead times will mean that we will see an extended period of low search interest and enquiries, with limited recovery starting in Q4 2020 for Tour Operators. This may well cause availability issues in 2021 as 2 years of adjusted demand is working to travel in the same shortened period. The impact of this supply constraint will need to be assessed as we see more data into Q3 2020.

The below graph depicts these two recovery scenarios from the baseline of 0% representing volumes prior to Covid-19. As you can see Bed/Flights delivery (dotted line) lags Tour Operator demand (solid line) in both cases. Our experience was a sharp drop-off in demand starting in the second half of February 2020 and rapidly accelerating into March, culminating with the lockdown of Southern Africa in late March. The bookings moved from existing 2020 travel dates can be seen to aid travel volumes recovery in the months following the restart of travel and will be highly sensitive to confidence levels discussed previously.

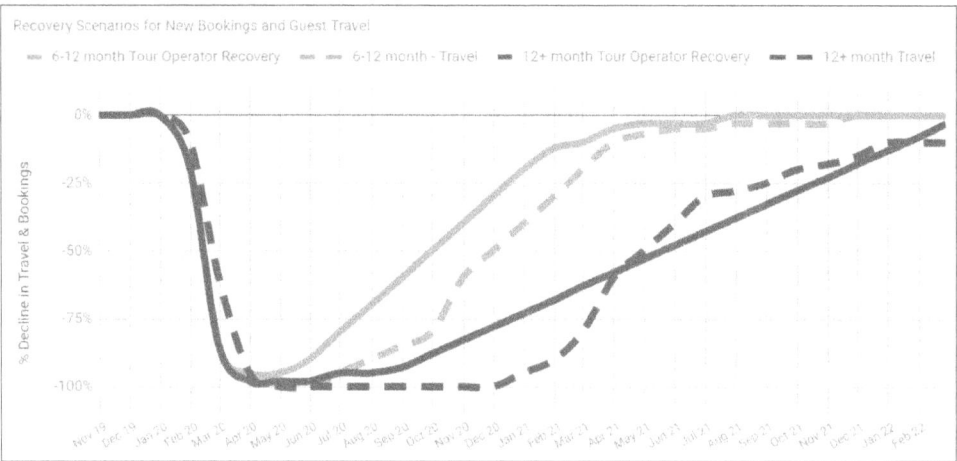

However fleeting or long-lived, no business will emerge from this crisis without significant change, and hence our attention is now focused on how best to adjust our operations and structures to ensure we can continue to serve our guests and suppliers in either of these scenarios. Whether your belief is that this crisis will be short- or long-lived, the road to recovery, to returning to pre Covid-19 booking numbers and sales will require different areas of focus, expertise and capacity.

In the absence of substantive Government intervention or rescue funding, now is the time that many of our partners and peers will need to focus on using this crisis to recalibrate our businesses. In the case of Rhino, that is to ensure that when we emerge, we are able to increase our market share and productivity as we play our role in the recovery of this industry we all love so much.

As our friend and mentor Colin Bell so aptly put it: "There is no question that when tourism does come back, Africa will be in a much better position than it was before Covid-19. Under tourism destinations it will be in more demand than before the crisis." Consequences of Covid-19 in Shaping our Industry.

Somewhat controversial and arguably self-serving, perhaps the most significant shift we will see as a result of this Covid-19 pandemic, is the accelerated channel distribution in favour of the B2C channel, as the value of direct client relationships and data required to understand and serve them comes to the fore in the management of clients through a crisis. Bed operators will note a stark difference between both the rate of cancellations and the standard terms and conditions being applied by the various channels, which are directly related to the ability to manage clients through a relationship of trust and on-the-ground expertise.

B2C Tour Operators share a unique connectedness with their clients through months of intimately planning and suggesting routes, logistics, activities and accommodations as we curate tailor-made experiences. That connectedness, while increasing workload, has the significant benefit in times of crisis of allowing us to continue that experience of weighing options and scenarios with our guests, thus ensuring we consider the best course of action. This requires consideration for and translating of the significant complexity in play behind the scenes to ensure all options available and thereby maintaining a large proportion of the forward book for when travel returns. In addition, as conditions improve history will show that B2C's led our recovery through proactively mobilising new, repeat and referral clients to connect with suppliers that have gaps in occupancy and specials as we do our part to rebuild occupancies faster than any other available channel. More than ever, on-the-ground knowledge and experience will be invaluable as clients, shaken by the disruptions caused in all areas of life by Covid-19, will need information and reassurance that we have their backs as they cautiously return to rediscover Africa.

Final Thoughts

As such, we are reminded that now is not the time to fear, falter or hide, for in this moment, however fleeting or long-lived, is our chance as a generation and industry to leave our mark. With that in mind, we recognise the need to redefine and restructure our business, even more than ever before; not only to create better value for our guests, our people and our partners, but to ensure we are able to survive this crisis. We recognise that it is in times of uncertainty that people remember those who were there and chose to make a difference. On that note, we would like to thank every one of our Rhinos, mentors, partners, peers and industry associations that have come together to work with a common purpose as we navigate this challenge together.

As this progresses, we all have the opportunity to spread hope, knowledge and humanity with one another, as everyone continues to seek ways to fill their time with purpose and a sense of connectedness. While no business will emerge from this crisis without significant change, we thank you for being part of the Rhino story. We're making history, and we're going to be okay as an industry – together.

Chapter 18

The story of African Bush Camps and the impact of COVID 19 on tourism, conservation and community

Beks Ndlovu

About African Bush Camps

African Bush Camps (ABC) is an owner-run, African-based safari portfolio spanning 15 luxury tented camps and lodges in Botswana, Zimbabwe and Zambia. The company promotes travel to Africa on a global scale while operating with a strong focus on conservation. It upholds an environmentally sustainable footprint that celebrates the culture of communities in the areas in which its properties operate.

Today, ABC employs more than 600 people across the world including hospitality staff and guides at the camps, those who manage its communication and administrative boat from the Cape Town headquarters and representatives residing outside of Africa.

ABC was founded in 2006 by Beks Ndlovu, a professional safari guide born and raised in the village of Lupane on the outskirts of Hwange National Park in Zimbabwe. From the start of operations, Ndlovu's mission has been to operate a safari hospitality portfolio that reincarnates the fantasy of 'Old Untouched Africa,' and its lifestyles with surrounding communities while treating guests to authentic and adventurous professional guide-led experiences that can only be found in the bush.

The African Bush Camps Foundation (ABCF) was also started in 2006. It is a not-for-profit organisation driven by conservation, education, and empowerment for the communities that surround the company's camp locations. With ABCs support, the Foundation has spearheaded 72 community projects across Botswana, Zimbabwe, and Zambia. Just over 40 of those projects are currently operating under the Foundation's wing.

Introduction

African Bush Camps has always been a fan of the African proverb, 'If you want to go fast, go alone. If you want to go far, go together'. Since we started ABC, I was driven by the coming-together of communities and likeminded individuals who sought to bring tourism back to the people of Africa. It is strange to think that today, this proverb, in its literal sense, has lost some of its impact as we are forced to distance ourselves from each other, physically. But the melancholy of this situation is again overturned by another proverb by American civil rights activist, Maya Angelou: 'Every storm eventually runs out of water'.

In the ironic situation where we find ourselves isolated in an unprecedented time brought about by the COVID-19 interventions, so too do we recognise that now, more than ever, we *are* in this together. Together, in the hope of overcoming the challenges posed by the virus' global outbreak, we are moving forward to fasten hope and trust in an industry most of us have spent our working lives building.

Considering the visible efforts by travel operators to continue keeping the industry 'alive', consistently developing smarter strategies to connect with future travellers, we are proving our vigilance and perseverance to come out of this stronger and even more prepared than our clientele could have imagined.

Life in Lockdown: Company, Community, Conservation

Company

Since the news of COVID-19s outbreak late December 2019, our team went into full response mode as we anticipated the brooding storm for 2020. At that time, the New Year still looked promising on our books. Our plans for expansion were on track and interest in our new developments saw a healthy increase. Considering our properties' locations, and the fact that most of our guests were international travellers, we needed to think on our feet and be a step ahead in precautionary health and hygienic measures. It was in February that we introduced new training guidelines for staff and put routine measurements in place to ensure we safeguard our employees and guests' wellbeing.

Our camps were 'lucky' as the first confirmed cases in Africa were closer to our headquarters in Cape Town, South Africa. We were fortunate that no cases were confirmed at our properties. We knew that was only the beginning of the storm. We knew we were in the wake of governments' strict regulations that would stir our travellers' confidence. It was only a matter of time before lockdown came into play.

From April, we entered a 'curl up' period and decided to 'hunker' down for four months while assisting clients to postpone their trips.

Our 'new normal' posed numerous threats for our business objectives and forced us to make some of the most difficult decisions. Since ABC has started in 2006, it has been a rule of thumb for us to invest in the upskilling of individuals, may it be within the company or those members with whom we associate through our Foundation.

I have experienced so many people finding their niche and extending their career checkpoints to bigger goal posts. I have seen people grow in their profession and as individuals. It was natural to keep our pot of brewing skills on the fire and continue motivating our employees to continue wanting more growth.

Realistically, as we, alongside our friends in the industry, are served with an exceptional challenge to support staff financially, we entered a stringent consultation process involving employees, and where we could reach common ground to keep the ABC family intact. All employees remain on our payroll with a reduced salary agreement as we enter our hibernation period.

Today, ABC's operational machine remains well oiled with staff reporting for rotating shifts at camps. There, we are tending to the maintenance and upkeep of our properties' structures. Staff are encouraged to broaden their knowledge, participate in other members' day-to-day routines and lend a hand with tasks they normally could not give as much attention to during guest visits. Hostesses, waiters, the chef's team and maintenance staff are urged to join the guides on game drives. Our guides also spend more time together in the field, studying the environments while continuing to learn from each other.

Community

For the Foundation, the playing field is slightly different. As part of our collaboration, for every bed booked per night with ABC, a fee automatically goes towards the Foundation's initiatives. While tourism is at a standstill, funds for the Foundation are also paused and the need for more creative outreach is in the hands of our coordinators. With the additional support we previously received from donors and partners, the Foundation has managed to set aside emergency funds for these types of situations.

The Foundation has, to date, built close relationships with community members and has been providing basic infrastructure to help improve living circumstances in the villages. This includes installing boreholes and water tanks for community gardens, cattle, and members' personal use. These efforts created the platform the Foundation needed to gain the community members' cooperation and acceptance of their aid. Now, while there are less resources to rely on, the Foundation's presence remains rife in the communities, with members turning to those provisions that are now in more demand.

Considering our future projects and bouncing back to doing what the Foundation does best, we are ensured of the confidence we need to continue working together with the villages and retake the tasks we started.

Conservation

When it comes to conservation, it really comes down to the power of collaboration. The sharing of information, resources and clubbing with competitors and tourism in times of crises – essentially, putting competition aside and choosing to cooperate to help each other come out head above water on the other side. The power of collaboration has been a major focus for me in the last four years. Hence the birth of the *Conservation and Wildlife Fund* (Hwange). Zimbabwe has been well known for innovative and professional approaches to its precious wildlife. In this country there is strong technical expertise and reasonable infrastructure, plus much enthusiasm and goodwill by many conservation players. But financial help is the big need; the world at large has to help pay for the costly protection of a truly global asset – Africa's wildlife. ABC is one of the managing partners and as the Fund's chairman, it's a priority for me (and us) to form part of a body of collaborative operators, scientists and researchers who have come together to conserve the entire landscape.

The national parks encompass vast regions which are remote from traffic and unfenced. The halt in our industry and decline in visitor support naturally renders wildlife vulnerable. Desperate times call for desperate measures. For those residing on the outskirts of the parks and who find themselves in dire situations, the inaccessibility of electricity, water and basic food items accelerates the need for people to either hunt for their communities or for the purpose of sale. Our neighbour at our Bumi Hills Lodge in the Lake Kariba region in Zimbabwe, the Bumi Hills Anti-poaching Unit (BHAPU), works alongside the army and national park rangers to curtail the increasing spike in wildlife snags. Since the start of lockdown, we could clearly see the rise in poaching efforts.

Everything that has a consumptive nature can become destructive for the environment. It is our responsibility to continue sustaining some form of support for our partnering rangers, staff and guides in order to reach out to the communities.

Safari operators and their guides act as custodians of wildlife conservation and keep the spark bright when it comes to the positive influence we can have on our surroundings.

Life After Lockdown

'Uncertainty' has certainly earned its place in the dictionary this year. The world has been in a tug of war of feedback-and-response, trying to keep abreast of COVID-19s developments to again pull back on future steps. The virus' persistence has succeeded to filter the value of a year's time (even more) in a matter of weeks.

Where we can likely accept the longevity of the terms that have crossed our paths, the virus' aftereffects will probably surround us in everything we do. Social distancing is another term we will likely not put aside soon. Trade, modes of transport, how we interact in our work environment, our grocery shopping trips, and education at schools may never be the same but humans are resilient. We learn to adapt, and sometimes, if we are good at it, we flourish.

Resources and Conversation

We know the future will have us strapped for resources. In Zambia and Zimbabwe, governments are running low on support. And, while these countries may not be rich in capital, they are rich in resources. Private enterprises are in the position to actively participate and communicate their vested interest in the survival of protected areas and its people. Our fauna and flora belong to the world and we can only continue to urge people to travel and help us sustain the means to protect it.

Social Distancing in Practice

High-end safari operators prioritise the luxury of privacy, space and attention to detail to personalise the experience for their guests. Our largest camp has 24 rooms (mostly 6 rooms for a maximum of 12 beds) which only permits two people per room. Villas and family units are prepared with interconnecting passageways on request. Our vehicles transport a maximum of six guests and our partnering air travel operator has a limited capacity allowance. Considering recent developments and aligning those with anticipated changes, low-volume, high-impact tourism may be the way forward as opposed to mass tourism – where a large number of people gather within confined spaces.

Domestic versus an International Comeback

International revenue is what we aim to secure in the long term, considering its impact on conservation, community input, and development. The current reality is that we cannot rely on this revenue. We have no certain guarantee that international travel is going to bounce back immediately. Local tourism can enable us for the interim to keep the 'ball rolling'. Where we rely on local suppliers and service providers, supporting the local industry can be a sound way to help us build from the ground up before reeling in international travellers. It is a natural step in progression for us as a local operator. We need to be able to relaunch everything we do. If it is a matter of following a chronological order of business, starting afresh, that is what I believe we need to do.

Regarding international travel, we will likely experience a 'slow burn' in the restructuring of the industry. And since this is the case, we can use this time to rebuild our essence as a company on the local front.

Local Support

In the buildup towards our comeback as an industry, welcoming both domestic and international travellers to our home turf, we continue to actively work on the ground in our communities. For one, the recently completed health care centre in the Maunga Village in the Mosi-Oa-Tunya National Park just outside of Livingstone in Zambia, is a project that needs consistent input for essential needs to be attended to. The project will build accommodation for a permanent team of doctors and nurses who will provide critical healthcare services to 4 000 people living in rural Maunga. Locals currently have no reliable access to healthcare. Children and pregnant women are particularly at risk. A clinic has successfully been built and equipped, but now needs to be staffed. Improved healthcare in rural communities has far-reaching implications – improving the community's productivity and development potential.[1], [2]

While the health centre is an important project, the Foundation's work is spread among more than 40 projects in the communities surrounding ABCs properties. Different ways of getting involved are listed here:[3]

Recovering Together

We are in a 'curl up' period. Time is on our side to prepare our team as much as possible for that time we can only hope will bring favourable prospects and challenge the odds. For those in limbo about their travel plans, it can be good to relish in the time given to us to reflect, reconnect and rejuvenate our senses before reliving the world in a renewed glory. In South Africa, we are familiarised by the sights of penguins wobbling across traffic intersections in the Cape Peninsula's coastal towns, squirrels showing confidence on the streets of Cape Town's neighbourhoods. In Gauteng, kudus and giraffes are grazing the Jacaranda trees in the streets of Pretoria. This and so much more, in the wilderness of the Hwange National Park in Zimbabwe, on the riverbanks of the Khwai River in Botswana and the inclining waters of the Zambezi River that flows in the Victoria Falls, will be waiting for our explorers.

---

1. GlobalGiving. (n.d.). Healthcare for 4 000 Rural Zambian Villagers. Retrieved from: https://www.globalgiving.org/projects/healthcare-for-4000-rural-zambian-villagers/
2. African Bush Camps Foundation: (n.d.). African Bush Camps Foundation Community Empowerment. Retrieved from: https://africanbushcamps-gdg-j945n.raisely.com/
3. African Bush Camps Foundation: (n.d.). Community Development Through Responsible Tourism. Retrieved from: https://www.africanbushcampsfoundation.org/

Chapter 19

The story of Care for Wild: Keeping rhinos safe in a time of crisis

Sharon Gilbert-Rivett

The effects of the COVID-19 pandemic present enormous challenges for those caring for orphaned and injured wild animals in rehabilitation centres across South Africa, but at Care for Wild Rhino Sanctuary there's confidence that both the wildlife and people they work with will weather the storm…

In the heart of South Africa's Mpumalanga province, surrounded by the rolling landscape of the Mountainlands Game Reserve near Barberton, Petronel Nieuwoudt is making a difference in the lives of both animals and people. This is home to Care for Wild Rhino Sanctuary, a non-profit organisation established by Petronel in 2011 to care for and rehabilitate a wide range of orphaned, injured and distressed wild animals.

Since its establishment, the rapid increase in rhino poaching led to Care for Wild becoming the country's leading centre for the treatment and care of orphaned rhino calves and it is one of the most specialised and well-respected sanctuaries in the world. It works directly with local communities, using conservation as a valuable empowerment tool to provide jobs, training and education, helping to develop livelihoods and micro economies in the process.

The tangible benefits created by Care for Wild for the communities it works with, ensures that local people see real value in conservation and the work being done to protect and care for rhino and other wildlife species.

COVID-19 has presented new challenges, but Care for Wild has not flinched. "The global and local events related to the pandemic have unfolded at an alarming and overwhelming rate, but we are still committed to our vision and purpose, helping every animal injured or orphaned by the poaching crisis," says Petronel. "The wellbeing of our staff and their families, our communities, our rhinos and all other animals continues to be our primary concern," she adds.

Experience gained from Care for Wild's quarantine area meant that extensive hygiene measures were already in place prior to the pandemic. "This meant we conformed with government regulations, minimising the risk of the spread of infection," says Petronel. "Our staff meets daily as a team to discuss developments to the ever-evolving situation, planning our day and addressing the challenges it brings. Our team caring for and protecting the rhinos during this time are supported with multivitamins, immune-boosting lemon tea, good food, and fun, morale-building activities," she adds. Petronel started her career in the South African Police Service's Endangered Species Protection Unit where she held the rank of captain. She'd always loved wildlife and grew up on a farm, bringing injured, abandoned and sick creatures home to care for throughout her childhood. In 1999 she left the police service and started The Game Capture School before establishing Care for Wild, which has become her life's passion. Almost 20 years later, she's one of South Africa's leading animal welfare experts, thanks to her extensive experience in the hand-rearing, management and safe capture of infant, injured and orphaned animals.

"Care for Wild's vision is sustainable conservation through community involvement to secure a viable free-ranging population of both white and black rhino here in the Barberton area as a nucleus population for future generations of rhino," she explains. "It's our mission to rescue, rehabilitate and release orphaned rhinos and we do this by fulfilling a commitment to rapid rescue response, thorough rehabilitation and release back into the wild," says Petronel.

When it comes to the rescue of orphaned or injured rhinos, time is of the essence. Care for Wild has a dedicated helicopter available to track, find, secure and rescue rhinos and is supported by a highly qualified veterinary team and vehicles to transport the rhino to Care for Wild's holding facilities.

"Most of rhinos in South Africa are found in the Kruger National Park," says Petronel, adding that in spite of intense anti-poaching efforts, we are still losing a high number of rhinos throughout Africa to poaching, driven by the demand for rhino horn in the Far East. "We have a close relationship with SANParks (South Africa's national parks organisation) and have an official memorandum of understanding with them and the Kruger National Park. Most of the rhino orphans in our care come from the Kruger National Park where their mothers were poached," she explains.

The rescued rhinos are taken to Care for Wild's state-of-the-art holding facilities which gives them the critical care they need in the early and extremely fragile stages of their rehabilitation and care process. It's here that they are slowly integrated with other rhinos, forming their own "crashes" (the collective noun for a group of rhinos) and unique bonds. While here the rhinos receive a high standard of care, feed and veterinary support to ensure full rehabilitation and ultimate release back into the wild.

Of course, not all of the rhinos rescued are babies, and as Petronel explains, handling fully grown rhinos is no easy task! "It comes with many challenges," she says. "We need specially designed bomas and highly functional spaces to accommodate them and ensure their optimal safety, as well as the safety of those who care for them," says Petronel, adding that Care for Wild is in the process of building a brand new, cutting-edge facility specifically for this purpose.

Once the rehabilitation process is complete, all of the rescue rhinos are reintroduced back into their natural habitat which is protected from poaching and other threats. It's protected by a highly skilled security team consisting of rhino monitors, canine units, mounted patrols and an armed reaction unit.

The long-term sustainability of Care for Wild and its reserve depends on the effective inclusion of local communities and their full participation in helping to maintain and protect both. This is achieved through an extensive range of community programmes that directly benefit local people and create enormous value for what Care for Wild is doing and the animals it works with.

Care for Wild currently employs more than 300 youth from the communities around the reserve. "They are employed in partnership with Investec Bank through the Government YES programme," explains Petronel. "They are employed as field rangers, game scouts and nature reserve general assistants (conservation workers) and work on eradicating alien invasive plants, repairing road infrastructure, maintaining fences, preparing the annual fire breaks and responding to fires on the reserve and in the communities," she says.

The sanctuary has also established a large vegetable garden that provides fresh produce to the sanctuary's kitchens that supply around 70 cooked meals each day to all Care for Wild staff. The vegetable garden also supplies vegetables to the interns of the YES programme who work within the sanctuary. "Over the past year the garden has also been used to train several of the interns in all aspects of vegetable production. The long-term intention is to establish more of these gardens in the communities surrounding the sanctuary," says Petronel.

The first of these community-based gardens has been established within the Mandela Village community along the Noordkaap River. The garden covers an area of 0.60 ha and is managed by a community entity called the Sunrise Community.

"We also recently embarked upon an ambitious long-term commercial farming venture in partnership with the local Lomshiyo Community," says Petronel. "The project aims to develop 100ha of macadamia nuts, avocados, citrus and vegetables," she says, adding that the community will benefit through a number of avenues. "The profits will be shared after costs and taxes between Care for Wild and the Lomshiyo Trust. The farming operations will employ more than 40 young people and will also offer training in agriculture to the community in the future."

Petronel is positive about Care for Wild Rhino Sanctuary's future, even with the spectre of COVID-19 still looming large. "By the grace of God, our dedicated team will continue to care for and keep the rhinos safe," she says, sharing a message for everyone in the tourism sphere: "Please keep the team at Care for Wild close in your thoughts and prayers. Our purpose is, as always, to save rhino, to save people and to save tomorrow."

Chapter 20

#TOURISMINMYBLOOD: United in purpose to share, inspire and help one another during the crisis vortex

Greg Smith & Richard de la Rey

COVID 19 is unprecedented. It has affected the tourism industry negatively and its scope is far reaching, from a housekeeper in a small B&B to airlines and everything in-between. The industry is extremely resilient and we have faced many challenges (SARS, Swine Flu, 9/11 and let's not forget 2008) in the last 22 years. However, we have always managed to bounce back. The Travel and Tourism industry is in survival mode and we need to stick together and share ideas on how to best deal with this global crisis. During times like these, the human factor comes to the forefront. Travel is all about people and experiences. This is a time to re-connect with acquaintances, re-establish business connections and explore new opportunities that will be mutually beneficial to all parties in time to come.

One of the biggest challenges with Covid 19 is that the landscape changes daily. Doctors and epidemiologists sometimes have conflicting views to their own colleagues, and what the WHO has to say. The reason I mention this is because it affects our daily plans and strategies on how to move forward, not only as individuals, but from a business perspective too.

There have been countless webinars, workshops and online articles on how the tourism landscape is going to change. Some social media groups, such as #tourisminmyblood have been formed to focus on sharing positive stories and marketing initiatives through creating a platform for industry colleagues to help and support one another. Information is exchanged about a wide range of topics, from member surveys and technology platform recommendations, to health and safety tips for hotels and lodges post-Corona. We can learn from one another's experiences in how to cope and build strategies to survive the disastrous impact that the pandemic is having on the travel industry. It's not always easy to make head or tail of the right way forward, but there are quite a few common denominators that stand out.

Most clients are postponing trips. Tour operators are trying their utmost to get clients to postpone but this is not always possible. Lodges and hotels are also trying to convince direct clients to postpone and not cancel. In some cases lodges have offered a credit instead of a refund in order to not lose the booking altogether. Postponements do however create false hope in a sense as not all those who postpone will travel. The trick for agents, operators and establishments is to try and be as flexible as possible, as tourists will understandably be apprehensive when booking, as they themselves do not know when, or if, it will be possible to travel to the destination they have booked.

The general consensus is that without a doubt people will want to travel, and that the pent up demand will be huge. Some say international travel will be pushed out to the 4th quarter of 2020, however most say that we are looking at the first and second quarter of 2021. The confidence to travel again will depend largely on health and safety measures put in place and strictly adhered to. This will provide the traveller with some peace of mind as their health and safety will become a priority when travelling. Timing on regional and international travel is dependent on a few factors, such as borders opening, visa requirements, medical facilities in the host country, travel bans etc. Group travel will take much longer to materialise, if it materialises at all. Stimulus packages in some source markets will mean people will have money to travel. Older generation travel will decline for obvious reasons. It will take time before this picks up again. The 25 – 45 age group will travel and have the resources to do so, and we need to target them with a solid communications strategy.

Many have agreed that the freezing of all rates for 2021 is possibly the best route to go. To discount international rates would not be a good idea as it is a really difficult situation to get out of when you do increase rates again, as the market heads towards normality. Rather offer tactical long-stay rates and/or value adds. In the past many lodges and hotels have discounted international rates as a last-minute strategy to fill stressed inventory. However this, for the most part, is not a successful strategy as it has to be a countrywide offering as opposed to few individual establishments doing so. When marketing any packages such as stay/pay deals, long-stay packages and value adds it is recommended that you send out your 2021 rates. Don't wait until the 11th hour to send out packages, as you will get lost in the multitude of other lodges and hotels doing the same. You will also need to rethink terms and conditions and cancellation policies. You need to come up with a solution where the channel and the lodge or hotels have common ground. This is not the time for bullying but working together for the greater good or bigger picture, which is enticing tourists to travel to South Africa. In addition to this, offer value for money for the SADC market as we need to be cognisant of the fact that they will be our first port of call.

There will be a shift in what people are looking for when they travel. People will be looking for experiences and supporting social responsibility initiatives in order to "give back". There will definitely be a greater sense of responsibility. I think we will see much more mindful travel, a surge in retreats, special family holidays and a reconnection with our most-loved destinations. People will want to spoil themselves and their families and celebrate. There will be a larger uptake in health and relaxation holidays with family and friends. Visiting family and relatives travel will also take off.

Airlines will start with domestic travel and this has been confirmed. Regional travel and then long-haul travel will follow in that order, but timing is dependent on demand. Only time will tell. Borders obviously have to open to allow regional and long-haul travel. Once again, there is pent up demand. Relaxation of laws will happen haphazardly as things progress and more data is collected on the effects and implications of the virus. South Africa as a whole must work together to create demand, especially now that the rand is weak. If there is enough demand, more flights will follow. It is assumed that flight prices will drop in order to entice people to travel.

The local market in South Africa is a small pie with lots of competition, and operators that normally only dealt with inbound or outbound clientele are targeting the local market, which makes a lot of sense for reasons given above. You need to target local travel with local rates, as locals who normally travel overseas will travel in their own country first. This is also due to the expense of travelling internationally. Tourists will be looking for unique experiences in uncluttered environments.

Lodges and hotels should make sure they keep an online presence. Visuals are extremely important. Don't post on social media for the sake of posting. Make it count. Establishments will need to cover all their bases and promote their lodge, guest house, hotel or B & B on other platforms. 360 Virtual tours are a great way to promote your offering. Tourists will also be desperate to connect with nature and space. Bush and beach holidays will be very popular.

What will not be popular are buffets and anything that has a tricky hygiene aspect to it. Rather look to individual starter platters or platters for two, as an example of how to adapt. Use social media to promote the social seclusion and distancing without making an obvious connection to Covid; it's a buzz word that no one wants to hear on holiday. We are all aware of it. In saying this, the hotel industry in general will need to have a comprehensive, Covid-specific, health and safety plan in place and available to those tourists, operators and agents who request one.

All of the above cannot be done without some significant input from South African Tourism. South African Tourism will have to do their part and embark on some serious global media exposure to punt South Africa as a destination as Souh Africa will be competing against a myriad of destinations and we cannot afford to miss out.

It may be too early to say, and of course people are bound to have more frugal spending habits post-Covid-19, but there is potential for the rise in free independent travellers (FIT) business. With an influx of irresistible travel deals coming on line, we could even hope for some 'revenge spending' on travel. Either way, the travel industry has to be ready.

Chapter 21

Rise of the Warrior

Shanaleigh Hebbard

I keep hearing that everyone is in the same boat. But it's not like that. We are in the same storm, yes, but we are not in the same boat.

Your ship can be shipwrecked and mine not. Or vice versa.

For some, quarantine is optimal and full of moments of reflection, of reconnection and peace. Life is easy in flip flops, with a glass of Coke or a cup of tea in hand. For others, this is a desperate crisis. For others, it is facing real loneliness.

For some, it means peace, rest time and a bit of a holiday. For others, this is torture as they wonder how they are going to pay their bills? Others are concerned about the bread for the weekend and if the pasta will last for a few more days.

Some are in their "home office" doing all they can to protect the company they work for and still do an honest day's work from home. Others are looking through rubbish bins to survive. Some want to go back to work because they are running out of money but in the same breath, they are worried about the unseen virus and they have questions about it. Others want to kill those who break the quarantine.

Some need to break the quarantine to stand in a queue at the supermarket. Others just really want to escape. Others criticise the government for the queue at the shop and for all the uncertainty.

Some have faith in God and are patiently praying and waiting for miracles in 2020. Others say the worst is yet to come and that's probably our reality. Truth is, life, as we knew it before, is gone.

So, friends, we are not in the same boat.

We are going through a time when our perceptions and needs are completely different and each one will emerge, in his/her own way, from that storm. Some with a tan from their pool. Others with scars on their soul. It is very important to see beyond what is seen at first glance. Not just looking, more than looking, actually seeing.

See beyond the political party, beyond the nose on your face. Do not underestimate the pain of others if you do not feel it.

Do not judge the good life of others, do not condemn the bad life of others. Just don't be a judge.

Let us not judge the one who lacks, as well as the one who exceeds him.

We are on different ships and all looking to survive. Let everyone navigate their route with respect, empathy and responsibility. Stop the judgment and please just be kind. [1]

We have all been listening to endless webinars, attended countless zoom meetings and scrolled our screens reading one post after the other while trying our best to stay up to date with the latest figures, stats and all things COVID-19 with the stark reality of finding a spark of hope that can set us free from this new era of social distancing and getting to grips with the new lockdown level measures introduced. All the above has been necessary to tame the beast inside of us, to some degree. The beast I refer to is the "unknown". The feeling of knowing feels almost as good as doing in a world where we are asked to move around as little as possible and #staysafe. This "beast" has paralysed many into dark pits of despair and sleepless nights. The stories out there are gut-wrenching and leave one wondering how we will ever be able to get back up again, whole and ready to take charge when it will take a miracle from above to see the light at the end of the dark tunnel and the floodgates open to receive friends, family and tourists again. When I came across Nicki Peverett's[2] post on social media it didn't mention stats, figures or a recovery plan for a specific industry but it did speak to my heart and it instantly connected me to every person who is finding their way through the same storm no matter what boat we find ourselves in.

> *"We will not go back to normal. Normal never was. Our pre-corona existence was not normal other than we normalized greed, inequity, exhaustion, depletion, extraction, disconnection, confusion, rage, hoarding, hate and lack. We should not long to return, my friends. We are being given the opportunity to stitch a new garment. One that fits all of humanity and nature." – Sonya Renee Taylor*[3]

---

1 Peverett, N. (2020). Port Shepston Lions Club, We are not in the same boat. Retrieved from: https://www.facebook.com/241625045939607/posts/written-by-nicki-peverettfoodforthought-we-are-not-in-the-same-boati-keep-hearin/2437056849729738/

2 Ibid

3 Taylor, S.R. (n.d.). Over Grow the System. Retrieved from: https://m.facebook.com/OvergrowTheSystem/photos/a.218591438315581/1488703877970991/?type=3&source=48&__tn__=EHH-R

You see, behind every face lives a story that is unique to each person. No one's story is alike and yet it seeks the same ending that is universal at the core of mankind's ultimate story and intertwined with all fairy-tale endings – to live happily ever after. A story that tells the journey of one's life with many unforeseen twists and turns (e.g. COVID-19), roller-coaster ups and downs, sweet Hello's and sad Goodbye's and the coming and going of challenging and changing seasons. The journey is never straightforward and candidly beckoning one's free will to choose carefully and wisely between different paths through the untamed forest. It unequivocally challenges many as they timidly face the inevitable crossroads of life and decide which way to go, but the one constant feature in everyone's story is the main character, **YOU**! It's often said that no matter how long you've travelled in the wrong direction, you can always turn around. "Finally, there is a way out!" you might shout in desperate relief but just remember **You** take **You** with **You** every single time **You** change directions or turn around. Although external factors such as COVID-19 gets the blame for all hopes and dreams being shattered it's important to remember that **You** either contribute towards the problem or you are a voice that offers a solution to create a better vision for the future, which ultimately determines the outcome of mankind's future.

The relentless search for the right path is not the only challenge. Getting distracted by comparing your path to someone else's and veering off onto little side roads with signs along the journey saying "Path of least resistance – This Way" are designed to appeal and ignite all your senses into believing the crumbs of lies that lead to destination *"nowhere"* only to succumb into the blaming, shaming and naming game as you desperately try to get yourself off the path and justify why you haven't arrived at your final destination yet. Fortunately for you, your current situation isn't your final destination. The quest is not only about reaching your final destination bruised and battered, but it's also about finding joy in the journey as hard and hopeless as it seems, being present and letting go of any baggage that's too heavy of a burden to carry whilst every morsel of your scattered being becomes whole again. That's the essence of one's journey. So often one's story is a repeat of a similar journey just with a different path, different people, different places and different circumstances. Life will repeat the same lessons until you get it. You will never run out of paths to choose from but when you consciously decide to find the path that leads to love, peace, freedom, happiness, health and joy you have to believe and have unwavering faith that it already exists. You also have to visualise what type of person this path is looking for and then become that person that the path will welcome on. Feel it, taste it, touch it, see it, hear it and become it in every cell of your being before you can even think of taking the first step. Often we embark on this journey of desperately trying to find our path when it is dark – when we are caught and tangled up in fear, anger, resentment, denial, jealousy which only leaves you scared, afraid, hopeless and tired. The light that you are looking for is not outside of you – it lies within and it's patiently waiting for you to switch it on by engaging in some deep soul-searching and surrendering to the dark for it to light up and show you the way!

Now a story also won't be complete without a hero and a villain. What you don't know is that you are the hero or the villain at any given time in your own story – it all depends on which one you are feeding and making stronger or starving and making weaker. For some, their story has just begun and for many their story has ended, often too soon with blank pages and empty spaces left, only to fill the void. Some feel stuck and others wish their story were different. Only a handful prays their story never ends. But the saddest story ever told is the shortest one. The one where you decide that no one cares, that you are not enough and that your story doesn't matter. The end. The real stories are the ones that change the world and inspire the masses. Those are told only by the brave, the ones who know that freedom lies beyond the pain and the only way to break through it is to face it and embrace it, softly and gently, until you let it go and find the lesson in the story that becomes your message of hope, courage, forgiveness and love whilst never settling for anything less than your highest self knows to be true.

In the late '60s a show debuted called "Mister Roger's Neighbourhood". Mr Roger was a specialist in child emotional development and he was acknowledged and praised for being a genuinely kind person. One of his plentiful beautiful life lessons was to "remember others are not as different as their appearances may suggest. He knew that despite our differences, we all have basically the same fears and desires at our core, and understanding that leaves so much room for empathy." One of his most famous quotes reads: "Frankly, there isn't anyone you couldn't learn to love once you've heard their story". He reminded us all to embrace our individual power: "Never underestimate the impact that your mere existence can have on another human being," he said. "There is something of yourself that you leave at every meeting with another person." What beautiful lessons will your story teach others on this journey called life? Imagine your life was creating a story from where the seeds of ambition, dreams and desires which once lay dormant began to sprout. Where the lessons learnt, embraced and accepted were enough to break through the compact surface of the ground and as you grew and finally bloomed into something spectacular not only for the pure joy of the moment under the glorious sun but for everyone to get a sense of the fragrance of freedom and forever remember the sweet smell of someone who finally had found themselves at some point along the journey even more so on this unprecedented journey of COVID-19.

Chapter 21: *Rise of the Warrior*

"What we know matters but who we are matters more."
– Brene Brown[4]

Shared with permission from Joel Barker, futurist, author and film maker, there's a story I would like to share with you.[5] It was inspired by the writing of Loren Eiseley. Eiseley was a very special person because he combined the best of two cultures. He was a scientist and a poet. And from those two perspectives, he wrote insightfully and beautifully about the world and our role in it.[6]

> Once upon a time, there was a wise man, much like Eiseley himself, who used to go to the ocean to do his writing. He had a habit of walking on the beach before he began his work. One day he was walking along the shore. As he looked down the beach, he saw a human figure moving like a dancer. He smiled to himself to think of someone who would dance to the day. So he began to walk faster to catch up. As he got closer, he saw that it was a young man and the young man wasn't dancing, but instead, he was reaching down to the shore, picking up something and very gently throwing it into the ocean.
>
> As he got closer, he called out, "Good morning! What are you doing?" The young man paused, looked up and replied "Throwing starfish into the ocean."
>
> "I guess I should have asked, Why are you throwing starfish into the ocean?" "The sun is up and the tide is going out. And if I don't throw them in they'll die." "But young man, don't you realize that there are miles and miles of beach and starfish all along it. You can't possibly make a difference!"
>
> The young man listened politely. Then bent down, picked up another starfish and threw it into the sea, past the breaking waves. "It made a difference for that one!"
>
> His response surprised the man. He was upset. He didn't know how to reply. So instead, he turned away and walked back to the cottage to begin his writings.
>
> All day long as he wrote, the image of the young man haunted him. He tried to ignore it, but the vision persisted. Finally, late in the afternoon, he realized that he the scientist, he the poet, had missed out on the essential nature of the

---

4   Brown, B. (2013). *Daring Greatly: How the Courage to Be Vulnerable Transforms the Way We Live, Love, Parent, and Lead.* London: Penguin Books.

5   Eiseley, L. (2020). *The Star Thrower Story.* Retrieved from: https://starthrower.com/pages/the-star-thrower-story

6   Wikipedia. (n.d.) Loren Eiseley. Retrieved from: https://en.wikipedia.org/wiki/Loren_Eiseley

young man's actions. Because he realized that what the young man was doing was choosing not to be an observer in the universe and make a difference. He was embarrassed.

That night he went to bed troubled. When the morning came he awoke knowing that he had to do something. So he got up, put on his clothes, went to the beach and found the young man. And with him, he spent the rest of the morning throwing starfish into the ocean. You see, what that young man's actions represent is something that is special in each and every one of us. We have all been gifted with the ability to make a difference. And if we can, like that young man, become aware of that gift, we gain through the strength of our vision the power to shape the future.

And that is your challenge. And that is my challenge. We must each find our starfish.[7]

To find our starfish we need to share our stories. Stories that require vulnerability on our part because "vulnerability is the birthplace of innovation, creativity and change".[8] Vulnerability does not mean weakness. As Brene Brown would say "Vulnerability sounds like truth and feels like courage. Truth and courage aren't always comfortable, but they're never a weakness".[9]

What story will you share with your children and/or grandchildren about the COVID-19 era? What stories will you tell your colleagues when you return to the office? When those first guests arrive at the airport, lodge, hotel, Airbnb or campsite. When that first game drive leaves the camp. When the tour guide meets the guest at the airport. When the hostess greets her new guests. When the butler serves a welcome drink. They are going to want to know your story. What will you tell them? The story that we are busy writing now will shape the future for generations that will follow us. Will our stories inspire future generations and instil within them a sense of deep gratitude for when humanity faced a crisis we all connected with empathy, kindness and love to leave a legacy and a lesson behind that we needed each other more than we ever thought we would and our planet, wildlife and its resources must be looked after, preserved and nurtured because earth is our only home. The place we get to call home.

---

7   Barker, J. (2019). *The Star Thrower Story*, A Short Film. Retrieved from: https://www.youtube.com/watch?v=a0m6KJwwyNk

8   Brown, B. (2012). *Listening to shame*. Retrieved from: https://www.youtube.com/watch?v=psN1DORYYV0

9   Brown, B. (2013). *Daring Greatly: How the Courage to Be Vulnerable Transforms the Way We Live, Love, Parent*, and Lead. London: Penguin Books.

Less than two years ago, I stared at my laptop screen for a good 10 minutes, frozen and unable to write my first e-mail after being appointed to assist with logistics and supplier relations for our company's student travel programme. It was a straightforward e-mail, but it carried the gravitas of me finally breaking through the terrier barrier that had kept me safe and in my comfort zone for far too long.

To fully understand the complexity of this statement it requires some context of when my journey and love affair with Africa's wildlife and natural landscapes began. If you are interested in my story, please visit my blog on www.shongile.co.za

In conclusion

COVID-19 knocked us down as individuals, businesses and industry sectors but it's our responsibility to get up and come out the other side better versions of ourselves.

One of the biggest obstacles to overcome will be the mind-set. The biggest disability you can have is a bad mind-set. Who do you want to be when this is over? Don't get sucked up into the outside fear and wait to make a decision. Now is the time to gain a new mind-set and to focus on innovation. Realise that this is a scary and unique time. The greater the challenge the greater the opportunity. Will I wait for someone to give me my cheese or will I find new cheese to offer? Communicate the problem in the language of the consumer, not the expert, and remember a crisis like COVID-19 presses us into growth – a chance to pivot in life.

Value creation is key. Problems become gifts once we learn from them. Use your special abilities to give back to your community. People will remember that you were there for them. Emotions of gratitude and love outweigh negative emotions, so refocus your bad thoughts to put yourself in a position to create and be productive. Lead with love and compassion.

We have all been given a gift – Time. What will you do with this time you've been given?

Your story matters. Change your story from "why me? to **"THE WARRIOR IN ME"**.

Focus on getting one customer one result. Focus on what you have and not what is happening to you. Practise gratitude daily and remember we all have a story. Facts tell but stories sell.

There are more voices out there, more stories that will inspire, more insights and strategies to share that could help a business or employee during this very challenging time we find ourselves in. I am inviting business owners and employees in the tourism and travel industry to share your story. Your story matters. Your story could make a difference.

I invite everyone in the tourism industry to share your stories, strategies, solutions, your status, your ambitions and lessons learnt during this COVID-19 period by visiting www.shongile.co.za. Continue to share your stories on as many digital platforms as possible whether it be social media, newsletters, websites and initiatives mentioned throughout this book. Your story could be a starfish moment in someone's life, family, business, community and/or country.

To find out which Southern and Eastern Africa countries are travel ready please visit www.shongile.co.za

> *"Our job is not to deny the story, but to defy the ending – to rise strong, recognize our story, and rumble with the truth until we get to a place where we think, YES! This is what happened. And I will choose how the story ends."*
> *– Brene Brown*[10]

---

10 Brown, B. (2015). *Rising Strong: How the ability to reset transforms the way we live, love, parent and lead*. New York: Random House.

REFERENCES

Chapter 1

Du Toit-Helmbold, M. (2020). COVID-19: *A time to reveal our true character and resolve*. Retrieved from: https://www.destinate.co.za/blog/entry/covid-19-a-time-to-reveal-our-true-character-and-resolve

Du Toit-Helmbold, M. (2020). *Helping Brands Survive and Build Resilience*. Retrieved from: https://www.destinate.co.za/blog/entry/helping-brands-survive-and-build-resilience

Du Toit-Helmbold, M. (2020). *Travel Trends Report for 2020*. Retrieved from: https://www.destinate.co.za/blog/entry/travel-trends-report-for-2020

Chapter 3

National Department of Tourism Republic of South Africa (NDTRSA). (2018). Tourism Destination Planning Manual National Department of Tourism. Retrieved from: https://www.tourism.gov.za/AboutNDT/Branches1/Knowledge/Documents/Destination%20Planning%20Manual-%20September%202018.pdf

Tshivhengwa, T, (2020). TBCSA presents calculated, driven and gradual re-opening of tourism to parliament's tourism portfolio committee. Retrieved from: https://www.satsa.com/tbcsa-lobby-for-gradual-re-opening-of-tourism-to-parliaments-tourism-portfolio-committee/

Tourism Update. (2020). COVID-19 relief – what the SA govt is offering. Retrieved from: http://www.tourismupdate.co.za/article/199253/COVID-19-relief-what-the-SA-govt-is-offering/5

Tourism Update. (2020). Letter to the editor: Government's flawed tourism model. Retrieved from: http://www.tourismupdate.co.za/article/199251/Letter-to-the-editor-Government-s-flawed-tourism-model

Tourism Update. (2020). Little awareness of tourism's economic effect, says Saunders. Retrieved from: http://www.tourismupdate.co.za/article/199269/Little-awareness-of-tourism-s-economic-effect-says-Saunders/17

UNWTO. (2020). International Tourist Arrivals Could Fall by 20-30% in 2020. Retrieved from: https://www.unwto.org/news/international-tourism-arrivals-could-fall-in-2020

World Tourism Organization (UNWTO). (2018). UNWTO Tourism Highlights: 2018 Edition. Retrieved from: https://www.unwto.org/global/publication/unwto-tourism-highlights-2018-edition, p4.

World Tourism Organization (UNWTO). (2020). International Tourist Arrivals Could Fall by 20-30% in 2020. Retrieved from: https://www.unwto.org/news/international-tourism-arrivals-could-fall-in-2020

World Tourism Organization (UNWTO). (2020). International Tourist Arrivals Could Fall by 20-30% in 2020. Retrieved from: https://www.unwto.org/news/international-tourism-arrivals-could-fall-in-2020

Chapter 5

Siret, M. (2020). Coronavirus: What global travel may look like ahead of a vaccine. Retrieved from: https://www.bbc.com/news/world-52450038

Chapter 9

IATA *Airlines* Magazine. (2020). Aviation Relief for African Airlines Critical as COVID-19 Impacts Deepen. Retrieved from: https://www.iata.org/en/pressroom/pr/2020-04-23-02/

Chapter 10

Box.com. (n.d.). Check-in, bag drop. Retrieved from: https://app.box.com/s/y346wk48dtqi74swq1kimaoc2p9zhcni
Box.com. (n.d.). Airport curbside. Retrieved from: https://app.box.com/s/fcl8jhuyek6pyj6ugsj7v34uqsns1xna
Box.com. (n.d.). Boarding area. Retrieved from: https://app.box.com/s/5lb8fihv6drd0nqhe0h30uu6fu7w2psm
Box.com. (n.d.). In-flight experience. Retrieved from: https://app.box.com/s/kwz8zpflhjnbp8k0xaksyqca2ml8gk6o
Box.com. (n.d.). Jetbridge. Retrieved from: https://app.box.com/s/h2d1moe3el4c9yv5do8icdvio1pcks2v
Box.com. (n.d.). Online check-in. Retrieved from: https://app.box.com/s/ers6i2r4udwux9rwkhu9hsbax6y8sop9
Box.com. (n.d.). Security. Retrieved from: https://app.box.com/s/h7haeg0341ku922izm720ou7ejq00ety
Box.com. (n.d.). The end of the in-flight magazine. Retrieved from: https://app.box.com/s/tqmqbyxyxf37qmfnn6fk9rhc7wjnyeen
Box.com. (n.d.). Timeline before flight. Retrieved from: https://app.box.com/s/0lax3x0und13pqrfz0rksb9hpbt7qbnn
Box.com. (n.d.). Timeline during flight. Retrieved from: https://app.box.com/s/egkqursgq0i5btwo1xpmlvk4tfcqm6v3
Box.com. (n.d.). Upon landing. Retrieved from: https://app.box.com/s/krzar5spljewcmoz20gu50hf147n21yr

Chapter 11

ALG Transport & Infrastructure Newsletter. (2020). *Covid-19 aviation briefing. African Aviation Industry.* Retrieved from: https://algnewsletter.com/

Chapter 12

Travel and Tourism Research Association (TTRA). (2020). Initial TRINET Responses to COVID-19 Tourism (v. April 2, 2020). Retrieved from: https://ttra.com/wp-content/uploads/2020/04/TRINET-COVID-19-Recovery.pdf
Travel & Tourism Transformed. (n.d.). Travel, Tourism & Hospitality in a COVID-19 World. Retrieved from: https://www.tourismtransformed.com/

Chapter 13

Couto, R. (2007). *Behind-the-Pages interview with Paul't Hart on his award-winning book: The Politics of Crisis Management: Public Leadership Under Pressure.* Silver Spring: International Leadership Association.
Crous, W. (2020). *Managing Organisations During the COVID-19 Vortex: Comprehensive guidelines for leading your organisation through the vortex.* Bryanston: KR Publishing.
Jordan-Meier, J. (2017). *Showing leadership in crisis.* Leadership Perspectives Webinar. Silver Spring: International Leadership Association.
Kurtz, C. F., & Snowden, D. J. (2003). The new dynamics of strategy: sense-making in a complex and complicated world. *IBM Systems Journal, 42*(3): 462-483.
Luthans, F., Youssef, C. M., & Avolio, B. J. (2007). *Psychological capital. Developing the human competitive edge.* Oxford: Oxford University Press.
Snowden, D. J., & Boone, M. E. (2007). A leaders' framework for decision making. *Harvard Business Review*, November: 1-8.
Veldsman, T. H., & Johnson, A. (2016). The future of leadership. In T. H. Veldsman and A. J. Johnson (eds.). *Leadership. Perspectives from the Front Line.* Johannesburg: Knowres, pp. 869-879.

Chapter 14

Brown, B. (2018). *Dare to lead.* New York: Random House.

Cloud, H. (2010). *Necessary Endings.* London: Ebury Publishing.

Cooper, J. (2017). *Transformation 2.0: Leading at the boundaries of the unknown...* Retrieved from: http://tiltinternational.com/uploads/3/5/9/8/35981559/transformation2017leaflet.pdf

Crous, W. (2020). *Managing Organisations During the COVID-19 Vortex: Comprehensive guidelines for leading your organisation through the vortex.* Bryanston: KR Publishing.

Heifetz, R., Grashow, A., & Linsky, M. (2009). The Practice of Adaptive Leadership: Tools and Tactics for Changing Your Organisation and the World. *Journal of Applied Christian Leadership*, 4(1): 16.

Snowden, D., & Boone, M. (2007). *A leader's framework for decision making. Harvard Business Review*, 85(11): 68-76

Taleb, N. N. (2007). *The Black Swan.* New York: Random House. Retrieved from: http://citeseerx.ist.psu.edu/viewdoc/download?doi=10.1.1.695.4305&rep=rep1&type=pdf

Chapter 15

Brooks, S. K., Webster, R. K., Smith, L. E., Woodland, L., Wessely, S., Greenberg, N., & Rubin, G. J. (2020). The psychological impact of quarantine and how to reduce it: rapid review of the evidence. *Lancet*, 395: 912–20.

Crous, W. (2020). *Managing Organisations During the COVID-19 Vortex: Comprehensive guidelines for leading your organisation through the vortex.* Bryanston: KR Publishing.

Organizacion Mundial de la Salud. (2020). *Mental Health and Psychosocial Considerations During COVID-19 Outbreak.* Retrieved from: https://www.who.int/docs/default-source/coronaviruse/mental-health-considerations.pdf?sfvrsn=6d3578af_8

Watson, R. (2017). *What's Next: Top Trends.* Retrieved from: https://toptrends.nowandnext.com/2017/05/08/map/

World Health Organization. (2001). *Mental disorders affect one in four people.* Retrieved from: https://www.who.int/whr/2001/media_centre/press_release/en/

Chapter 17

Ryan, D. & Rapaport, G. (2020). Thought Leadership. Retrieved from: https://blog.rhinoafrica.com/2020/04/08/how-rhino-africa-is-navigating-covid-19/

Chapter 18

African Bush Camps Foundation: (n.d.). African Bush Camps Foundation Community Empowerment. Retrieved from: https://africanbushcamps-gdg-j945n.raisely.com/

African Bush Camps Foundation: (n.d.). Community Development Through Responsible Tourism. Retrieved from: https://www.africanbushcampsfoundation.org/

GlobalGiving. (n.d.). Healthcare for 4 000 Rural Zambian Villagers. Retrieved from: https://www.globalgiving.org/projects/healthcare-for-4000-rural-zambian-villagers/

Chapter 21

Barker, J. (2019). *The Star Thrower Story. A Short Film.* Retrieved from: https://www.youtube.com/watch?v=a0m6KJwwyNk

Brown, B. (2012). Listening to shame. Retrieved from: https://www.youtube.com/watch?v=psN1DORYYV0

Brown, B. (2013). *Daring Greatly: How the Courage to Be Vulnerable Transforms the Way We Live, Love, Parent, and Lead*. London: Penguin Books.
Brown, B. (2015*). Rising Strong: How the ability to reset transforms the way we live, love, parent and lead*. New York: Random House.
Eiseley, L. (2020). *The Star Thrower Story*. Retrieved from: https://starthrower.com/pages/the-star-thrower-story
Peverett, N. (2020). Port Shepston Lions Club, we are not in the same boat. Retrieved from: https://www.facebook.com/241625045939607/posts/written-by-nicki-peverettfoodforthought-we-are-not-in-the-same-boati-keep-hearin/2437056849729738/
Taylor, S.R. (n.d.). Over Grow the System. Retrieved from: https://m.facebook.com/OvergrowTheSystem/photos/a.218591438315581/1488703877970991/?type=3&source=48&__tn__=EHH-R
Wikipedia. (n.d.) Loren Eiseley. Retrieved from: https://en.wikipedia.org/wiki/Loren_Eiseley

INDEX

#TOURISMINMYBLOOD, 171

A

ability to reopen and host, 146, 149
adaptability and opportunity, 23
affected regions, 83
Africa, 9, 11–13, 15–18, 45–46, 48–49, 51–57, 63–65, 79, 81–83, 145–147, 149–156, 158–159, 161–162, 166–168, 172–173
African air market, 84
African Aviation Industry, 79
African markets, 9, 90
African regions, 88
Africa's capacity, 87
age of sanitised travel, 67–68, 70–73, 75
air transport, 34, 62–64, 80–81, 84, 86, 92
air transport sector, 80, 92
airline passenger, 67
airlines capacity, 83
airport curbside, 68
airport operator responsiveness, 93
airport recovery profiles, 91
airports capacity cut-off by market, 83
airports require public support, 92
attracting domestic guests, 31, 34
authenticity, 55, 119, 143
aviation industry, 62–63, 79, 81
aviation nations, 89

B

beds and activities, 146, 149–150, 152
before the flight, 76
boarding area, 71
breakfast social distancing, 33
build resilience, 2, 5, 7
building a new model, 23
building tourism resilience, 34
business growth and sustainability, 39

C

care for wild, 167–170
check-in, 31–33, 44, 67–70, 72, 99

bag drop, 69
collaborative business environment, 56
communications, 6, 44, 96, 100, 172
community, 34, 55, 57, 59, 96, 99, 101, 103, 105, 107, 115, 120, 161–163, 165–166, 168–170
company, community, conservation, 162
complexity and chaos, 123
confinement, 79
conservation, 144, 161–162, 164–165, 167–169
conservation and tourism, 144
consumers, 7, 19, 41–42, 46, 52, 98–99, 103
conversations through visioneering, 1
COVID-19, 2–3, 5–7, 9–11, 15–16, 18–21, 31–34, 41–44, 49–51, 62, 79, 81–82, 95, 129–130, 132–133, 135–137
COVID-19 impact on the tourism, 9
COVID-19 outbreak, 5, 9, 67, 79, 81, 86, 95, 132
crises, 95–96, 101, 104–105, 119–121, 125, 130, 133, 164
crisis, 2–3, 5–6, 10–13, 26, 61–64, 80–81, 86, 95–97, 104–121, 123–124, 128–129, 134–135, 150–152, 154–155, 158–159
crisis leadership excellence, 106–108, 120–121
crisis management plans, 104
crisis recovery checklist, 61, 95–96
crisis vortex, 123, 126, 171

D

deposit liabilities, 51
deposits, 46, 49–51
destination markets, 146, 149, 155, 157
different recovery scenarios, 86
different recovery shapes, 86
digital transformation, 24, 27–29
disruption due to the pandemic, 155
domestic versus an international comeback, 165
dramatic drop in demand, 81
during and after the flight, 77

E

economic climate, 53
economic sustainability, 24, 29
emerging market currency weakness, 153
ensuring safety & peace of mind, 61

F

flight restrictions, 79
flights, 9, 34, 81, 83–84, 87, 102, 145–146, 148–151, 158, 173
future of aviation and the traveller, 61

G

global air market, 79
global aviation recession, 79
global cut-off on seat offers, 79
global economic, 80
global outbreak, 80, 162
government relations, 100
guidelines for companies, 19

H

health crisis, 80, 86
helping brands survive, 2, 5

I

impact all sectors, 81
impact of COVID 19, 161
individualistic business environment, 58
industry response, 62
in-flight experience, 73
in-flight janitor, 74
in-flight magazine, 74
international resolutions and decisions, 84
investment plans, 91

J

jetbridge, 72

K

key elements to positively influence, 39
key source markets, 12, 146–147

L

life after lockdown, 164
life in lockdown, 162
lowered operating costs, 153

M

major African airports/cities, 91
managing uncertainty, 123
markets & travel purposes, 86

N

navigate and adapt, 78
navigating COVID 19, 145
navigating in, beyond and through a crisis, 107

O

online check-in, 67–68
overseas tour operators, 47, 51–52

P

pandemic, 10, 12, 15, 17–18, 45, 47, 91–92, 123–124, 126, 128–129, 137, 139, 155, 157–158, 167
partial lockdown status, 149
personal and workplace mental health, 129, 136
positive mental health, 137, 140
positive mental mind-set, 137
post COVID-19, 95
power of collaboration, 1, 164
pre-payment, 46, 49–51

R

realities of sanitised travel, 78
recovering together, 166

recovery checklist, 61, 95–96
recovery process, 92
recovery rate segmented by African regions, 88
Red Location Museum, 58–59
re-ignite demand, 13
resilience action planning, 31
Reticular Activating System (RAS), 139
revenue management, 39–40
rhinos safe, 167, 170
rise of sanitised travel, 67
rise of the warrior, 175
road trips, 36–37

S

SAA, 20, 89
sanitised travel, 67–68, 70–73, 75, 78
security, 11–13, 16, 20, 69–71, 103, 148, 155, 169
segmentation by region, 84
social distancing in practice, 165
social distancing measures, 31–32, 37
South African tourism, 15, 60
Soweto, 52–55, 58
stimulate the mind, 140–141
strategic actions, 97
strengthen enabling capability, 13
structural differences between flights, tour operations and beds and activities, 149–150
supply side of tourism, 12
sustainability, 24, 28–29, 39, 81, 92, 102–103, 114, 117, 169

T

thought leadership, 145
time of crisis, 17, 154, 167
timeline before a flight, 76
timeline during a flight, 77
touchless cabin, 74
tour operations, 146, 149–152
tourism, conservation and community, 161
tourism crisis, 95–96, 105
tourism industry, 4, 6, 15, 17–20, 24–28, 40–41, 53, 56–57, 60, 145, 171, 182

tourism recovery, 9
tourism value chain, 18, 45
tourism versus poorism, 53
township entrepreneurs, 60
township tourism, 54, 56–57
township tours, 55, 57
traditional transaction flow, 45
treatment and vaccine, 146
TRINET, 95–96, 105
true character, 2
trust and strong relationships, 45

U

unprecedented crisis, 80
upon landing, 75

V

viability risks, 85

www.ingramcontent.com/pod-product-compliance
Lightning Source LLC
Chambersburg PA
CBHW080431230426
43662CB00015B/2243